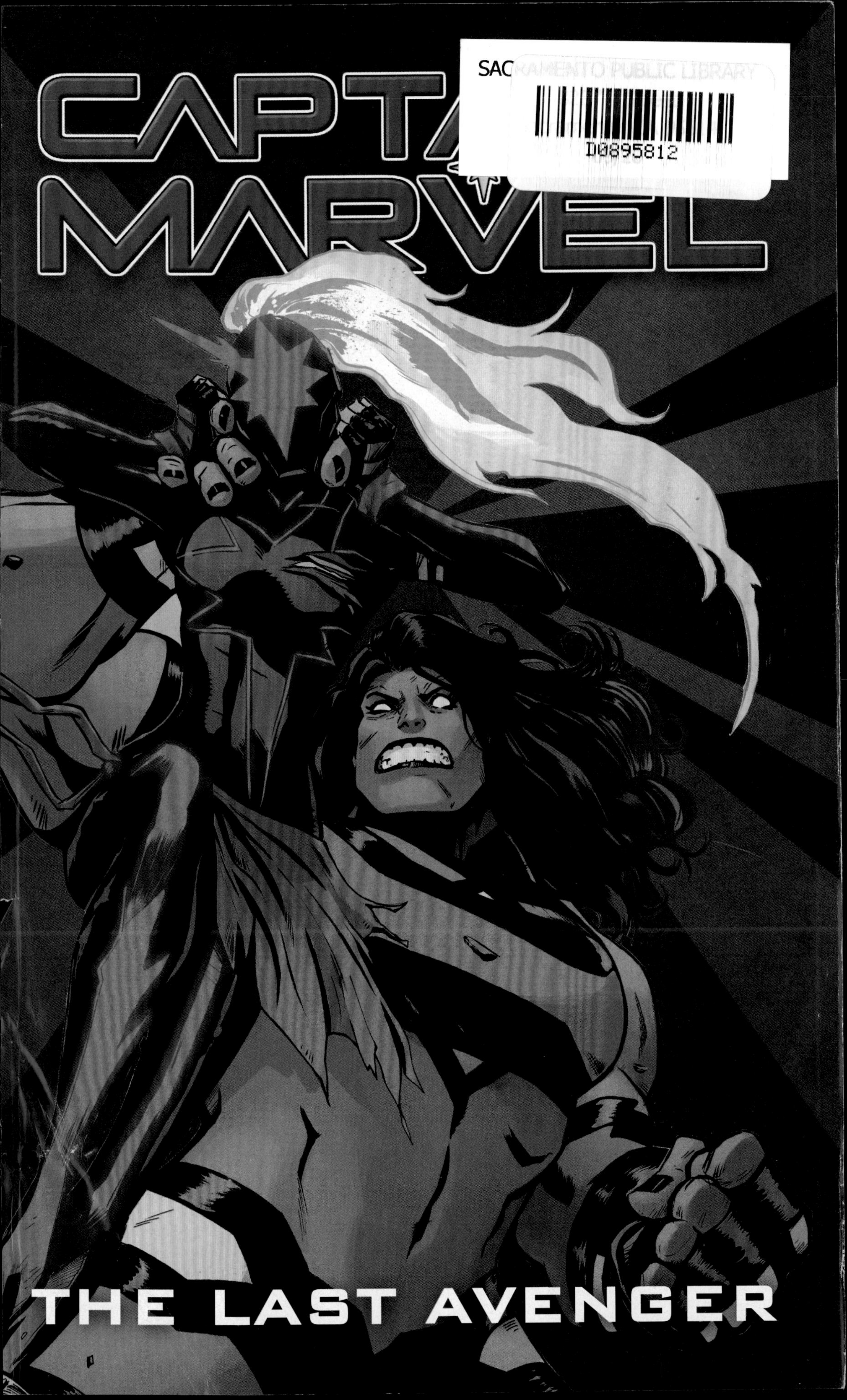
CAPT
MARVEL
THE LAST AVENGER

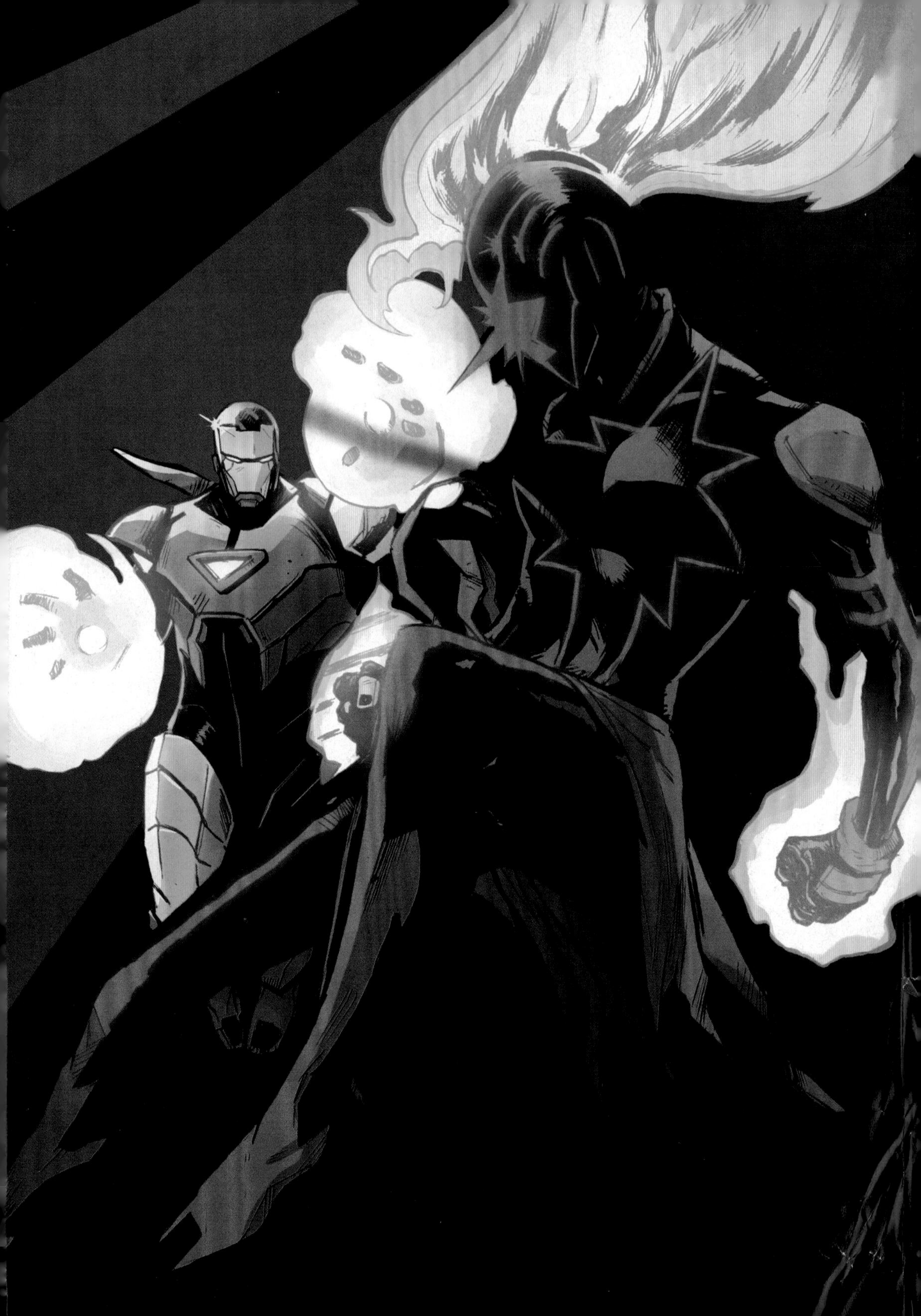

CAPTAIN MARVEL VOL. 3: THE LAST AVENGER. Contains material originally published in magazine form as CAPTAIN MARVEL (2019) #12-17. First printing 2020. ISBN 978-1-302-92308-2. Published by MARVEL WORLDWIDE, INC., a subsidiary of MARVEL ENTERTAINMENT, LLC. OFFICE OF PUBLICATION: 1290 Avenue of the Americas, New York, NY 10104. © 2020 MARVEL No similarity between any of the names, characters, persons, and/or institutions in this magazine with those of any living or dead person or institution is intended, and any such similarity which may exist is purely coincidental. **Printed in Canada.** KEVIN FEIGE, Chief Creative Officer; DAN BUCKLEY, President, Marvel Entertainment; JOHN NEE, Publisher; JOE QUESADA, EVP & Creative Director; TOM BREVOORT, SVP of Publishing; DAVID BOGART, Associate Publisher & SVP of Talent Affairs; Publishing & Partnership; DAVID GABRIEL, VP of Print & Digital Publishing; JEFF YOUNGQUIST, VP of Production & Special Projects; DAN CARR, Executive Director of Publishing Technology; ALEX MORALES, Director of Publishing Operations; DAN EDINGTON, Managing Editor; SUSAN CRESPI, Production Manager; STAN LEE, Chairman Emeritus. For information regarding advertising in Marvel Comics or on Marvel.com, please contact Vit DeBellis, Custom Solutions &

Born to a Kree mother and human father, former U.S. Air Force pilot **CAROL DANVERS** became a super hero when a Kree device activated her latent powers. Since then she's become an Avenger and Earth's Mightiest Hero.

But what the hell is she now?

CAPTAIN MARVEL

THE LAST AVENGER

KELLY THOMPSON
Writer

LEE GARBETT [#12-16] &
FRANCESCO MANNA [#17]
Artists

TAMRA BONVILLAIN [#12-16] &
CARLOS LOPEZ [#17]
Color Artists

VC's CLAYTON COWLES
Letterer

MARK BROOKS [#12-16] AND
PEPE LARRAZ & MARTE GRACIA [#17]
Cover Art

SARAH BRUNSTAD
Editor

WIL MOSS
Consulting Editor

TOM BREVOORT
Executive Editor

Collection Editor **JENNIFER GRÜNWALD**
Assistant Managing Editor: **MAIA LOY**
Assistant Managing Editor: **LISA MONTALBANO**
Editor, Special Projects **MARK D. BEAZLEY**
VP Production & Special Projects **JEFF YOUNGQUIST**

Book Designers **STACIE ZUCKER** and **ADAM DEL RE** with
JOE FRONTIRRE
SVP Print, Sales & Marketing **DAVID GABRIEL**
Editor in Chief **C.B. CEBULSKI**

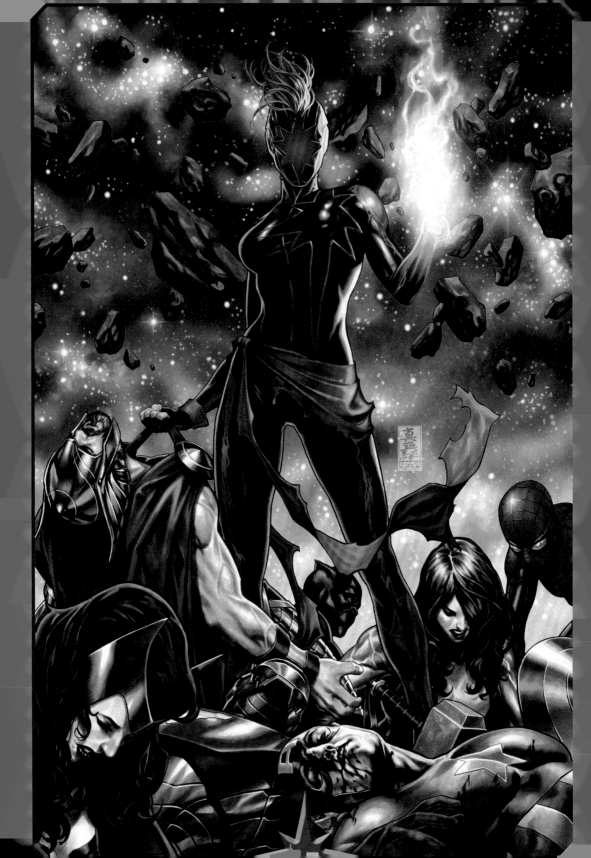

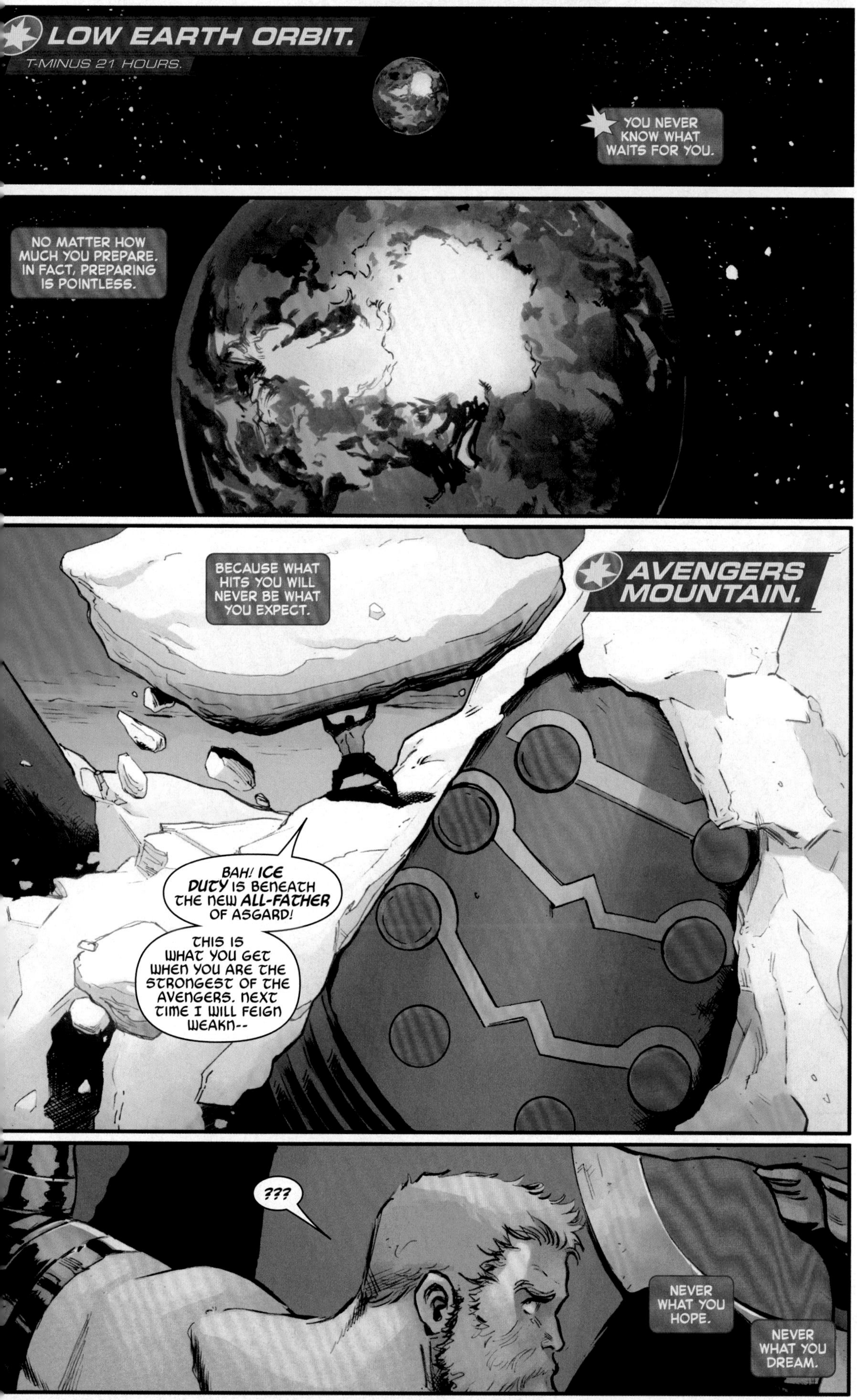
LOW EARTH ORBIT.
T-MINUS 21 HOURS.
YOU NEVER KNOW WHAT WAITS FOR YOU.
NO MATTER HOW MUCH YOU PREPARE. IN FACT, PREPARING IS POINTLESS.
BECAUSE WHAT HITS YOU WILL NEVER BE WHAT YOU EXPECT.
AVENGERS MOUNTAIN.
BAH! ICE DUTY IS BENEATH THE NEW ALL-FATHER OF ASGARD!
THIS IS WHAT YOU GET WHEN YOU ARE THE STRONGEST OF THE AVENGERS. NEXT TIME I WILL FEIGN WEAKN--
???
NEVER WHAT YOU HOPE.
NEVER WHAT YOU DREAM.

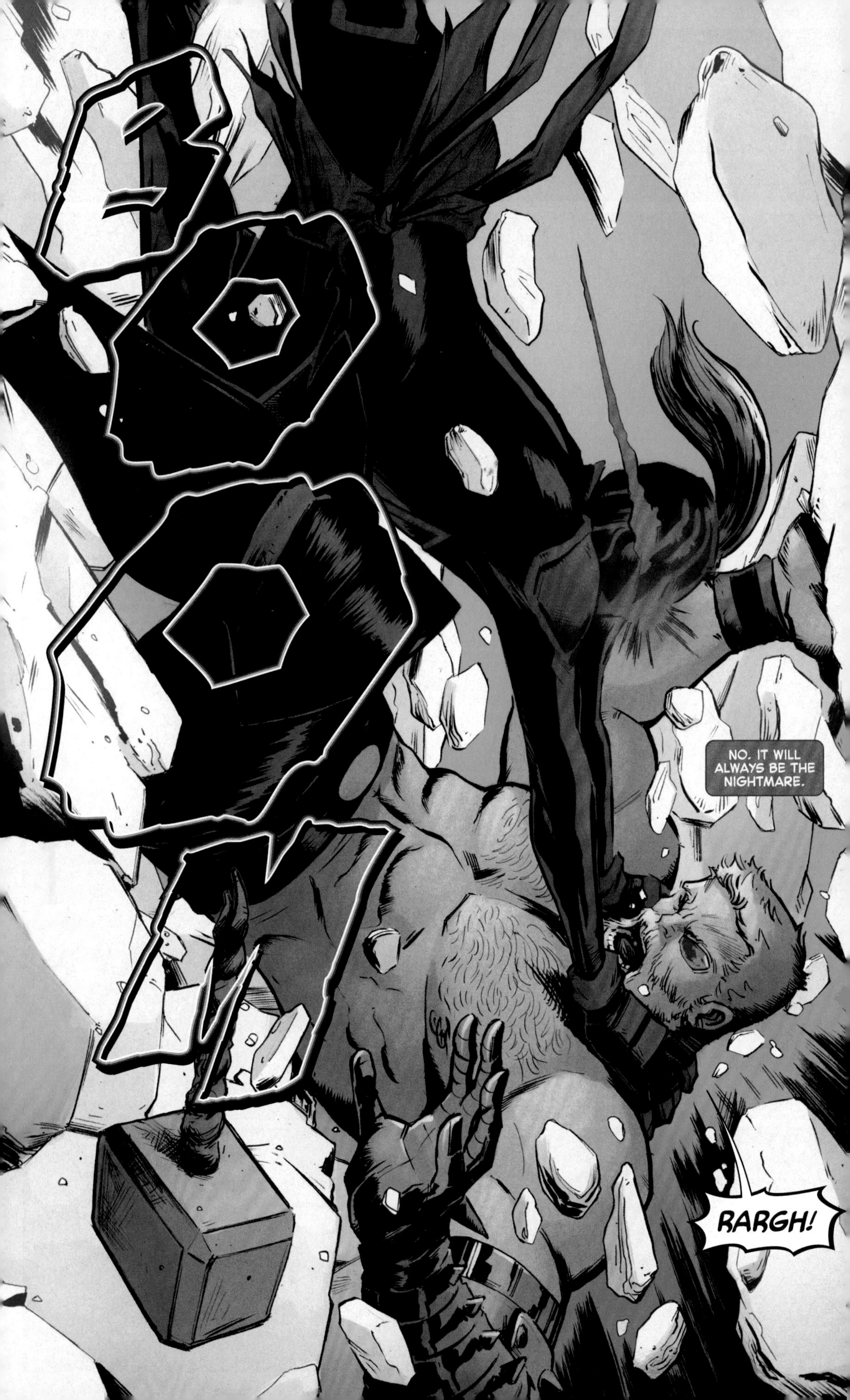
NO. IT WILL ALWAYS BE THE NIGHTMARE.
RARGH!

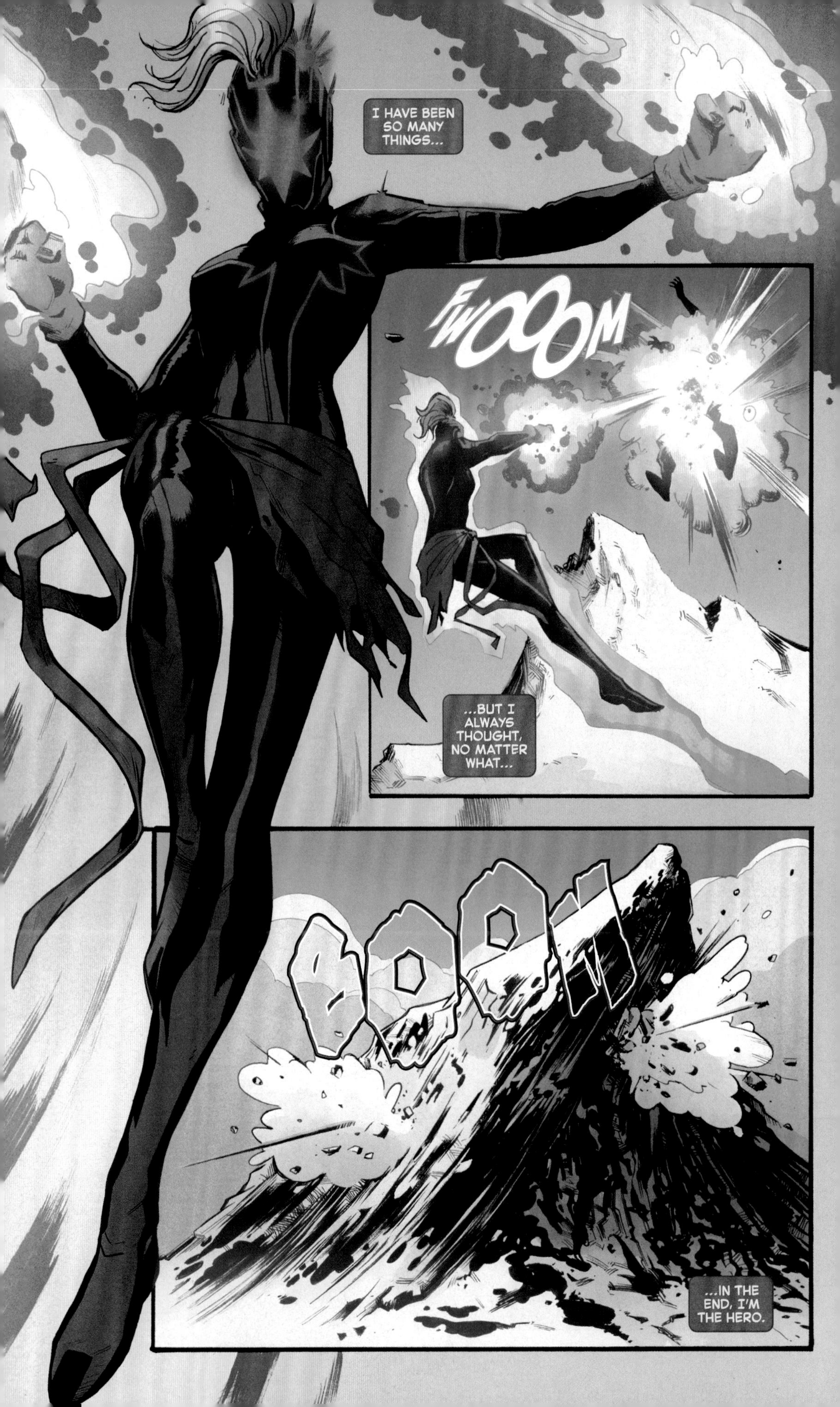
I HAVE BEEN SO MANY THINGS...
FWOOOM
...BUT I ALWAYS THOUGHT, NO MATTER WHAT...
BOOM
...IN THE END, I'M THE HERO.

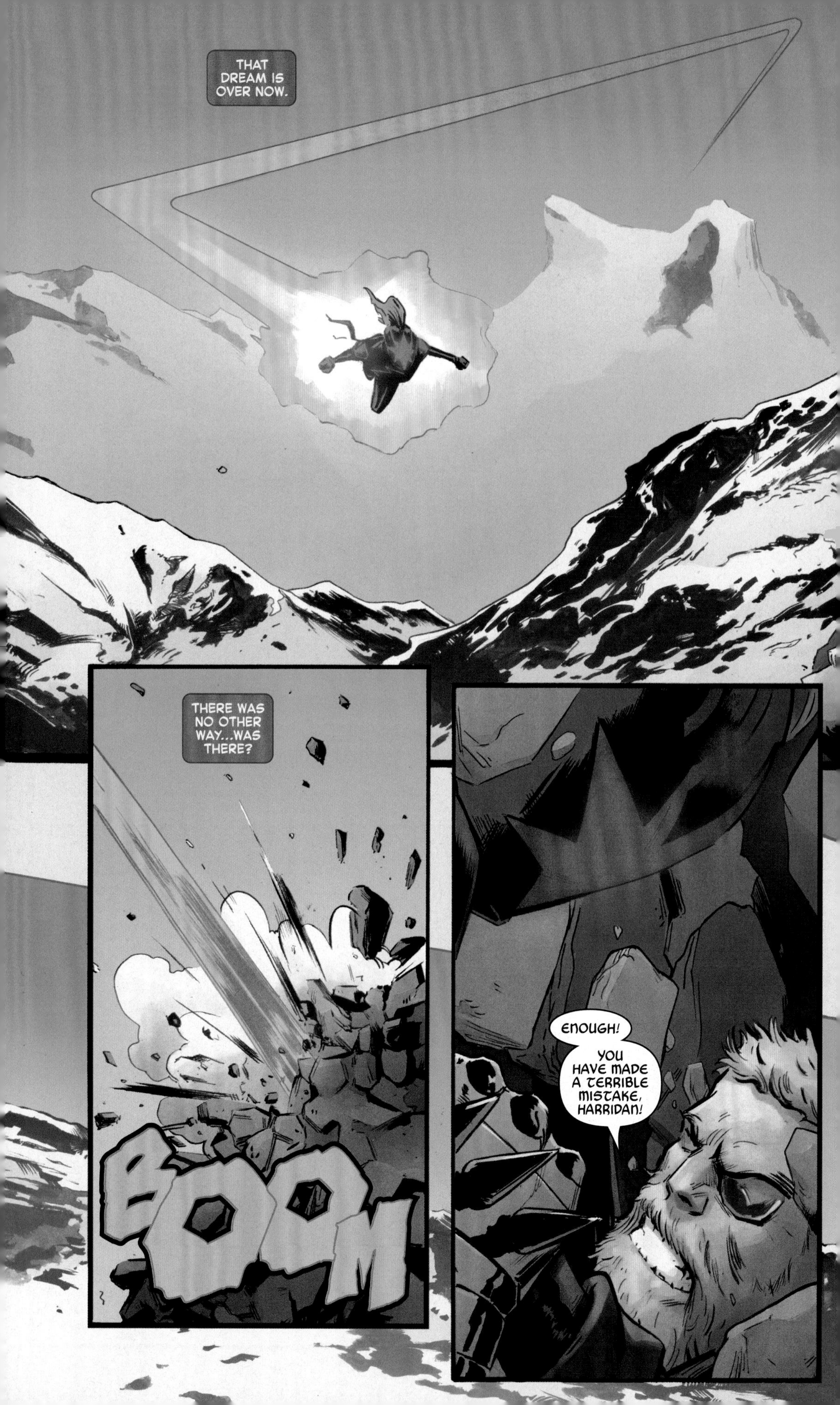
THAT DREAM IS OVER NOW.
THERE WAS NO OTHER WAY...WAS THERE?
BOOM
ENOUGH!
YOU HAVE MADE A TERRIBLE MISTAKE, HARRIDAN!

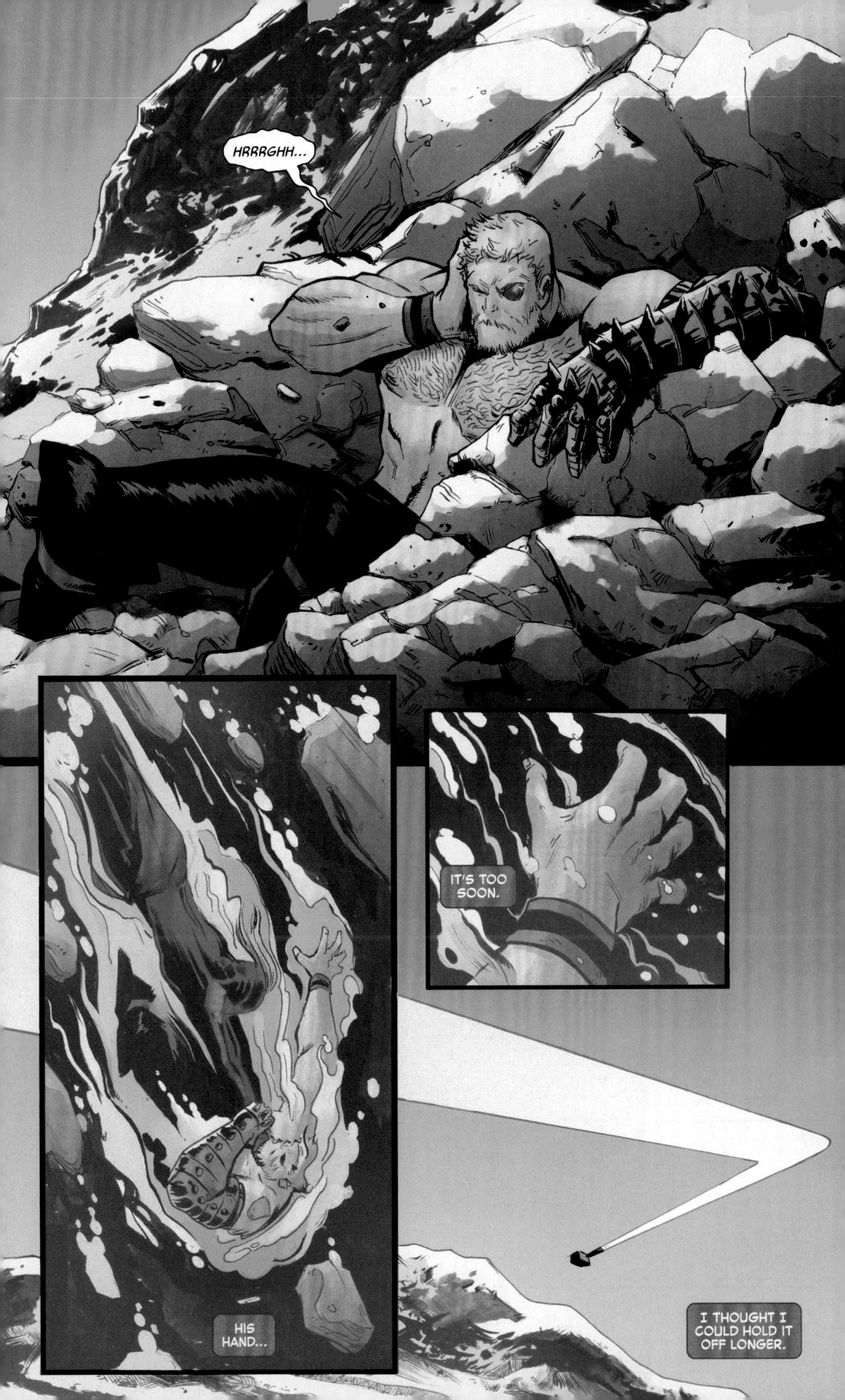
HRRRGHH...
IT'S TOO SOON.
HIS HAND...
I THOUGHT I COULD HOLD IT OFF LONGER.

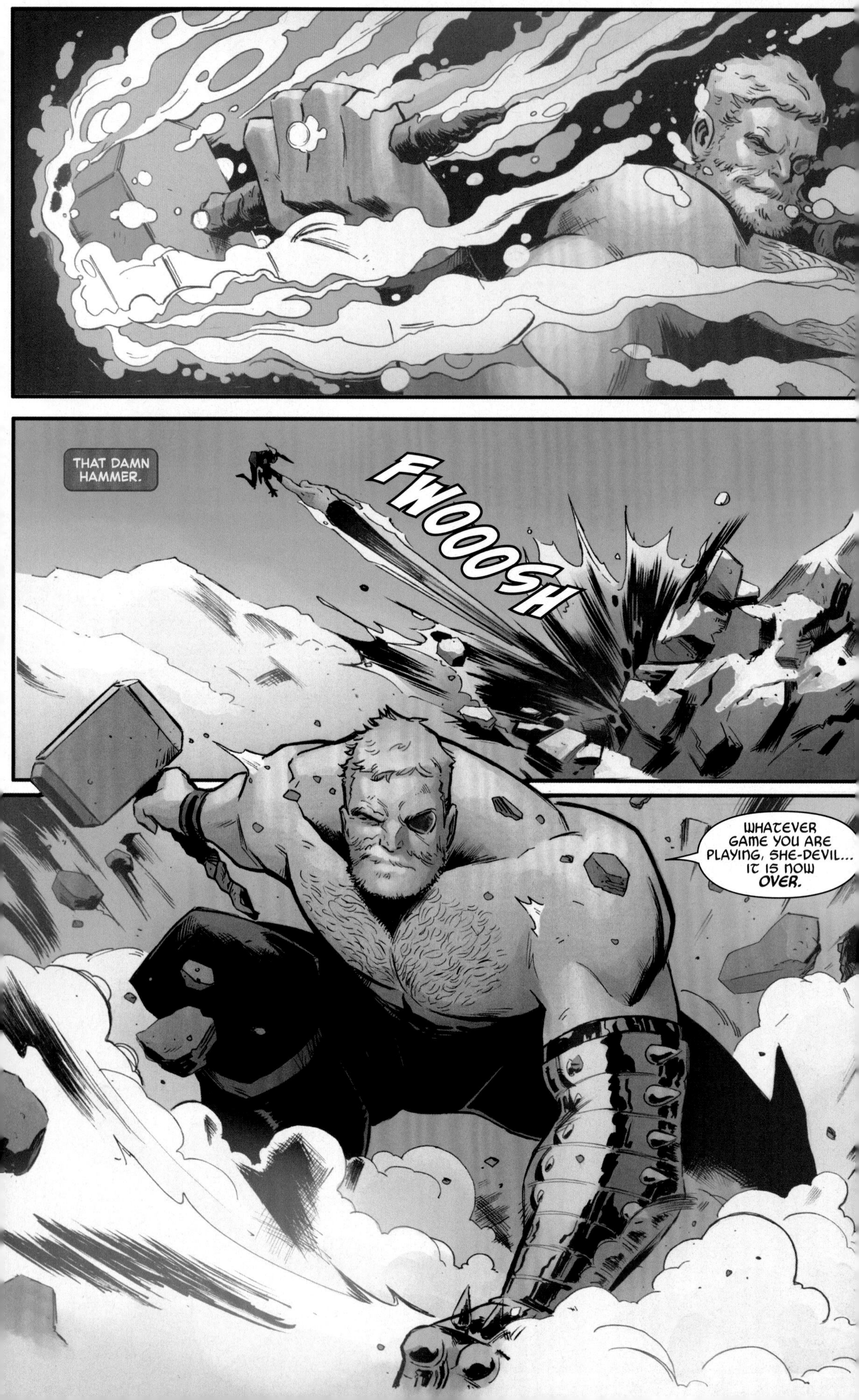
THAT DAMN HAMMER.
FWOOOSH
WHATEVER GAME YOU ARE PLAYING, SHE-DEVIL... IT IS NOW OVER.

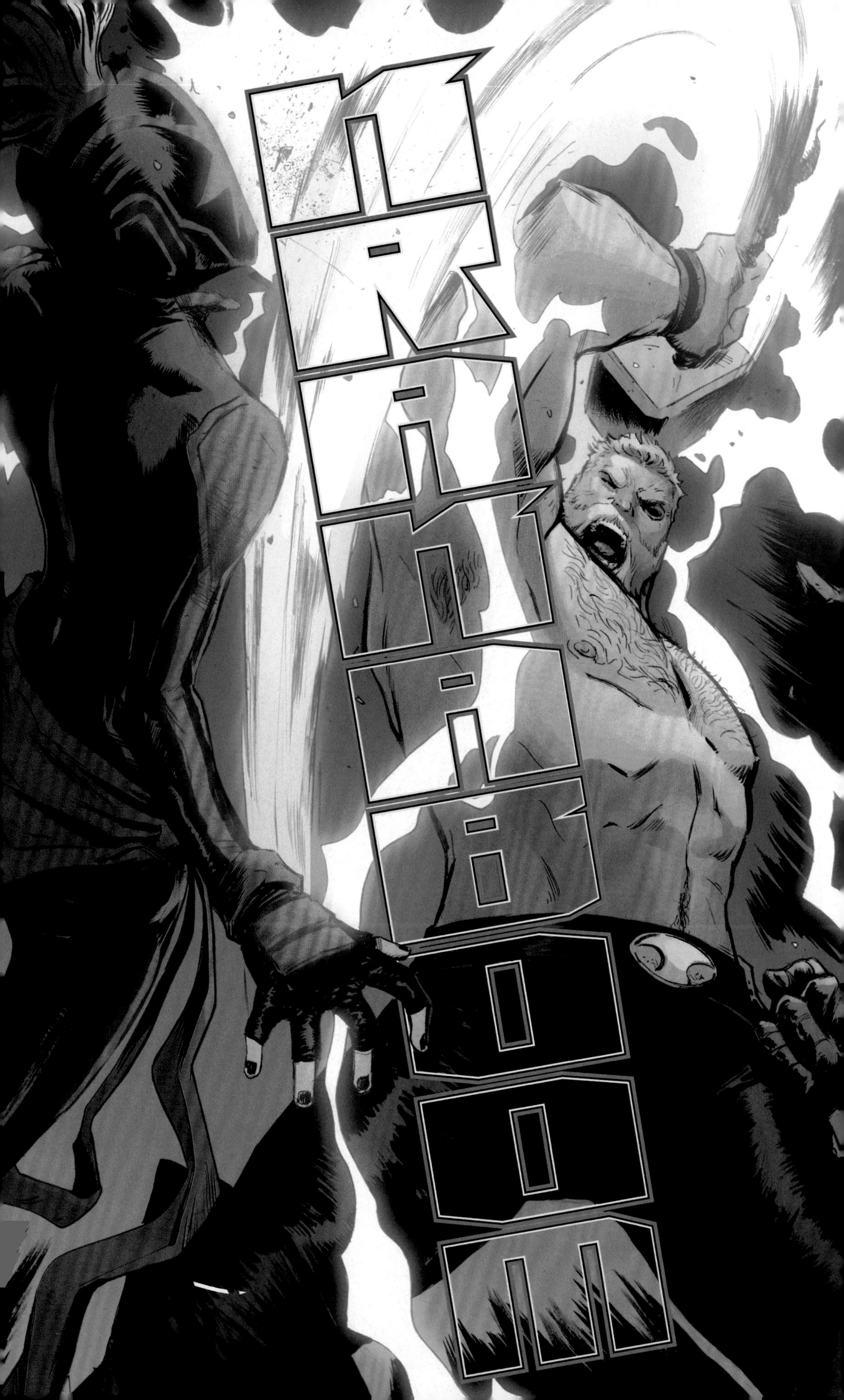
KRAAABOOM

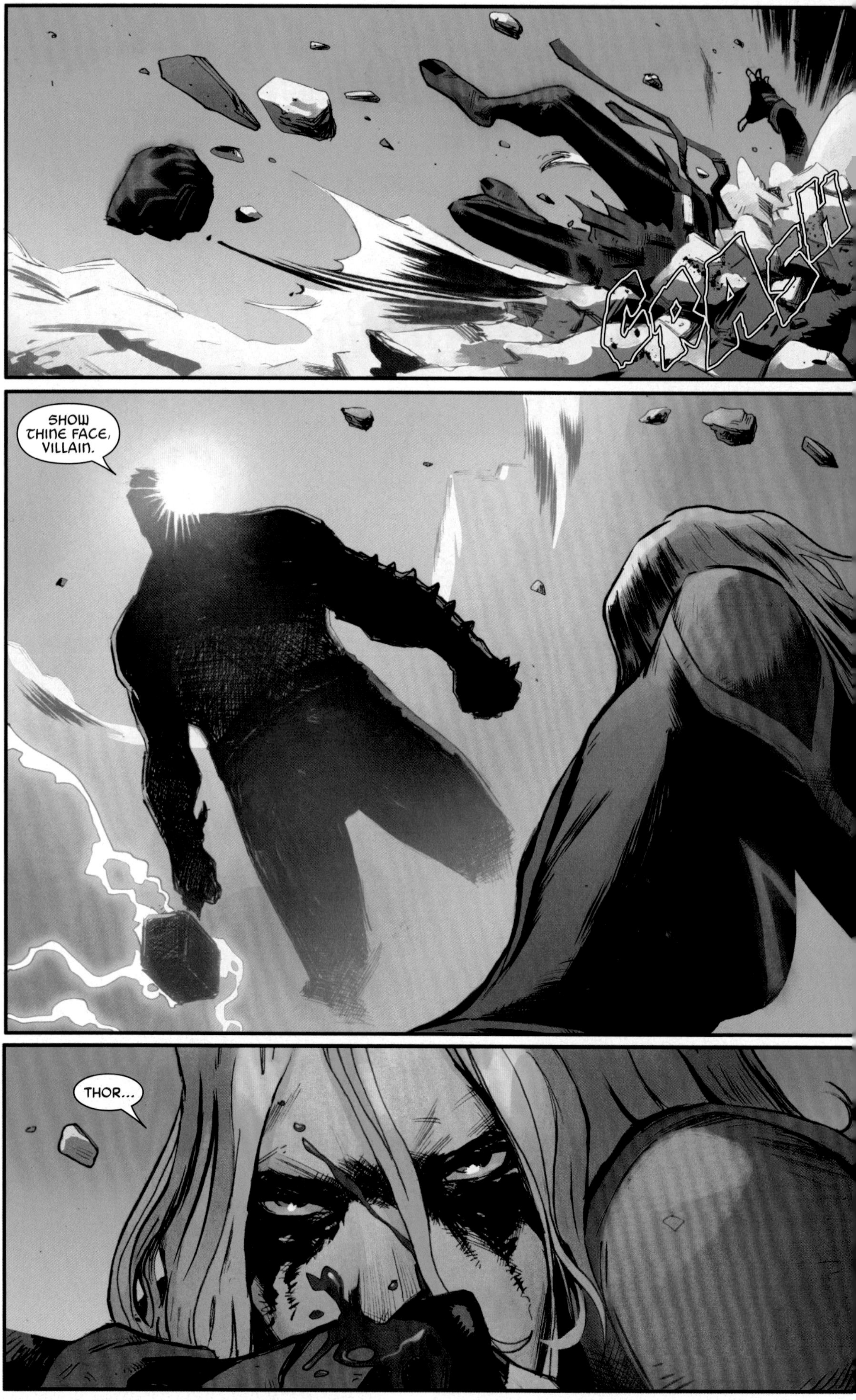
CRASH
SHOW THINE FACE, VILLAIN.
THOR...

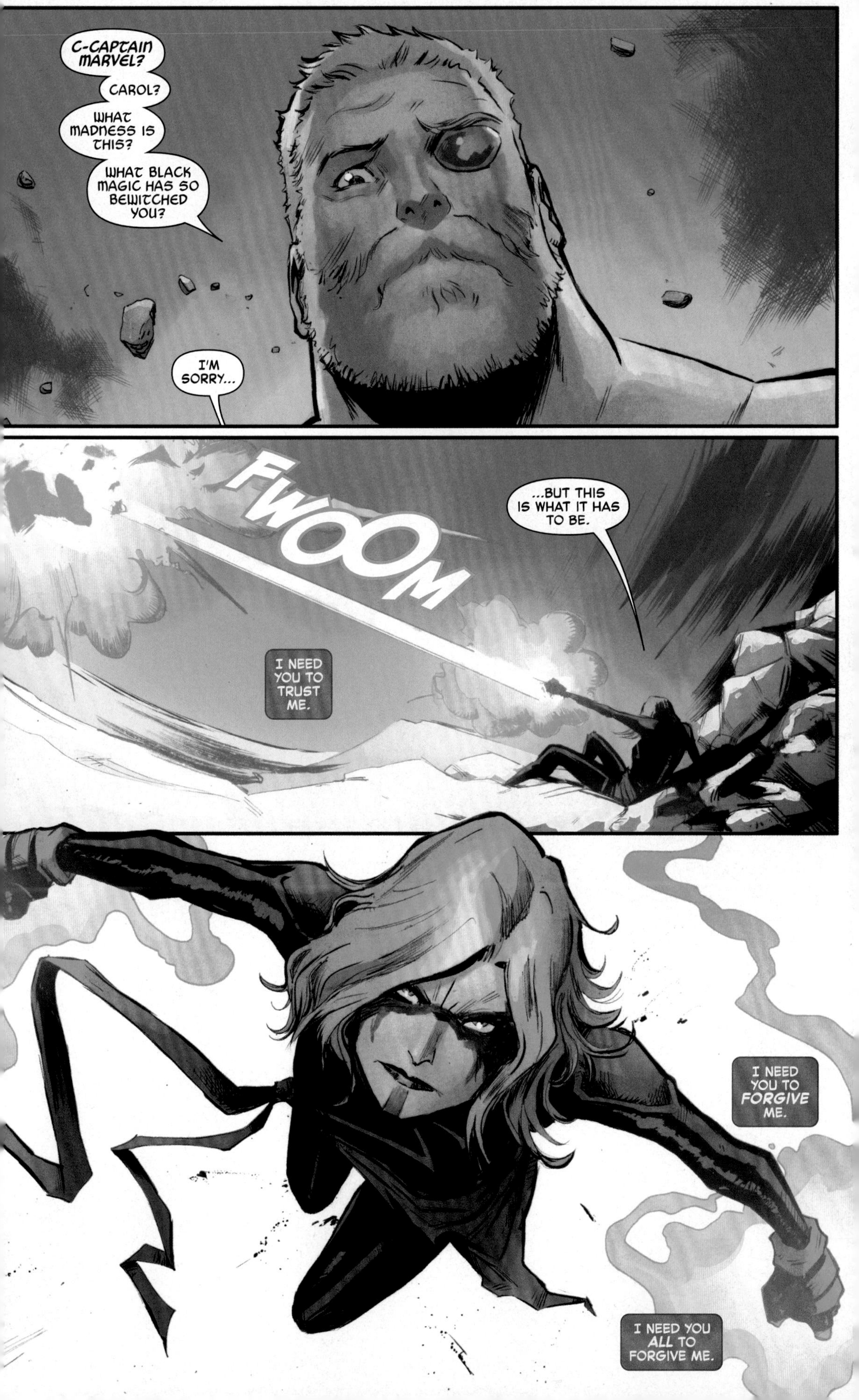
C-CAPTAIN MARVEL?
CAROL?
WHAT MADNESS IS THIS?
WHAT BLACK MAGIC HAS SO BEWITCHED YOU?
I'M SORRY...
FWOOM
...BUT THIS IS WHAT IT HAS TO BE.
I NEED YOU TO TRUST ME.
I NEED YOU TO *FORGIVE* ME.
I NEED YOU *ALL* TO FORGIVE ME.

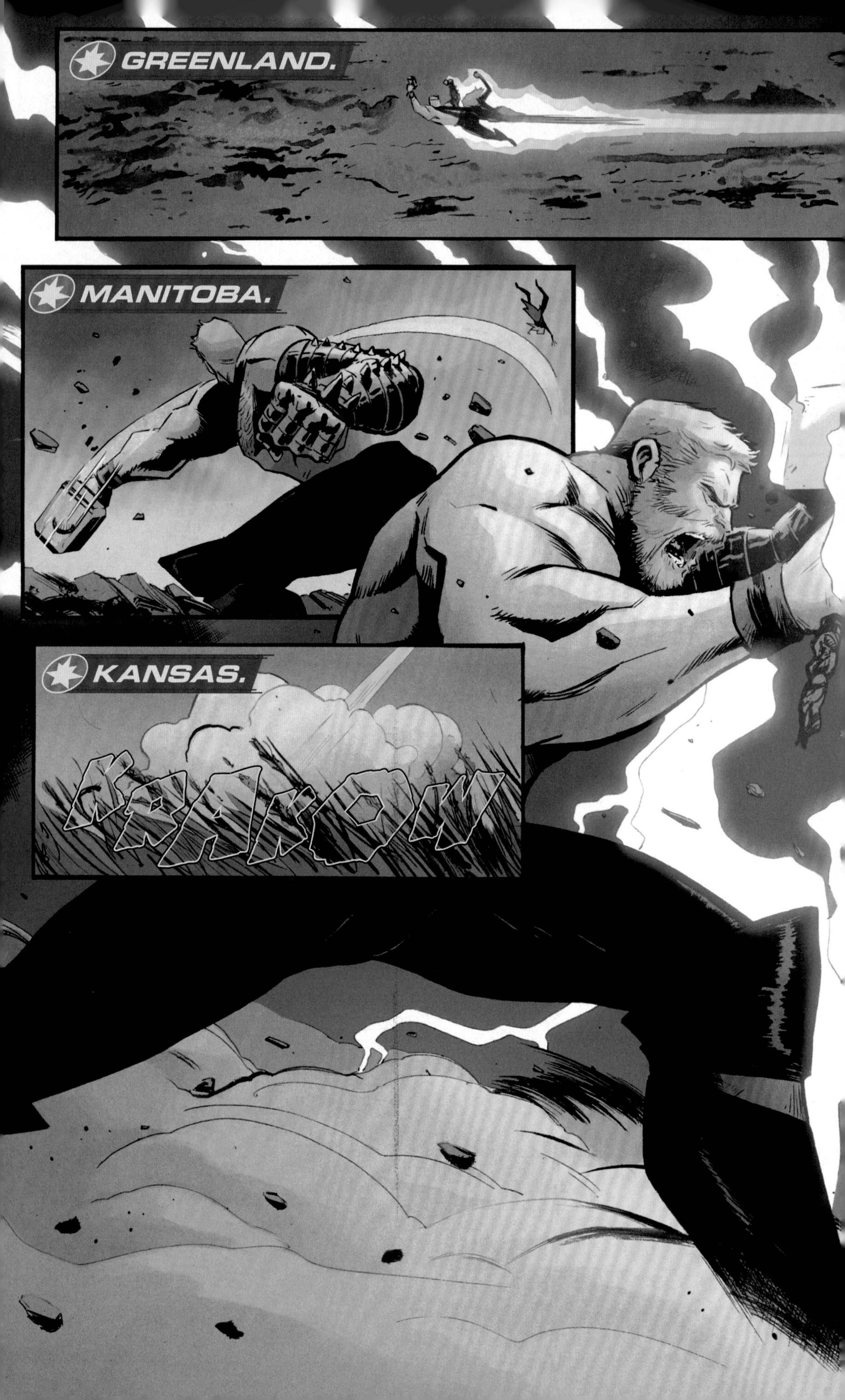
GREENLAND.
MANITOBA.
KANSAS.
KRAKOW

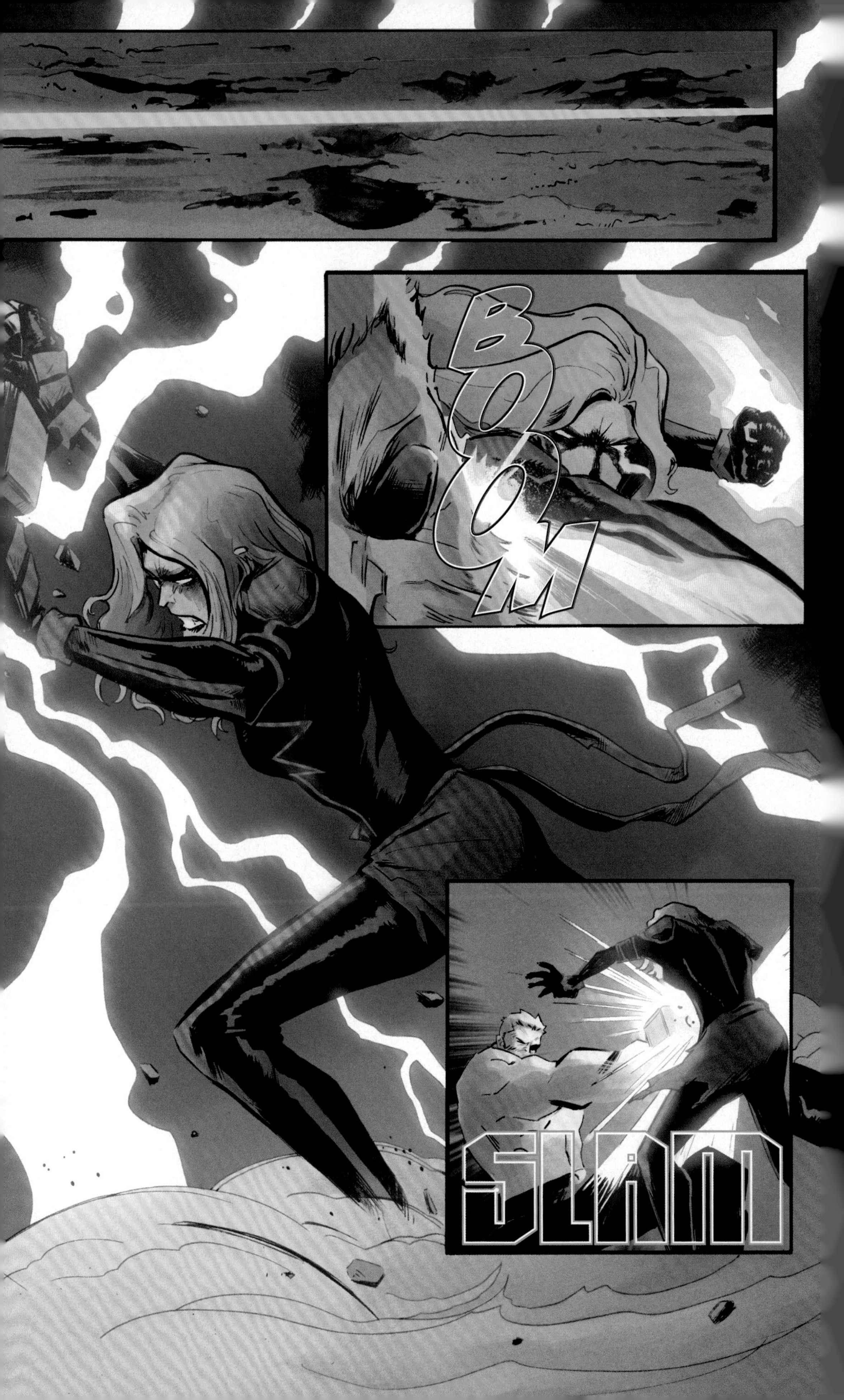
BOOM
SLAM

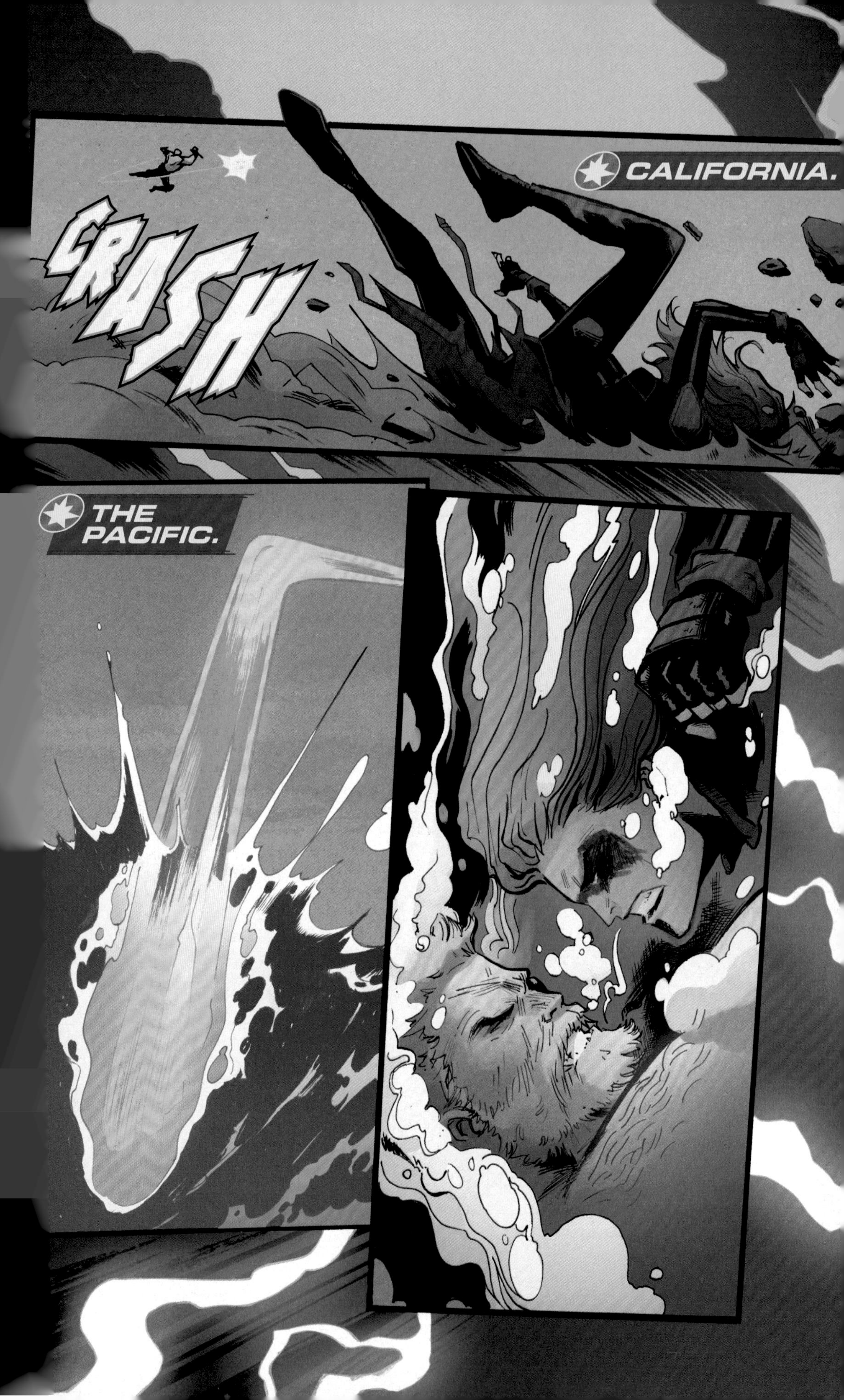
CALIFORNIA.
CRASH
THE PACIFIC.

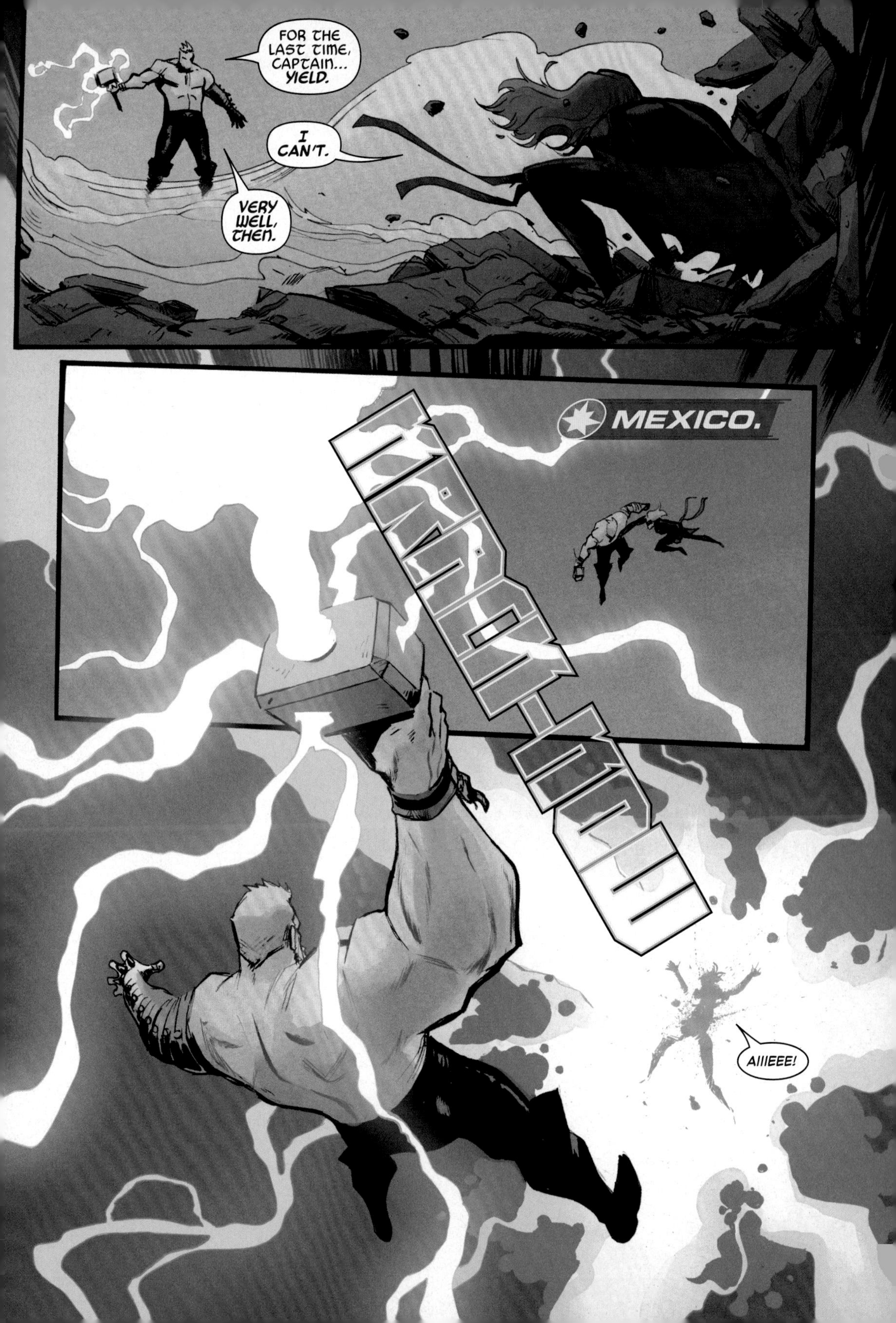

FOR THE LAST TIME, CAPTAIN... YIELD.
I CAN'T.
VERY WELL, THEN.
MEXICO.
AIIIEEE!

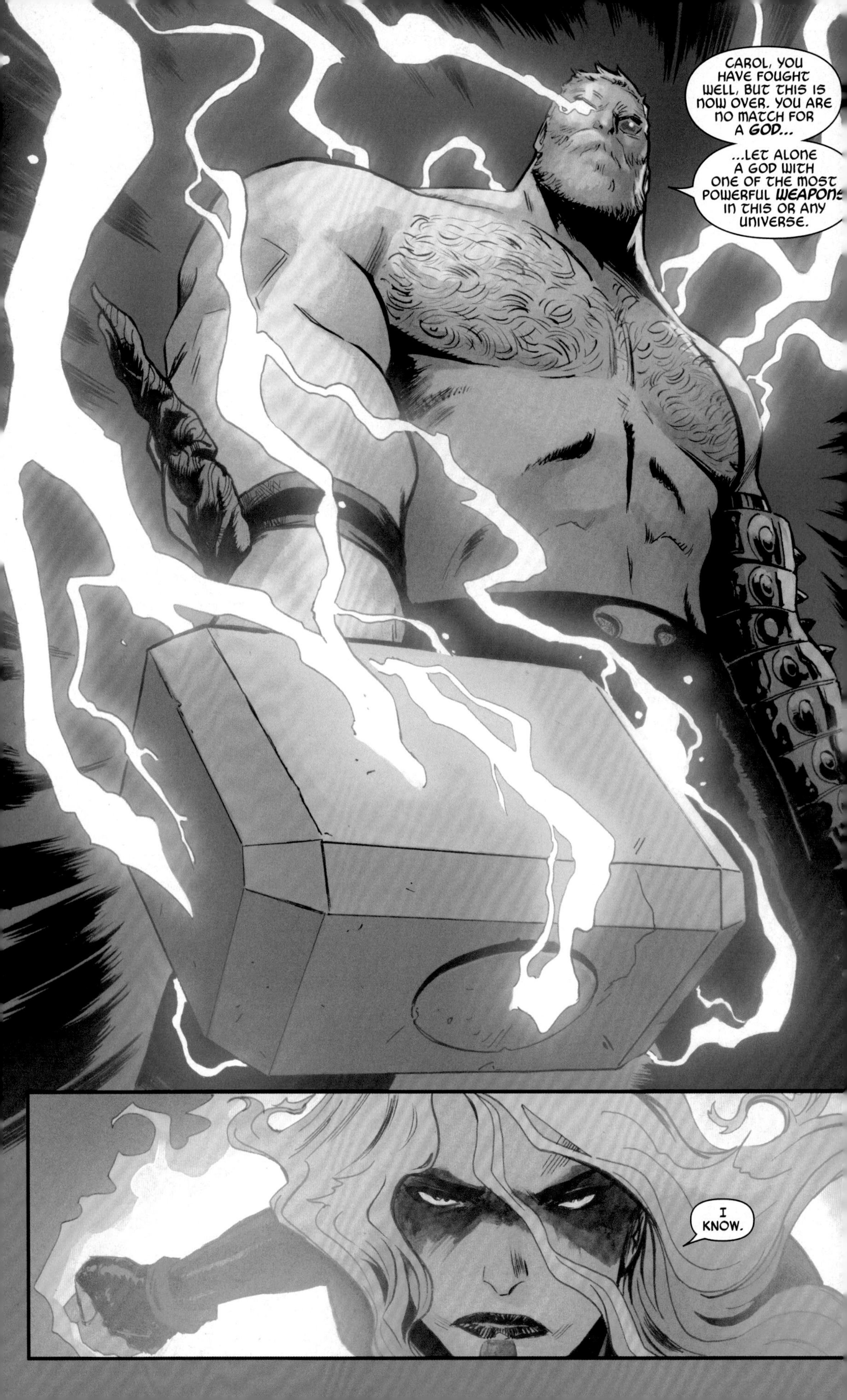
CAROL, YOU HAVE FOUGHT WELL, BUT THIS IS NOW OVER. YOU ARE NO MATCH FOR A GOD...
...LET ALONE A GOD WITH ONE OF THE MOST POWERFUL WEAPONS IN THIS OR ANY UNIVERSE.
I KNOW.

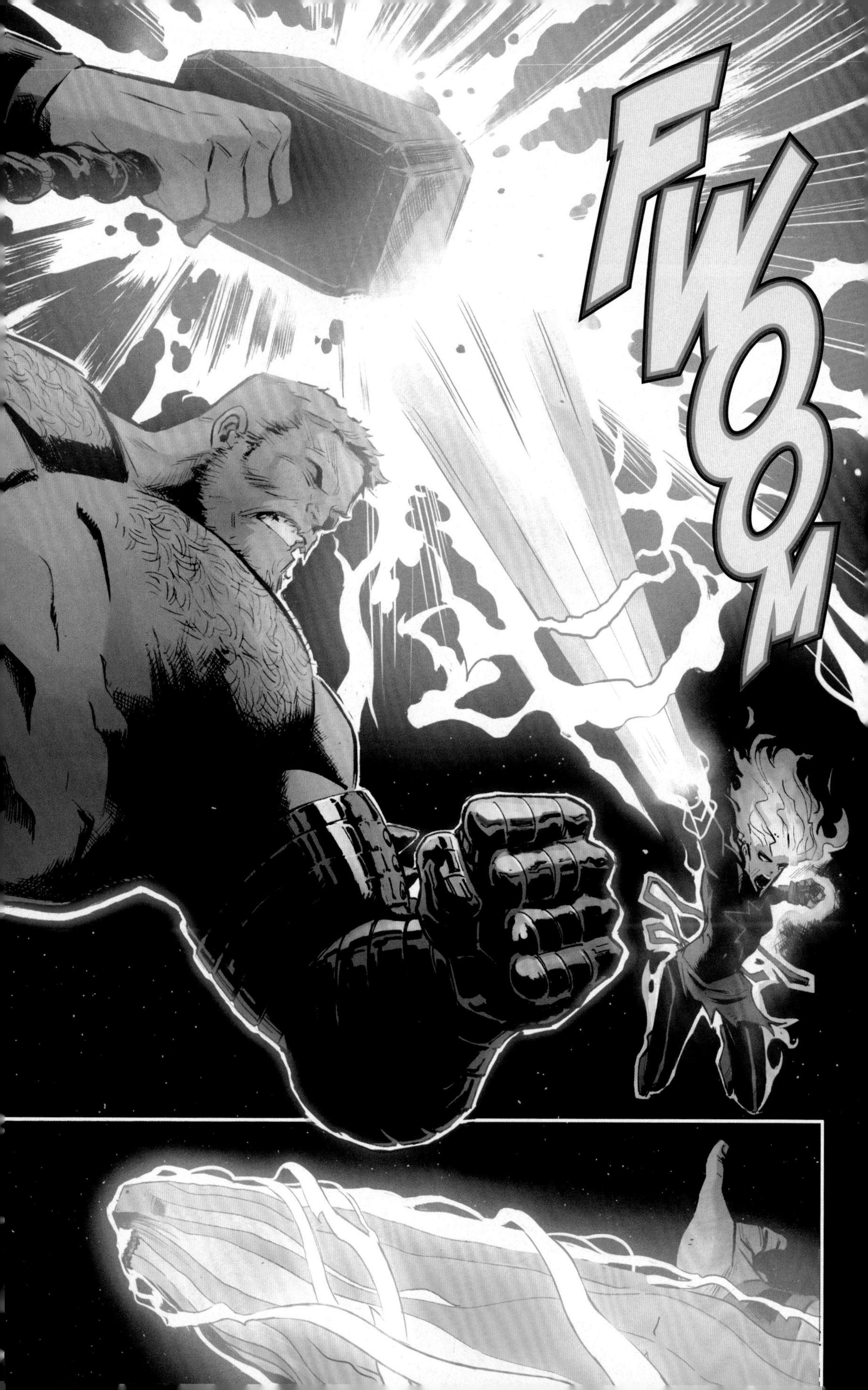
FWOOM

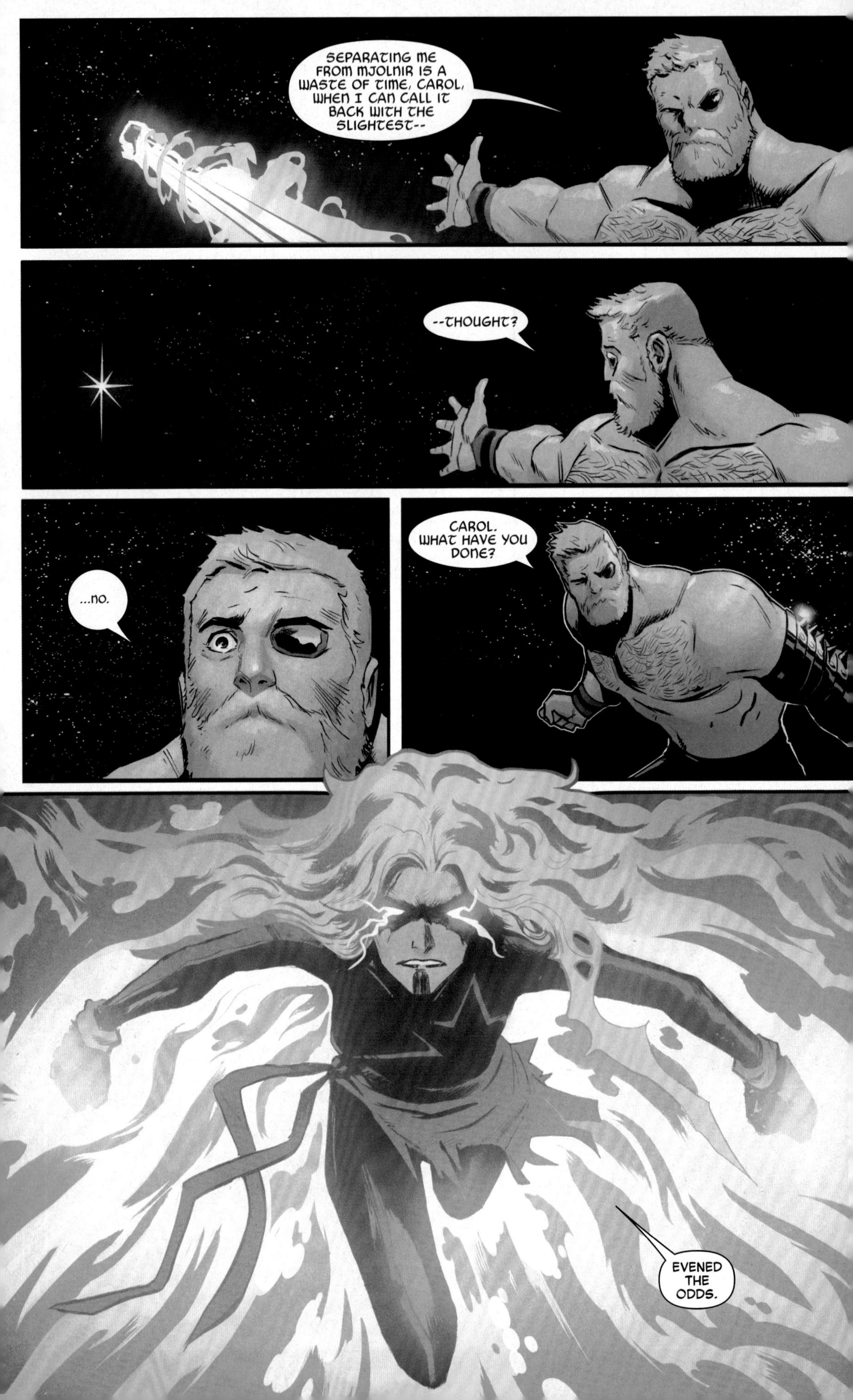
SEPARATING ME FROM MJOLNIR IS A WASTE OF TIME, CAROL, WHEN I CAN CALL IT BACK WITH THE SLIGHTEST--
--THOUGHT?
...no.
CAROL. WHAT HAVE YOU DONE?
EVENED THE ODDS.

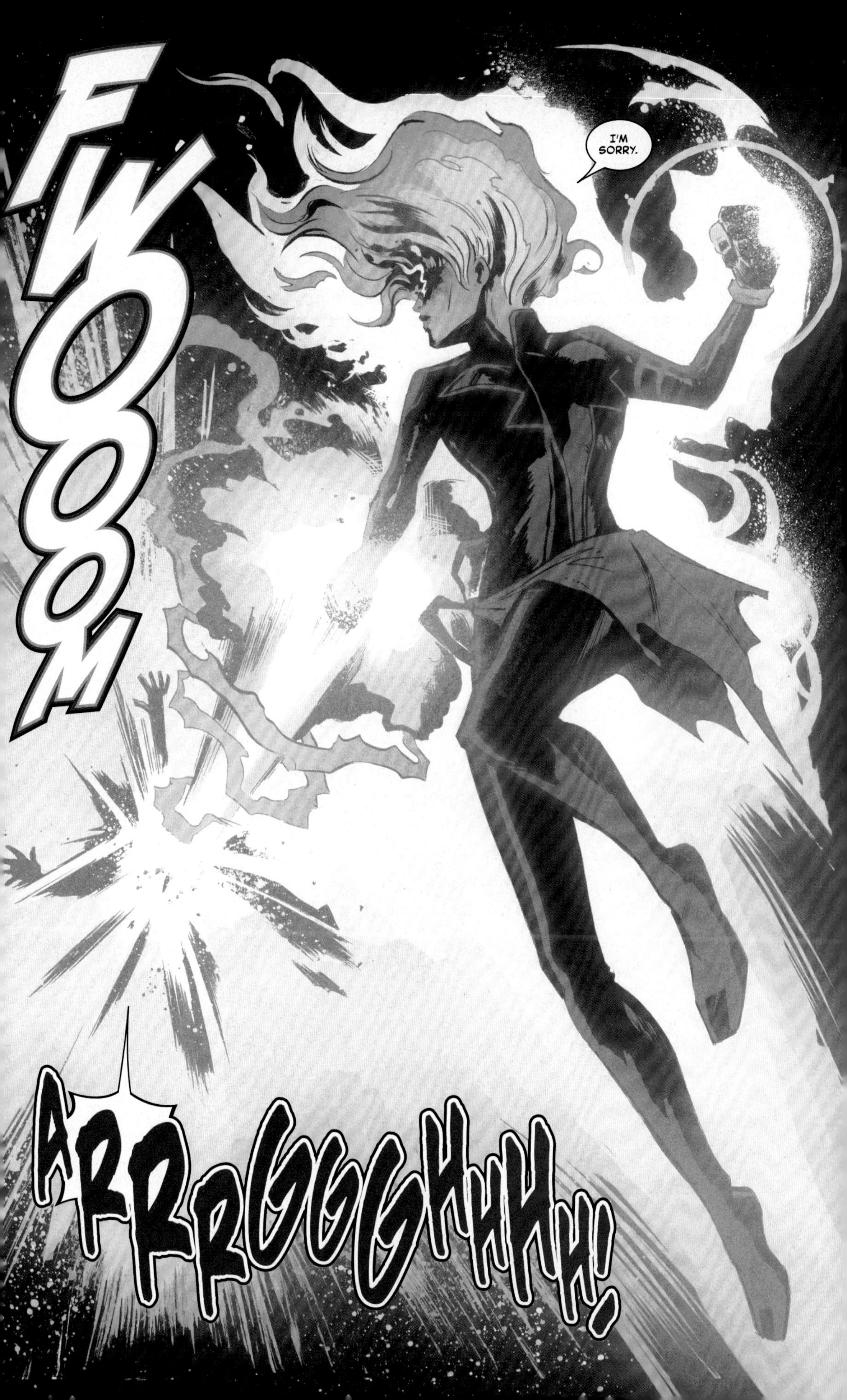
FWOOOM
I'M SORRY.
ARRRGGGHHHH!

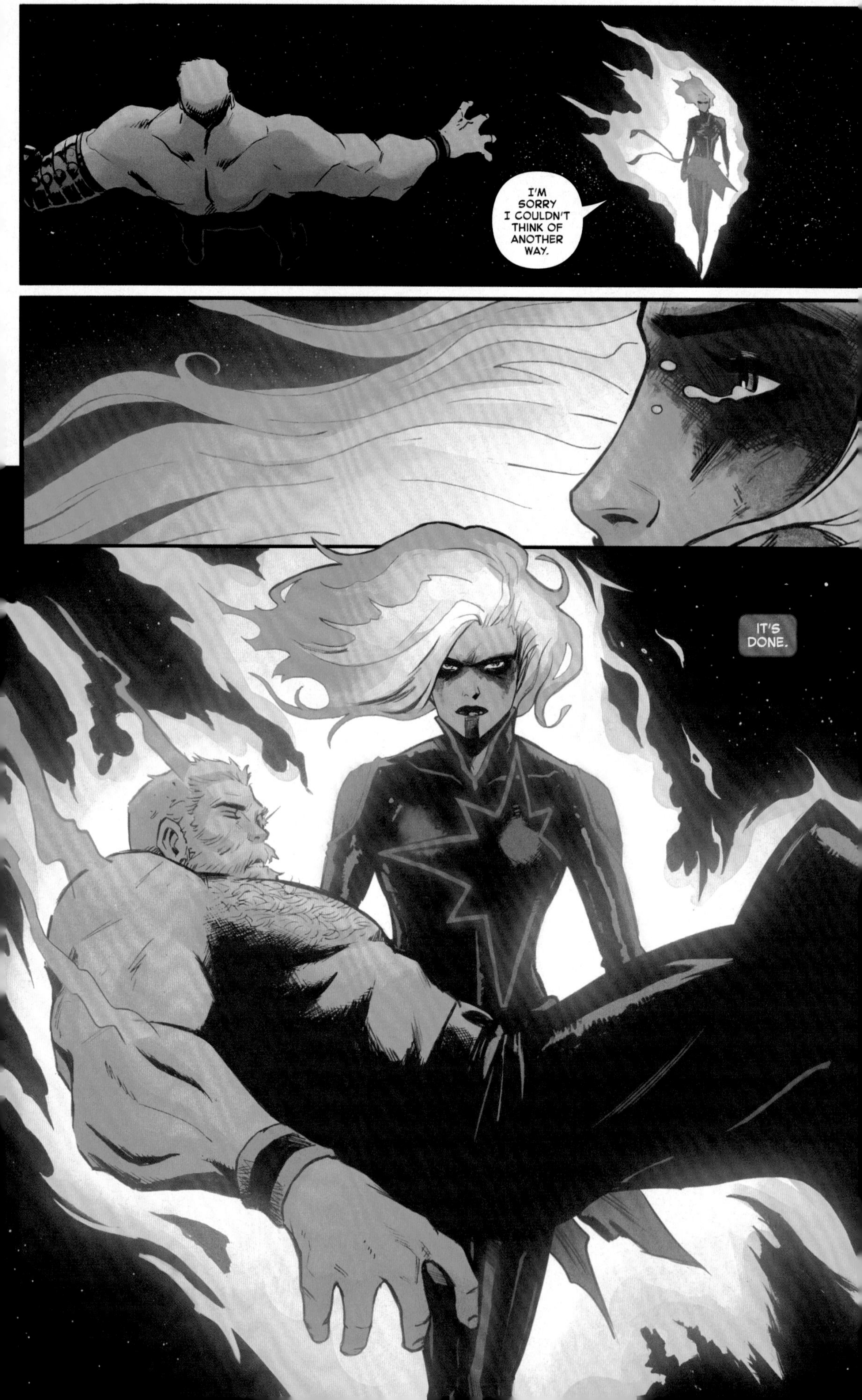
I'M SORRY I COULDN'T THINK OF ANOTHER WAY.
IT'S DONE.

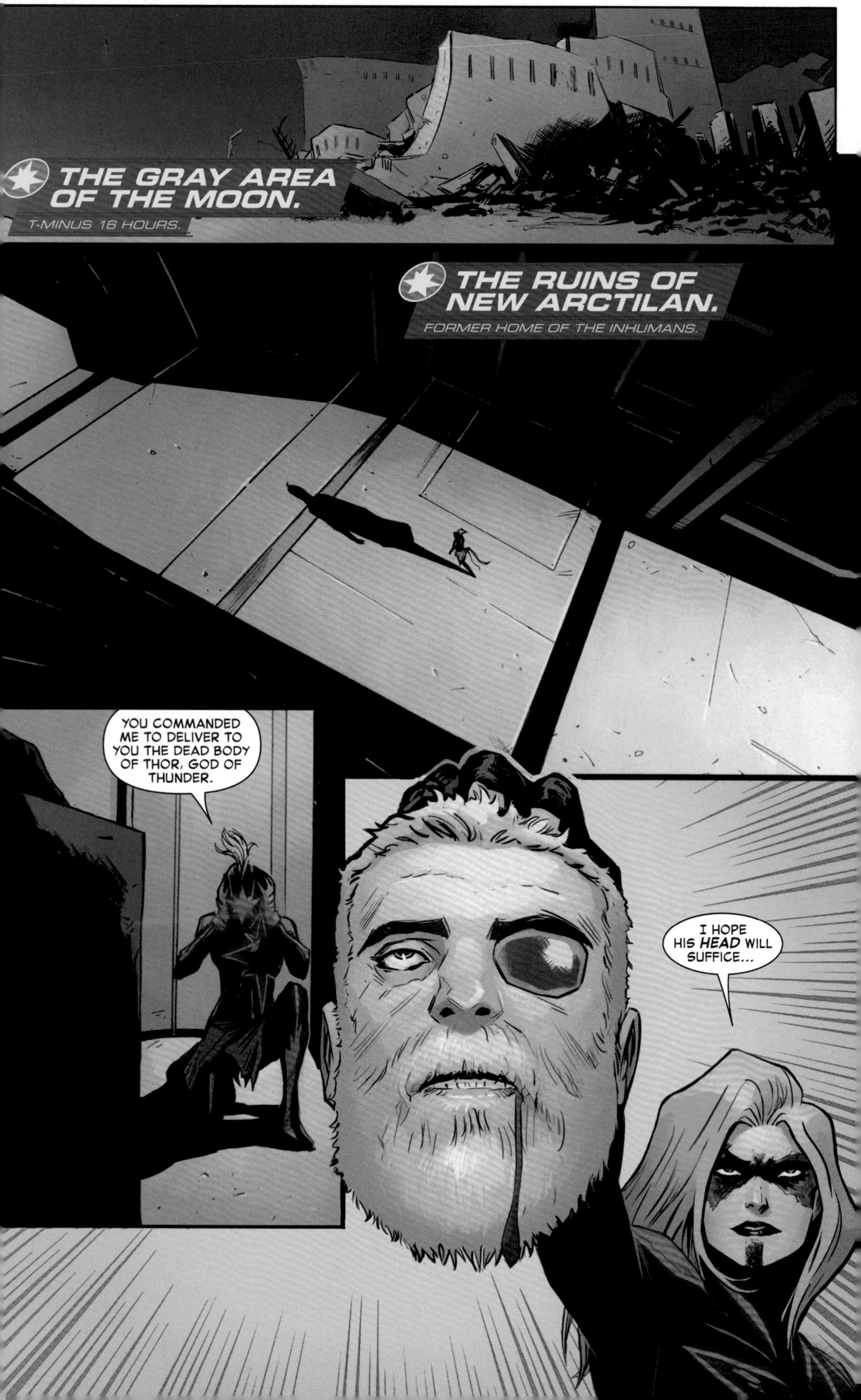
THE GRAY AREA OF THE MOON.
T-MINUS 16 HOURS.
THE RUINS OF NEW ARCTILAN.
FORMER HOME OF THE INHUMANS.
YOU COMMANDED ME TO DELIVER TO YOU THE DEAD BODY OF THOR, GOD OF THUNDER.
I HOPE HIS HEAD WILL SUFFICE...

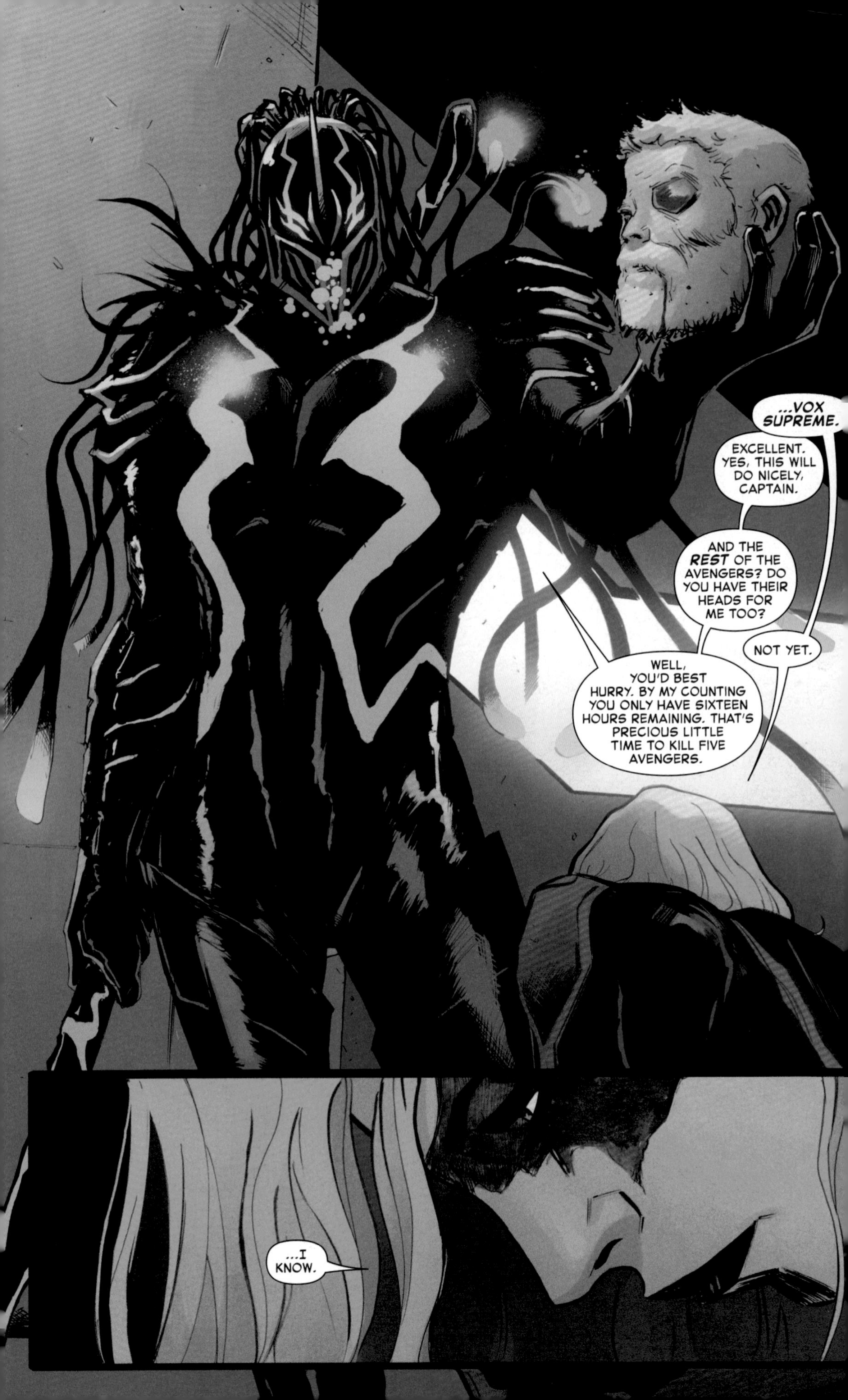
...VOX SUPREME.
EXCELLENT. YES, THIS WILL DO NICELY, CAPTAIN.
AND THE REST OF THE AVENGERS? DO YOU HAVE THEIR HEADS FOR ME TOO?
NOT YET.
WELL, YOU'D BEST HURRY. BY MY COUNTING YOU ONLY HAVE SIXTEEN HOURS REMAINING. THAT'S PRECIOUS LITTLE TIME TO KILL FIVE AVENGERS.
...I KNOW.

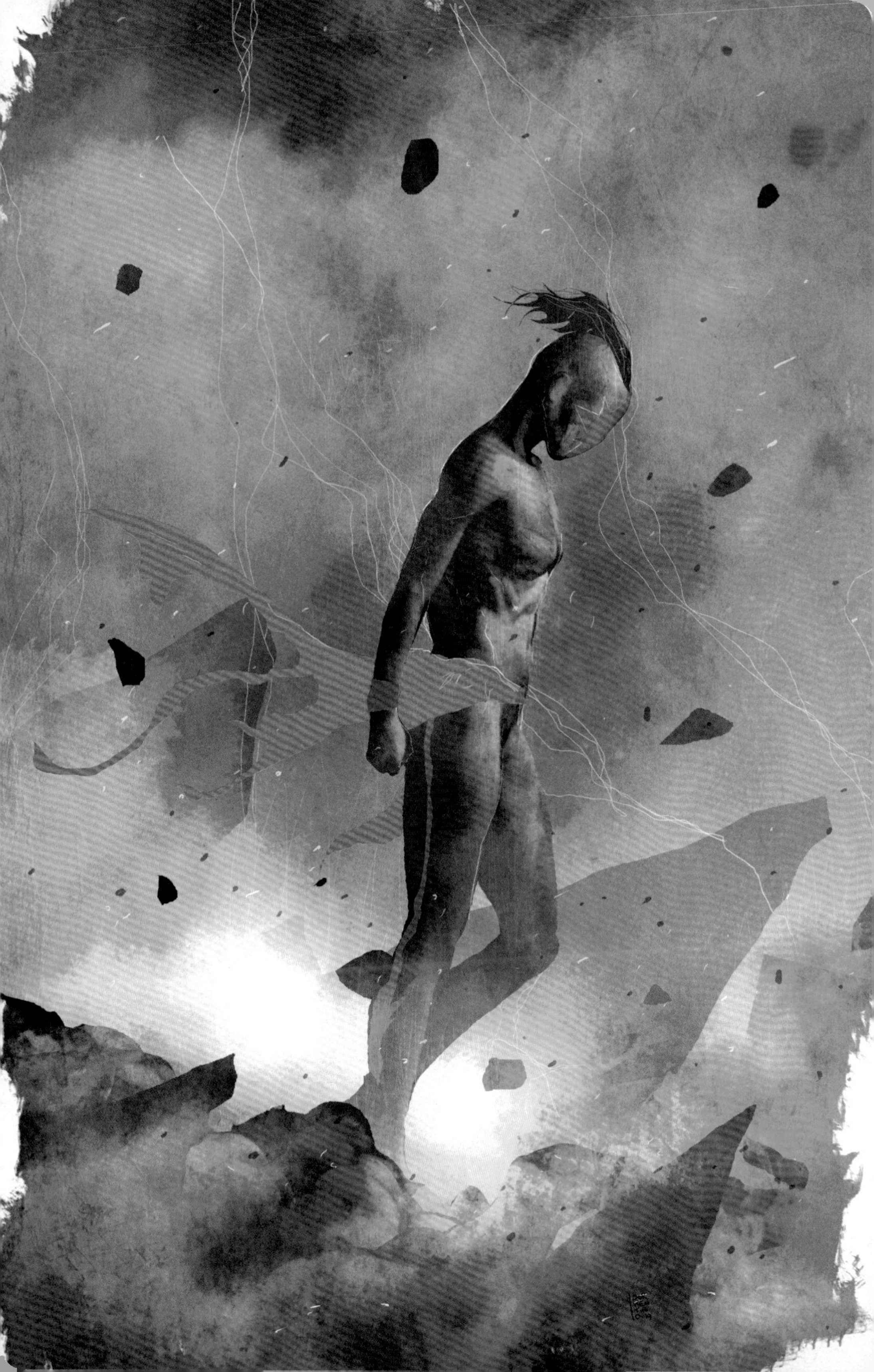

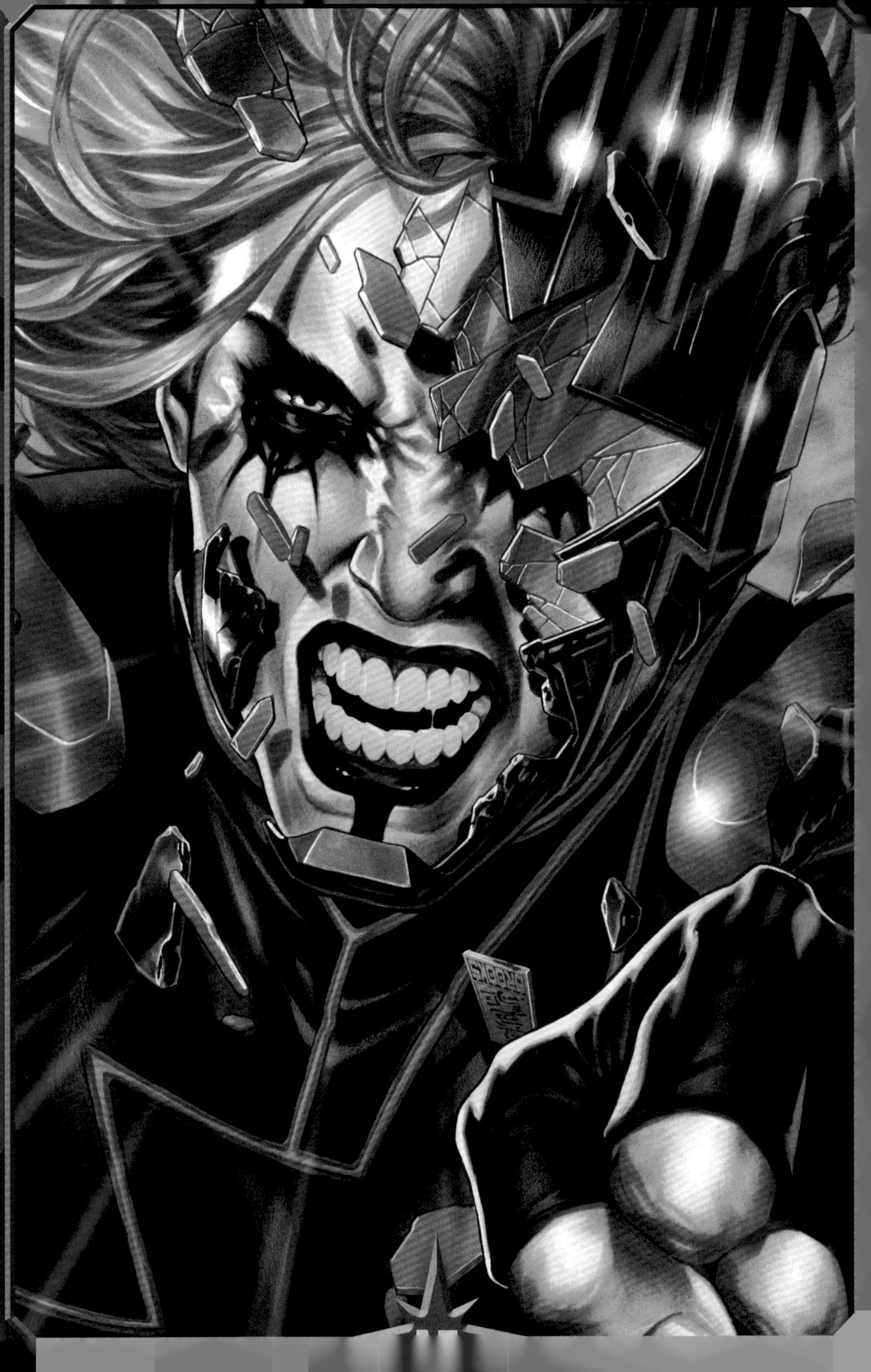

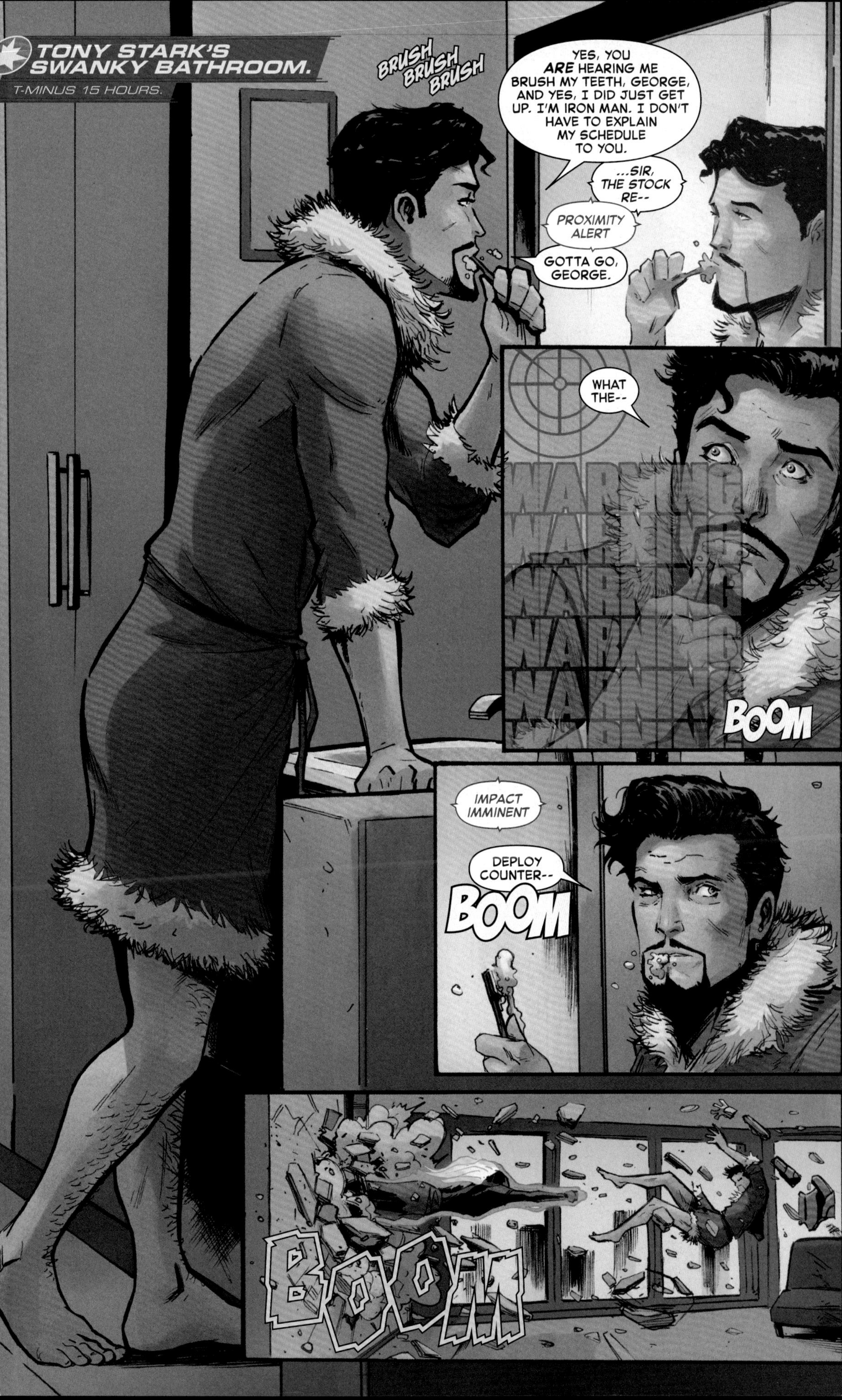
TONY STARK'S SWANKY BATHROOM.
T-MINUS 15 HOURS.
BRUSH BRUSH BRUSH
YES, YOU ARE HEARING ME BRUSH MY TEETH, GEORGE, AND YES, I DID JUST GET UP. I'M IRON MAN. I DON'T HAVE TO EXPLAIN MY SCHEDULE TO YOU.
...SIR, THE STOCK RE--
PROXIMITY ALERT
GOTTA GO, GEORGE.
WHAT THE--
WARNING
WARNING
WARNING
WARNING
WARNING
BOOM
IMPACT IMMINENT
DEPLOY COUNTER--
BOOM
BOOM

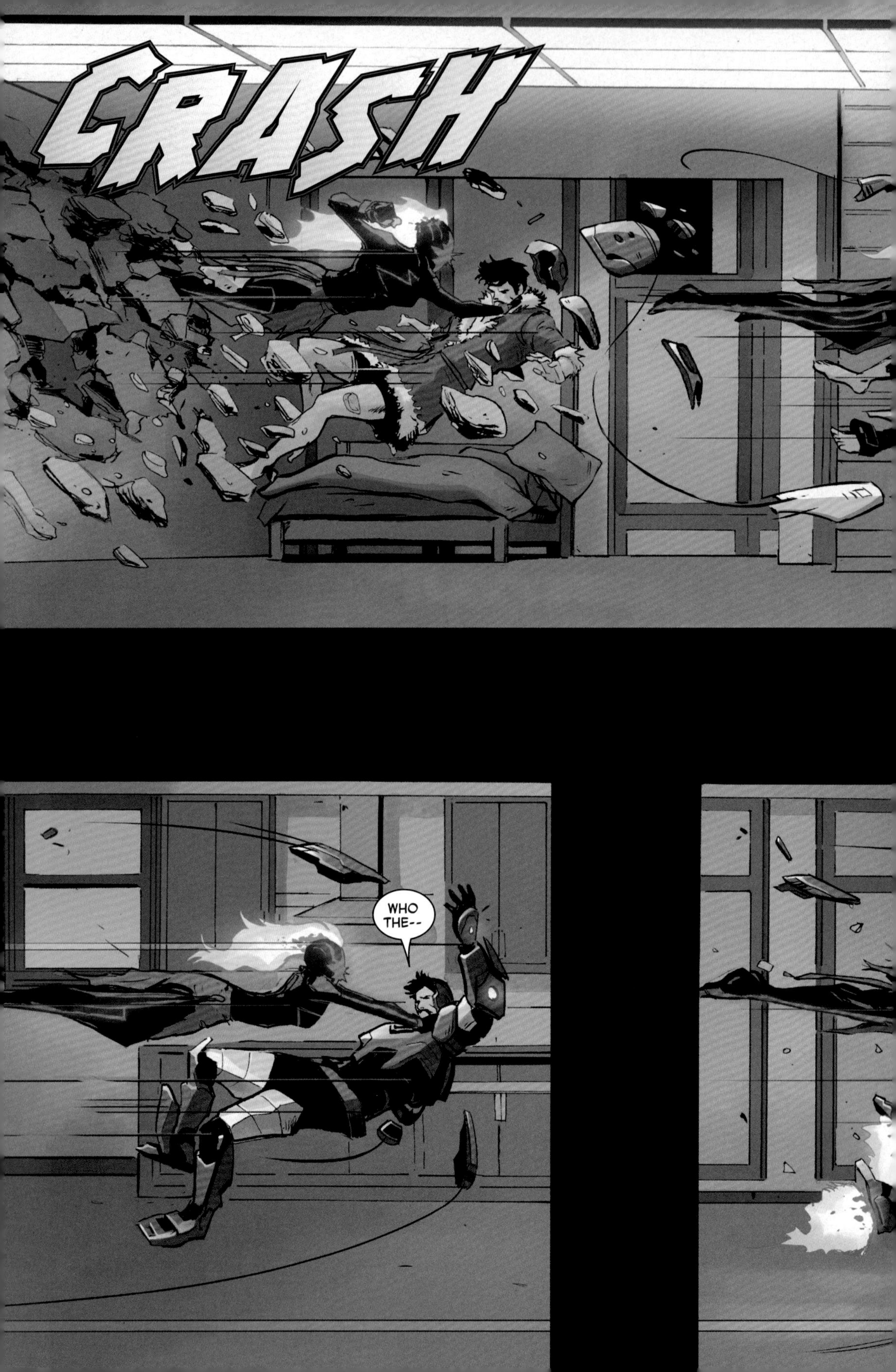
CRASH
WHO THE--

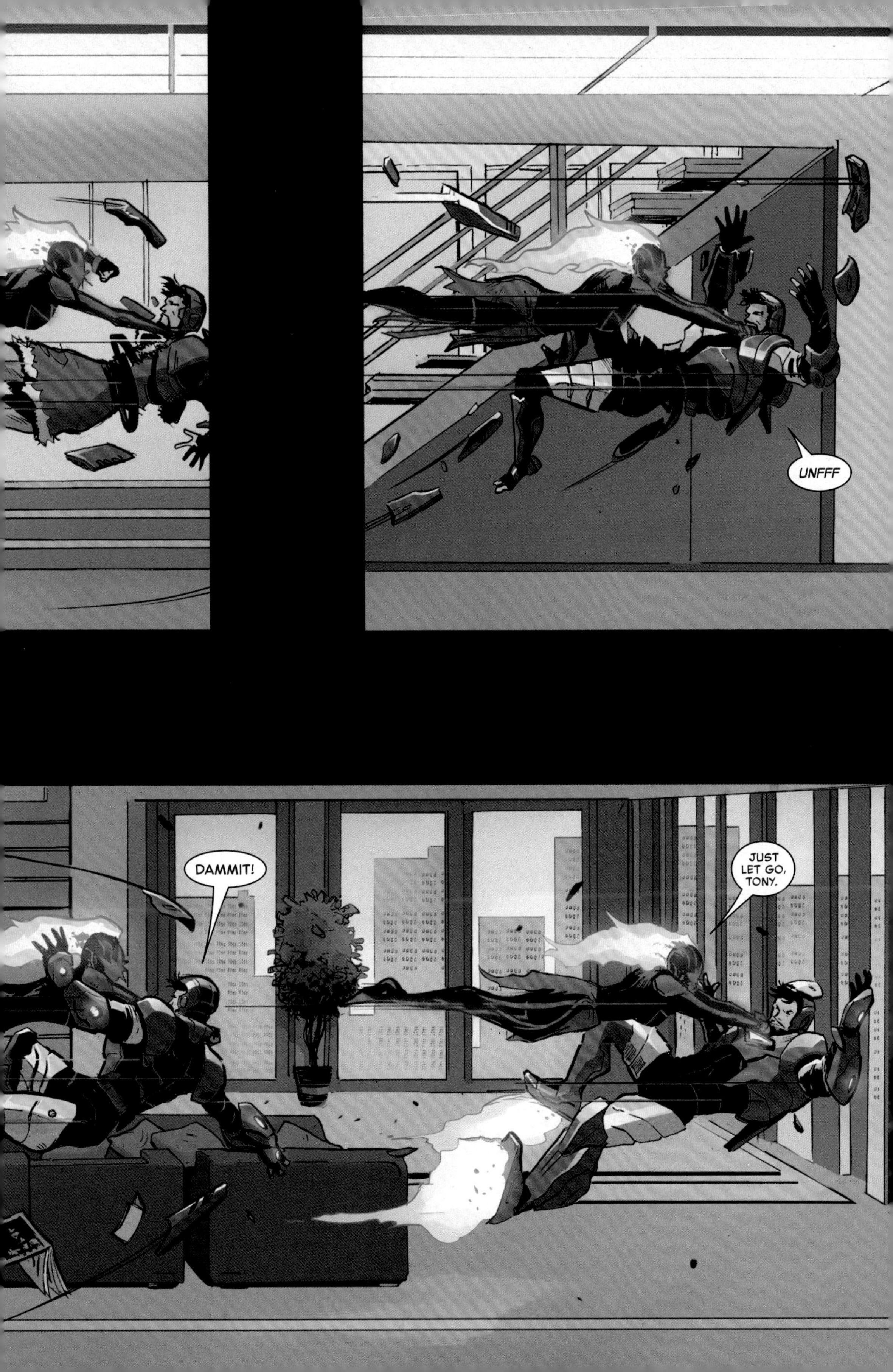
UNFFF
DAMMIT!
JUST LET GO, TONY.

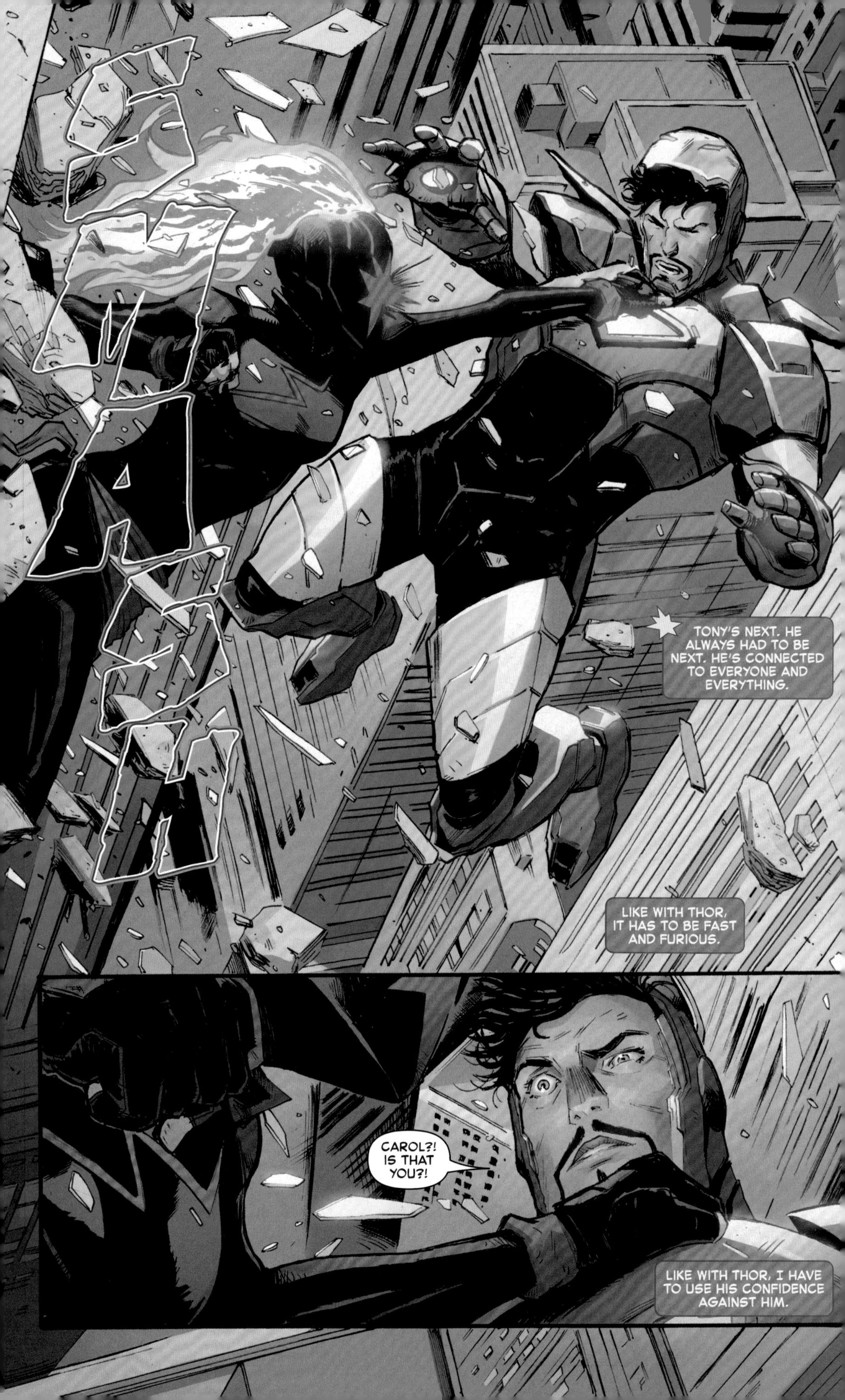
TONY'S NEXT. HE ALWAYS HAD TO BE NEXT. HE'S CONNECTED TO EVERYONE AND EVERYTHING.
LIKE WITH THOR, IT HAS TO BE FAST AND FURIOUS.
CAROL?! IS THAT YOU?!
LIKE WITH THOR, I HAVE TO USE HIS CONFIDENCE AGAINST HIM.

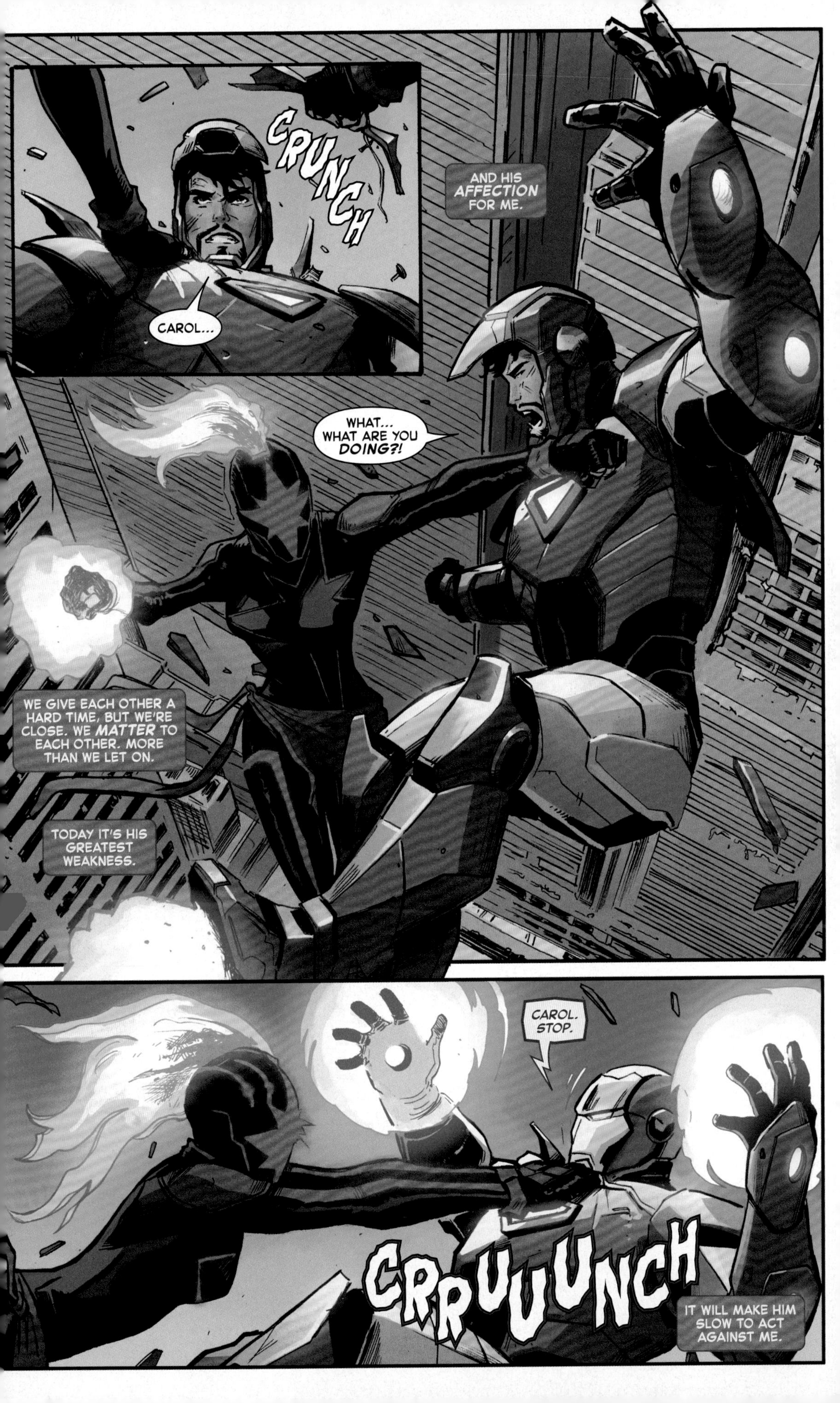
CRUNCH
CAROL...
AND HIS AFFECTION FOR ME.
WHAT... WHAT ARE YOU DOING?!
WE GIVE EACH OTHER A HARD TIME, BUT WE'RE CLOSE. WE MATTER TO EACH OTHER. MORE THAN WE LET ON.
TODAY IT'S HIS GREATEST WEAKNESS.
CAROL. STOP.
CRRUUUNCH
IT WILL MAKE HIM SLOW TO ACT AGAINST ME.

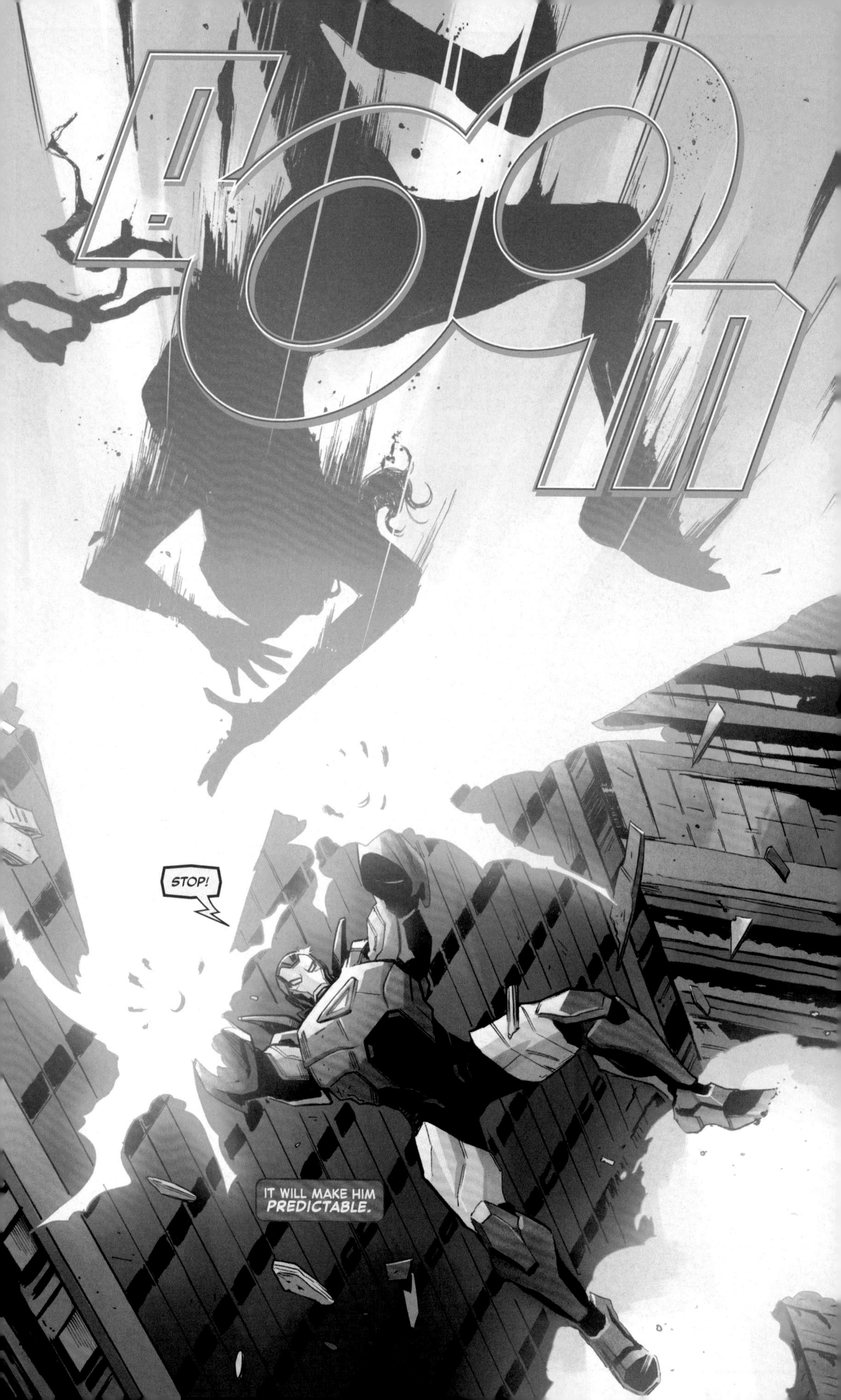
BOOM
STOP!
IT WILL MAKE HIM PREDICTABLE.

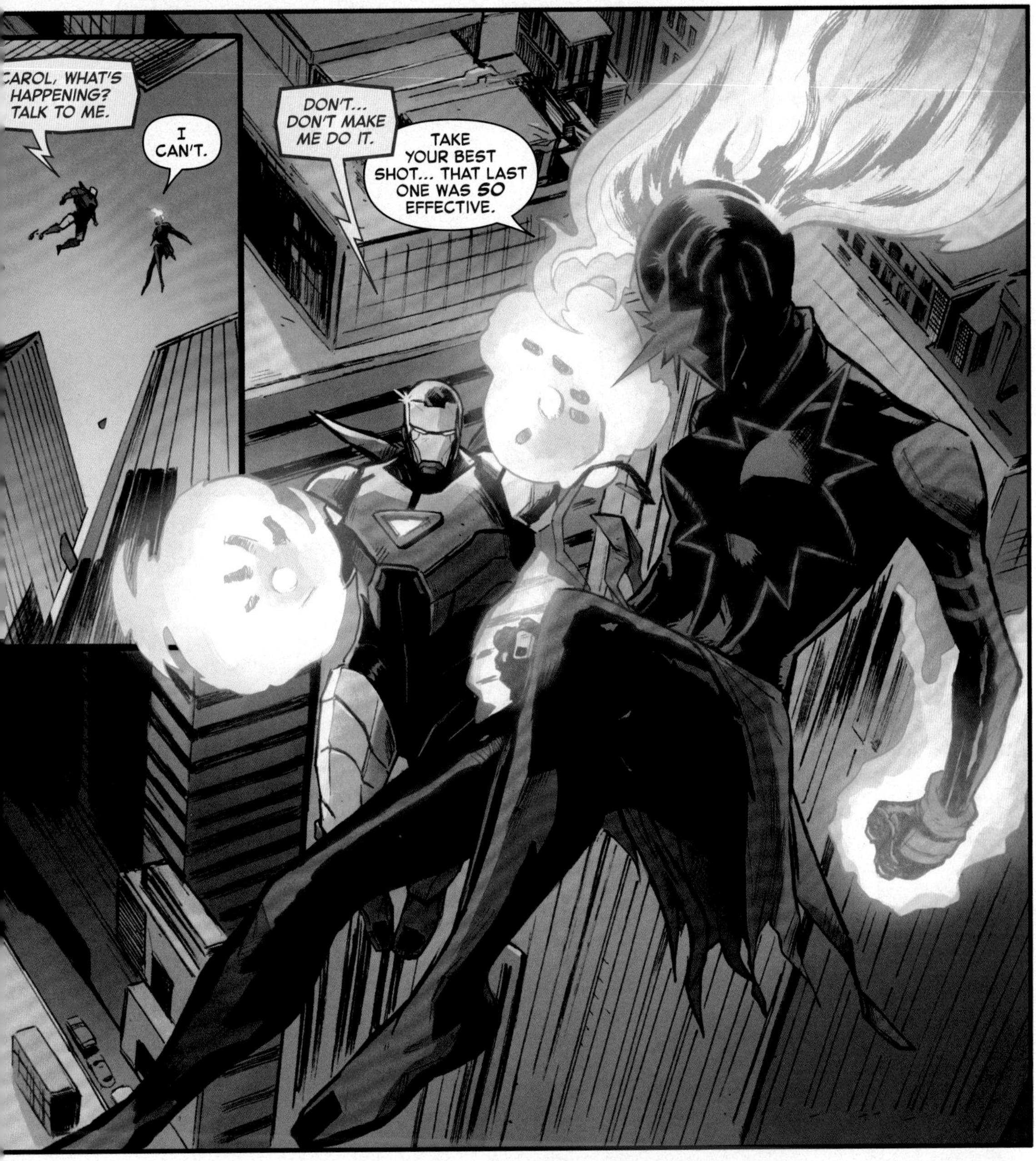
CAROL, WHAT'S HAPPENING? TALK TO ME.
I CAN'T.
DON'T... DON'T MAKE ME DO IT.
TAKE YOUR BEST SHOT... THAT LAST ONE WAS SO EFFECTIVE.

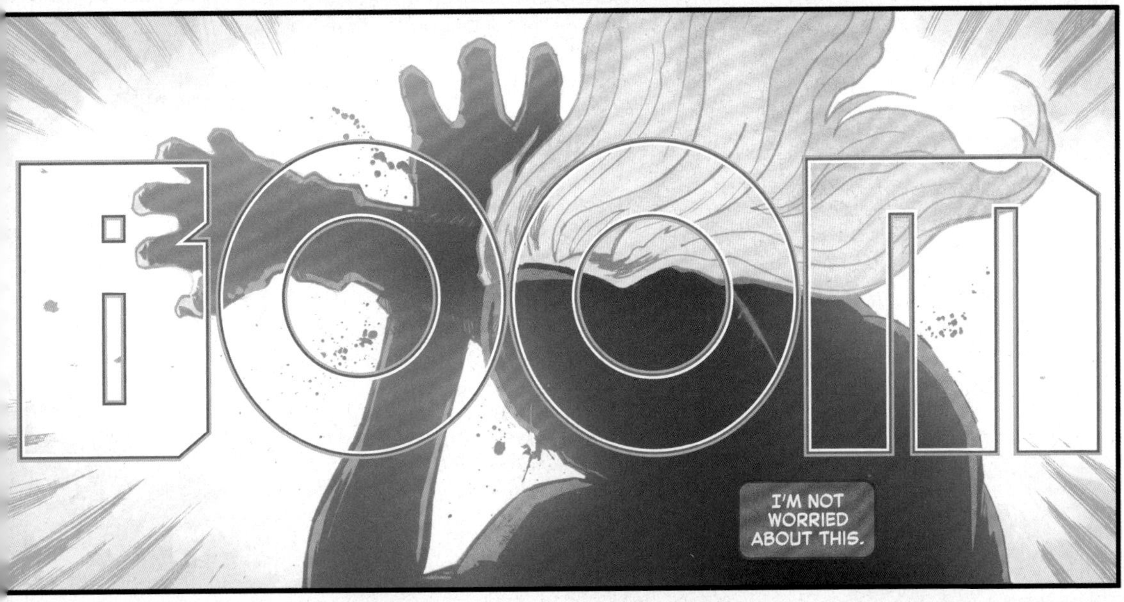
BOOM
I'M NOT WORRIED ABOUT THIS.

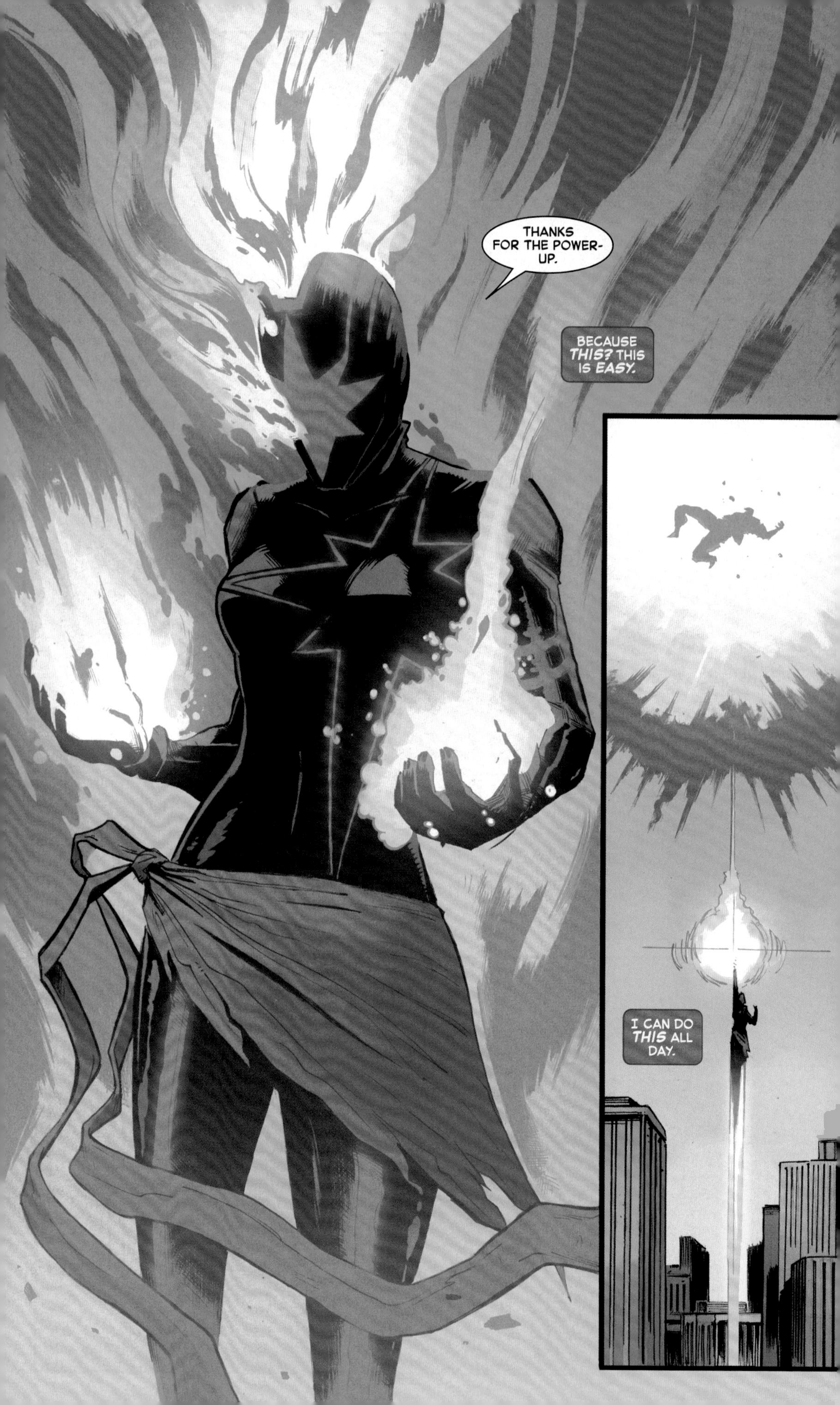
THANKS FOR THE POWER-UP.
BECAUSE THIS? THIS IS EASY.
I CAN DO THIS ALL DAY.

WHAT I'M WORRIED ABOUT IS *TIME*.

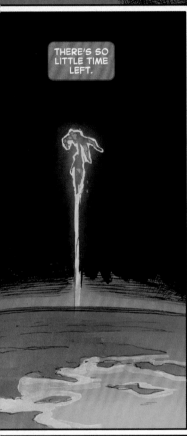

THERE'S SO LITTLE TIME LEFT.

HNNNG--CAROL--I DON'T KNOW WHAT'S HAPPENING...BUT YOU CAN'T WIN THIS. EVEN IF YOU CAN GET PAST ME...AND YOU CAN'T...YOU THINK THE *REST* OF THE AVENGERS WON'T TEAR YOU APART?

TONY. I ALREADY KILLED A GOD TODAY. YOU'RE JUST A GUY IN A FANCY SUIT.

I WORRY ABOUT TIME, AND ONE *OTHER* THING.

WRONG. I'M A GUY IN AN *AMAZING* SUIT...

...WITH AN *ARMY* OF ROBOTS.

THAT THING. THE ARMY THING.

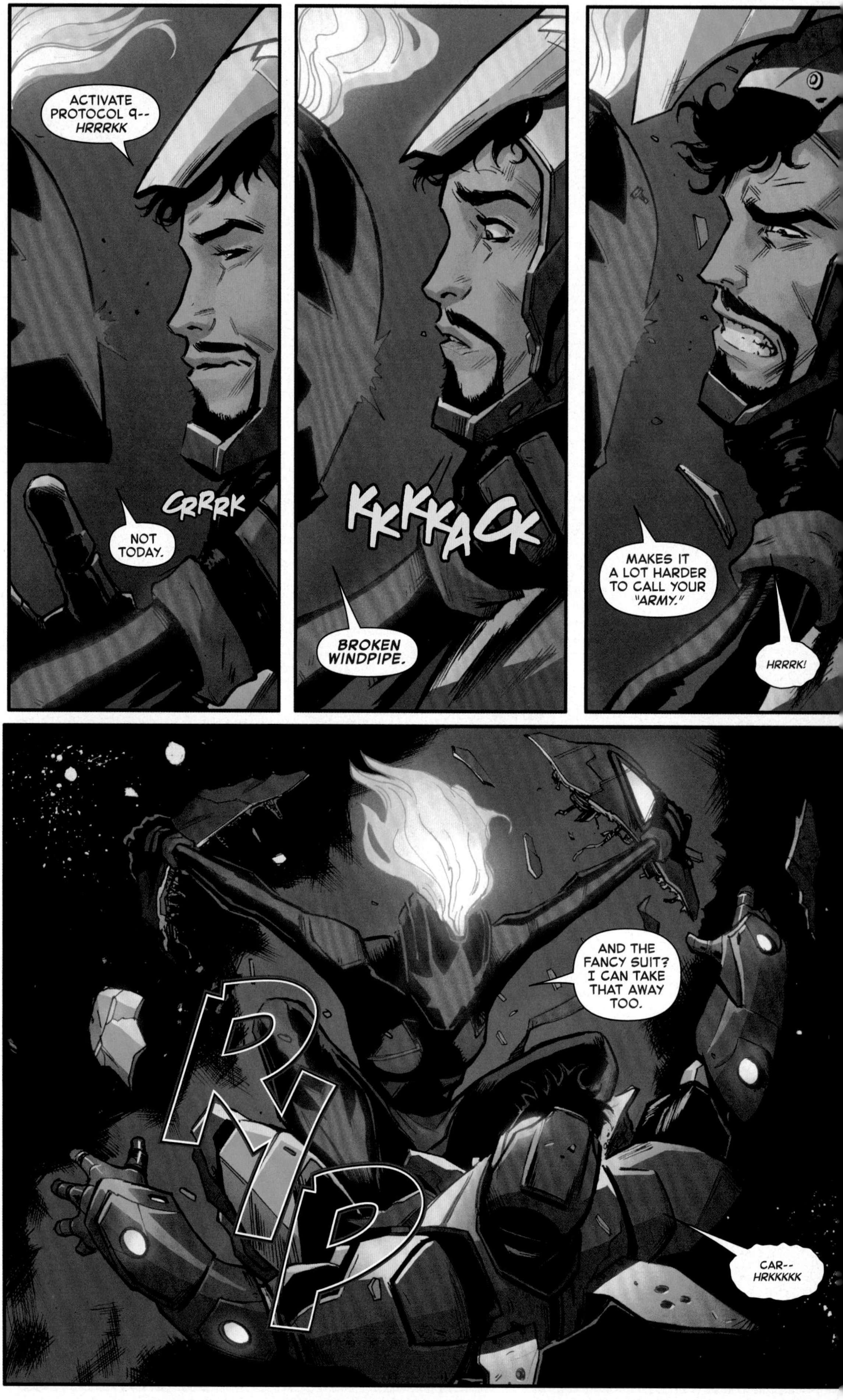
ACTIVATE PROTOCOL 9-- HRRRKK
CRRRK
NOT TODAY.
KKKKKACK
BROKEN WINDPIPE.
MAKES IT A LOT HARDER TO CALL YOUR "ARMY."
HRRRK!
RIP
AND THE FANCY SUIT? I CAN TAKE THAT AWAY TOO.
CAR-- HRKKKKK

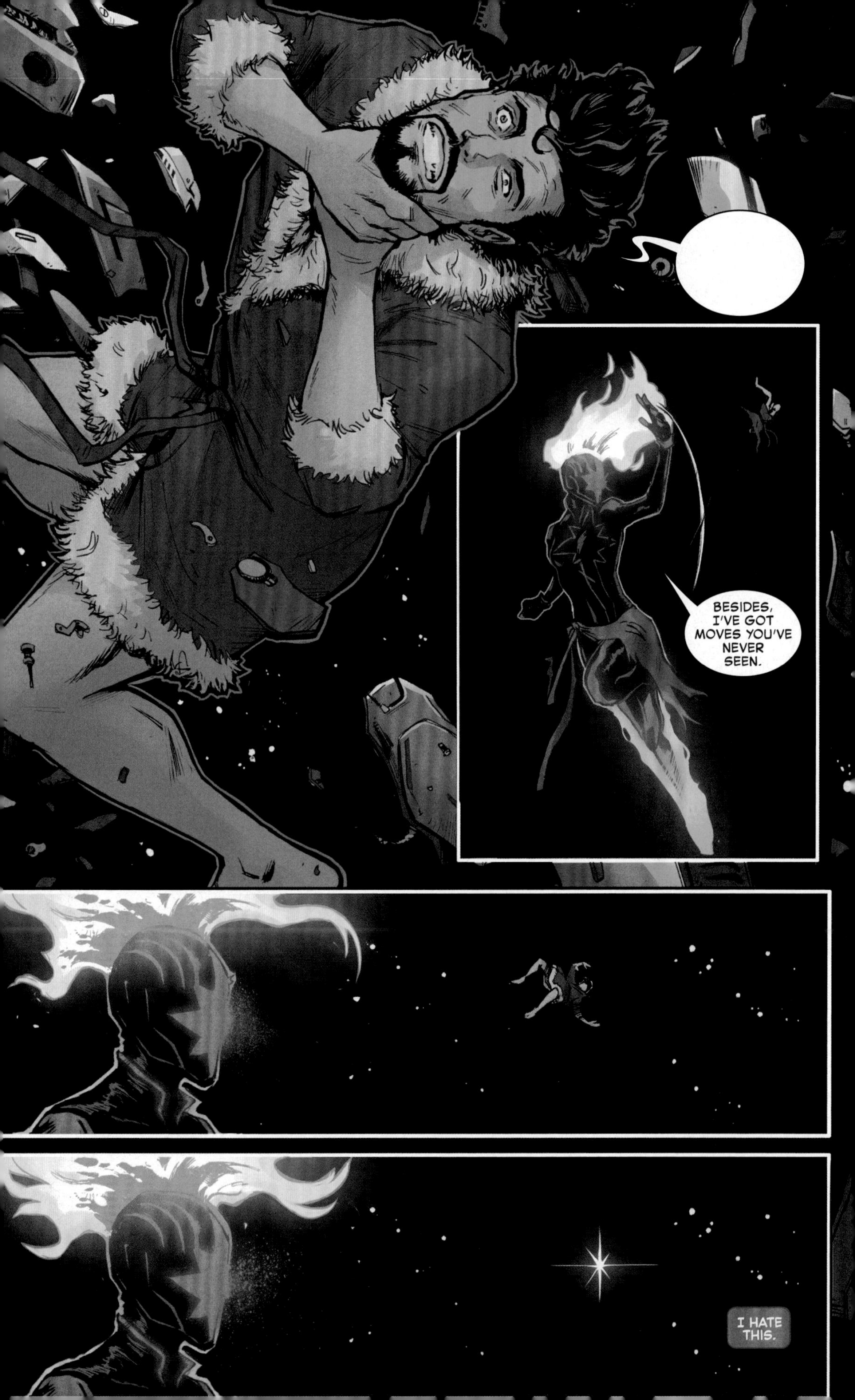
BESIDES, I'VE GOT MOVES YOU'VE NEVER SEEN.
I HATE THIS.

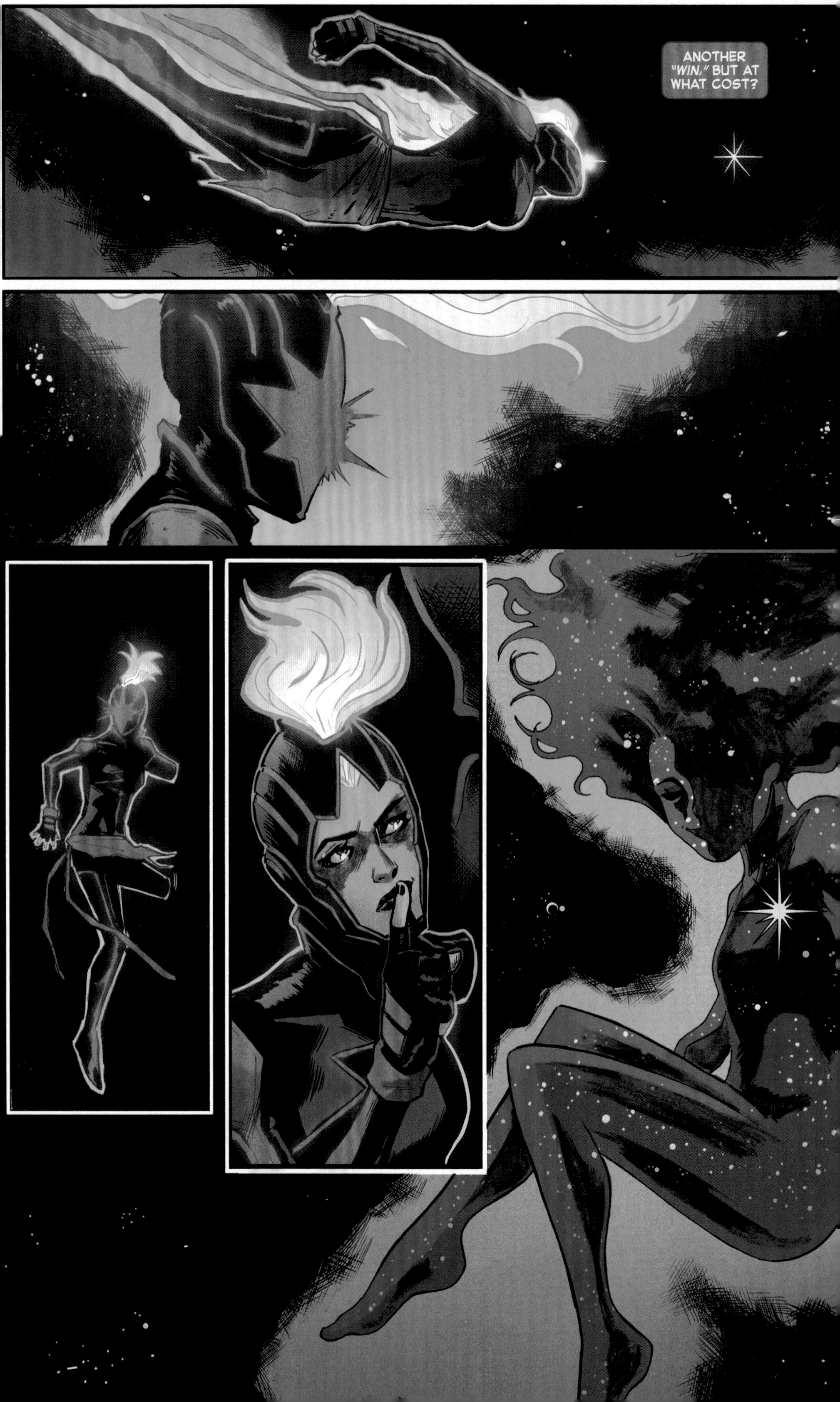
ANOTHER "WIN," BUT AT WHAT COST?

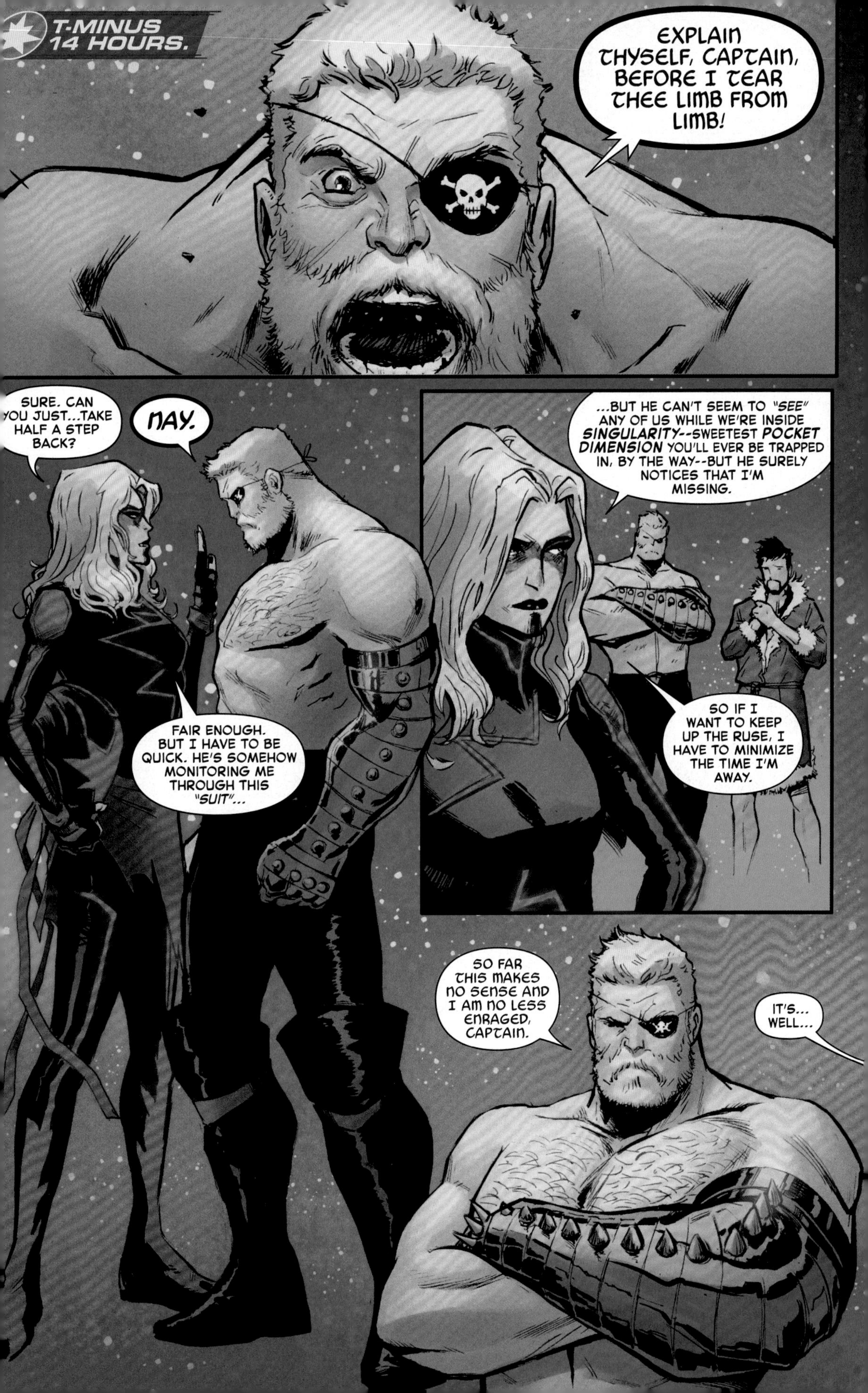

T-MINUS 14 HOURS.
EXPLAIN THYSELF, CAPTAIN, BEFORE I TEAR THEE LIMB FROM LIMB!
SURE. CAN YOU JUST...TAKE HALF A STEP BACK?
NAY.
FAIR ENOUGH. BUT I HAVE TO BE QUICK. HE'S SOMEHOW MONITORING ME THROUGH THIS "SUIT"...
...BUT HE CAN'T SEEM TO "SEE" ANY OF US WHILE WE'RE INSIDE SINGULARITY--SWEETEST POCKET DIMENSION YOU'LL EVER BE TRAPPED IN, BY THE WAY--BUT HE SURELY NOTICES THAT I'M MISSING.
SO IF I WANT TO KEEP UP THE RUSE, I HAVE TO MINIMIZE THE TIME I'M AWAY.
SO FAR THIS MAKES NO SENSE AND I AM NO LESS ENRAGED, CAPTAIN.
IT'S... WELL...

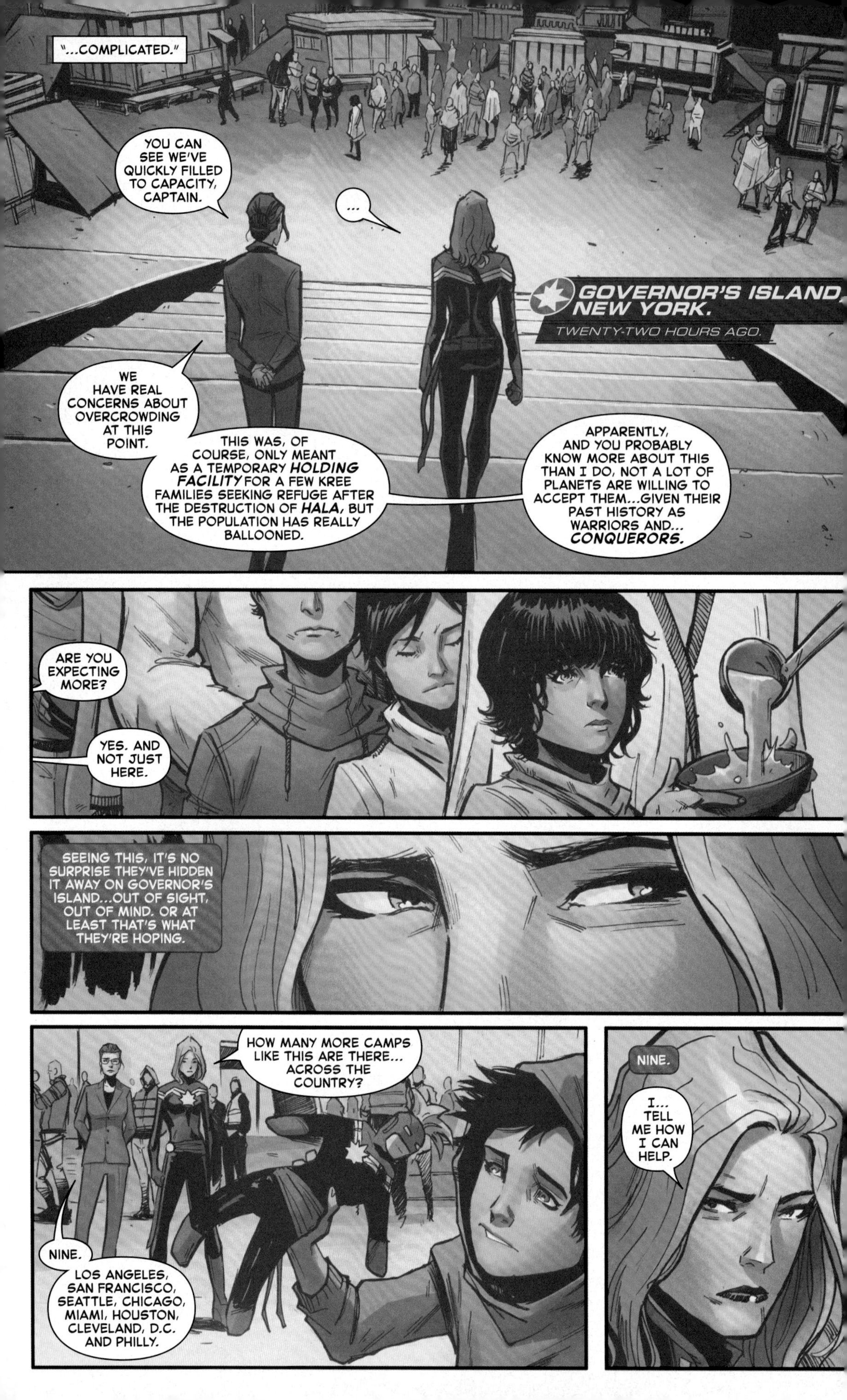
"...COMPLICATED."
YOU CAN SEE WE'VE QUICKLY FILLED TO CAPACITY, CAPTAIN.
...
GOVERNOR'S ISLAND, NEW YORK.
TWENTY-TWO HOURS AGO.
WE HAVE REAL CONCERNS ABOUT OVERCROWDING AT THIS POINT.
THIS WAS, OF COURSE, ONLY MEANT AS A TEMPORARY HOLDING FACILITY FOR A FEW KREE FAMILIES SEEKING REFUGE AFTER THE DESTRUCTION OF HALA, BUT THE POPULATION HAS REALLY BALLOONED.
APPARENTLY, AND YOU PROBABLY KNOW MORE ABOUT THIS THAN I DO, NOT A LOT OF PLANETS ARE WILLING TO ACCEPT THEM...GIVEN THEIR PAST HISTORY AS WARRIORS AND... CONQUERORS.
ARE YOU EXPECTING MORE?
YES. AND NOT JUST HERE.
SEEING THIS, IT'S NO SURPRISE THEY'VE HIDDEN IT AWAY ON GOVERNOR'S ISLAND...OUT OF SIGHT, OUT OF MIND. OR AT LEAST THAT'S WHAT THEY'RE HOPING.
HOW MANY MORE CAMPS LIKE THIS ARE THERE... ACROSS THE COUNTRY?
NINE.
LOS ANGELES, SAN FRANCISCO, SEATTLE, CHICAGO, MIAMI, HOUSTON, CLEVELAND, D.C. AND PHILLY.
NINE.
I... TELL ME HOW I CAN HELP.

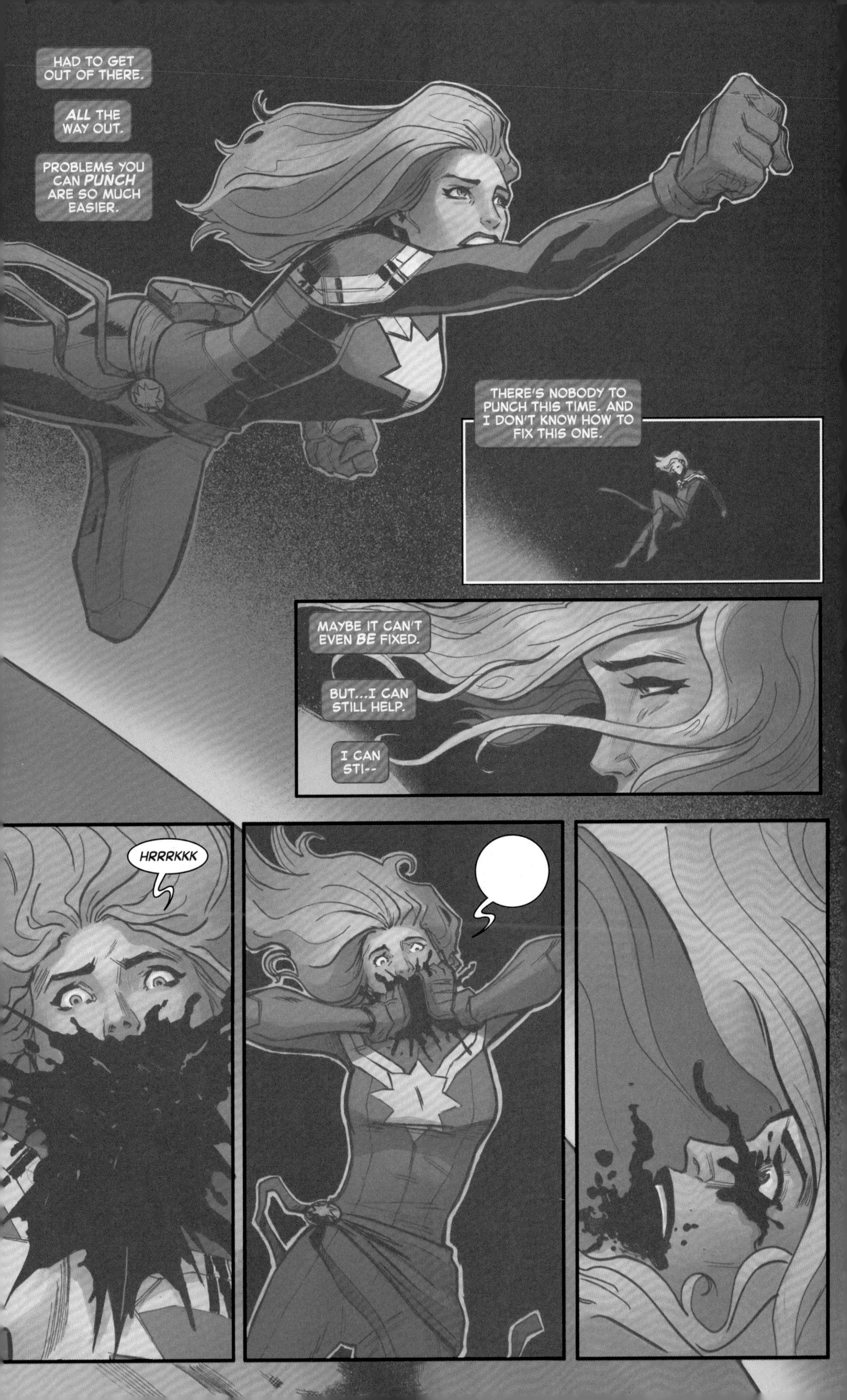
HAD TO GET OUT OF THERE.
ALL THE WAY OUT.
PROBLEMS YOU CAN PUNCH ARE SO MUCH EASIER.
THERE'S NOBODY TO PUNCH THIS TIME. AND I DON'T KNOW HOW TO FIX THIS ONE.
MAYBE IT CAN'T EVEN BE FIXED.
BUT...I CAN STILL HELP.
I CAN STI--
HRRRKKK

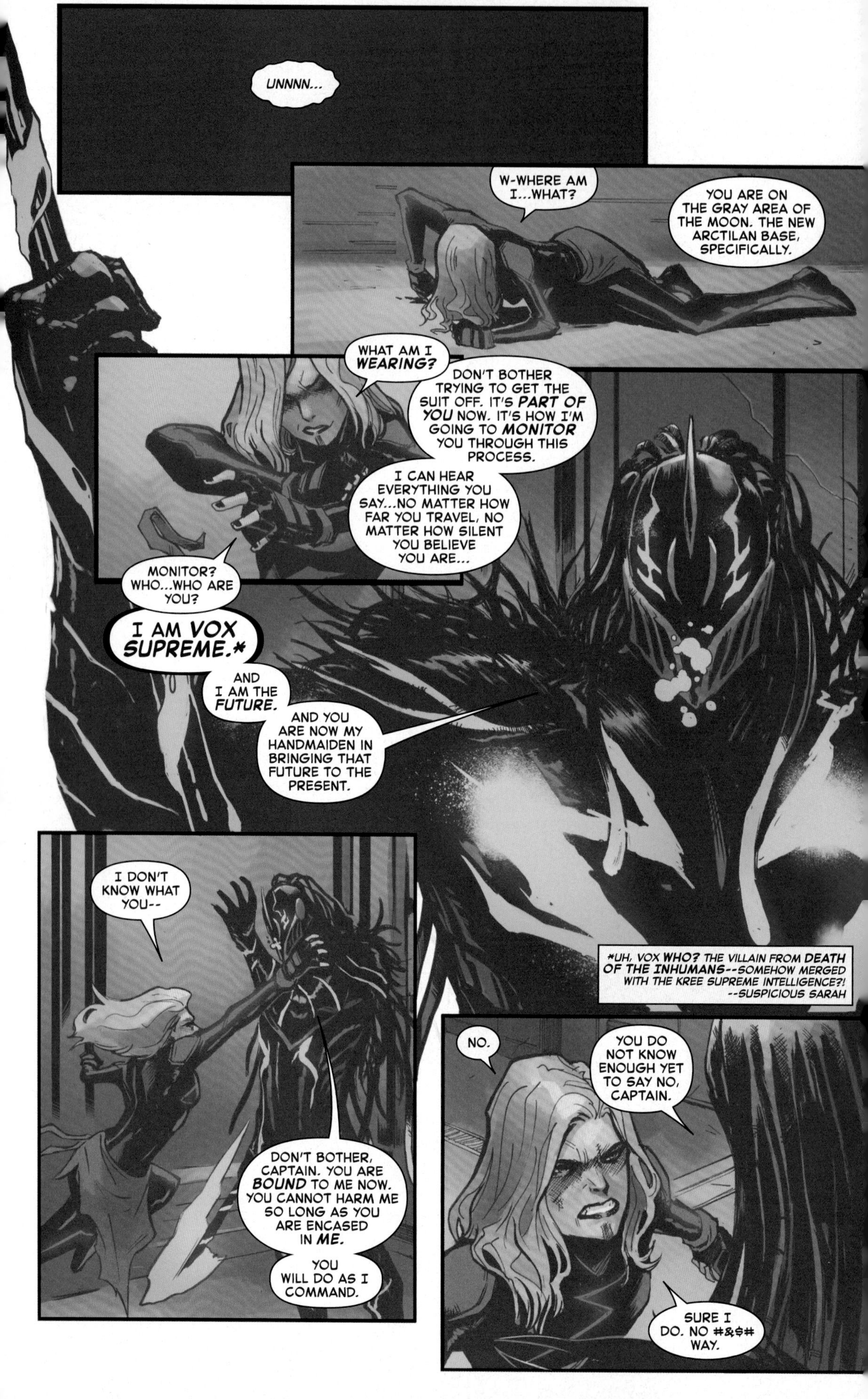
UNNNN...
W-WHERE AM I...WHAT?
YOU ARE ON THE GRAY AREA OF THE MOON. THE NEW ARCTILAN BASE, SPECIFICALLY.
WHAT AM I WEARING?
DON'T BOTHER TRYING TO GET THE SUIT OFF. IT'S PART OF YOU NOW. IT'S HOW I'M GOING TO MONITOR YOU THROUGH THIS PROCESS.
I CAN HEAR EVERYTHING YOU SAY...NO MATTER HOW FAR YOU TRAVEL, NO MATTER HOW SILENT YOU BELIEVE YOU ARE...
MONITOR? WHO...WHO ARE YOU?
I AM VOX SUPREME.*
AND I AM THE FUTURE.
AND YOU ARE NOW MY HANDMAIDEN IN BRINGING THAT FUTURE TO THE PRESENT.
*UH, VOX WHO? THE VILLAIN FROM DEATH OF THE INHUMANS--SOMEHOW MERGED WITH THE KREE SUPREME INTELLIGENCE?! --SUSPICIOUS SARAH
I DON'T KNOW WHAT YOU--
DON'T BOTHER, CAPTAIN. YOU ARE BOUND TO ME NOW. YOU CANNOT HARM ME SO LONG AS YOU ARE ENCASED IN ME.
YOU WILL DO AS I COMMAND.
NO.
YOU DO NOT KNOW ENOUGH YET TO SAY NO, CAPTAIN.
SURE I DO. NO #&$# WAY.

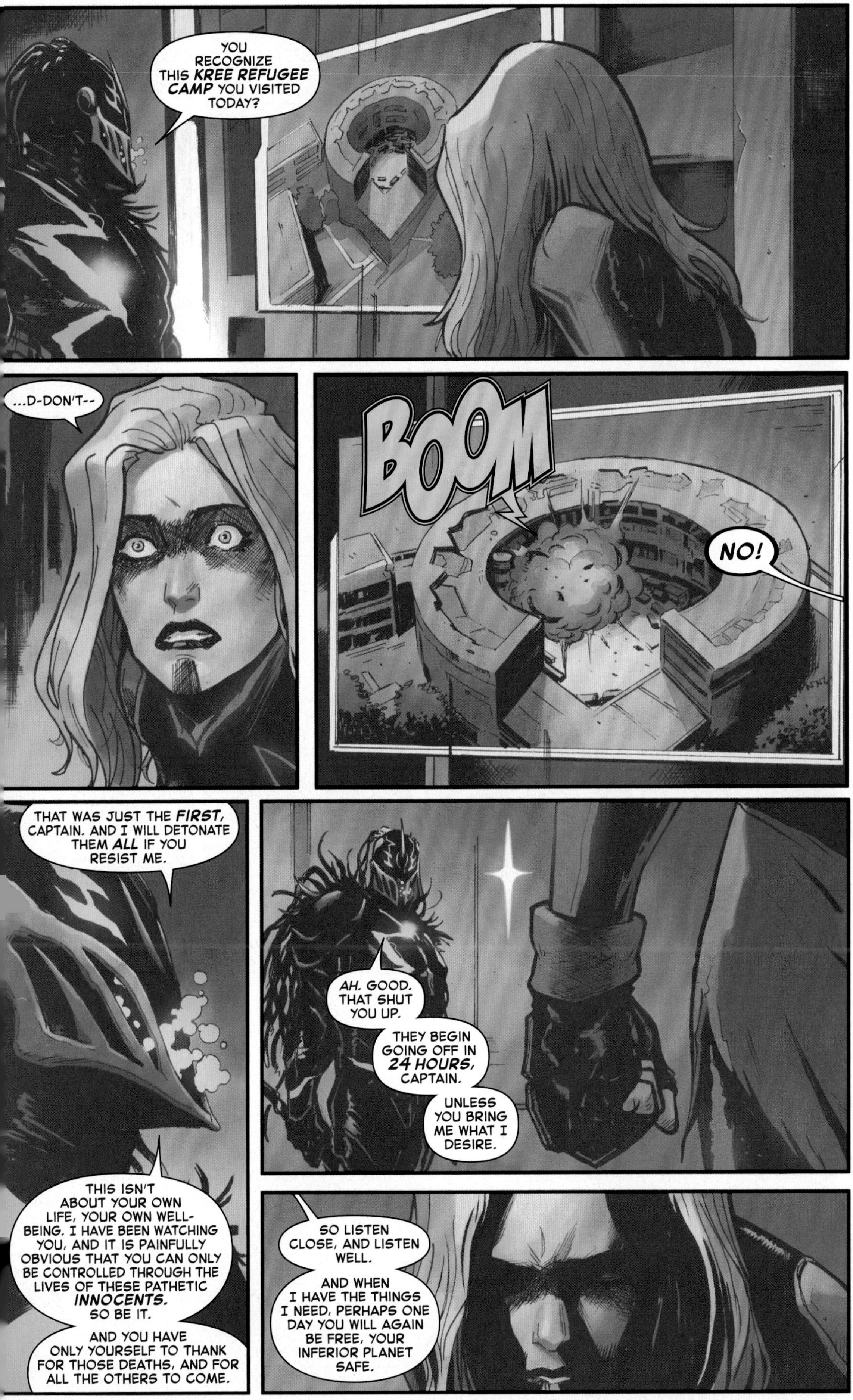

YOU RECOGNIZE THIS KREE REFUGEE CAMP YOU VISITED TODAY?
...D-DON'T--
BOOM
NO!
THAT WAS JUST THE FIRST, CAPTAIN. AND I WILL DETONATE THEM ALL IF YOU RESIST ME.
AH. GOOD. THAT SHUT YOU UP.
THEY BEGIN GOING OFF IN 24 HOURS, CAPTAIN.
UNLESS YOU BRING ME WHAT I DESIRE.
THIS ISN'T ABOUT YOUR OWN LIFE, YOUR OWN WELL-BEING. I HAVE BEEN WATCHING YOU, AND IT IS PAINFULLY OBVIOUS THAT YOU CAN ONLY BE CONTROLLED THROUGH THE LIVES OF THESE PATHETIC INNOCENTS. SO BE IT.
AND YOU HAVE ONLY YOURSELF TO THANK FOR THOSE DEATHS, AND FOR ALL THE OTHERS TO COME.
SO LISTEN CLOSE, AND LISTEN WELL.
AND WHEN I HAVE THE THINGS I NEED, PERHAPS ONE DAY YOU WILL AGAIN BE FREE, YOUR INFERIOR PLANET SAFE.

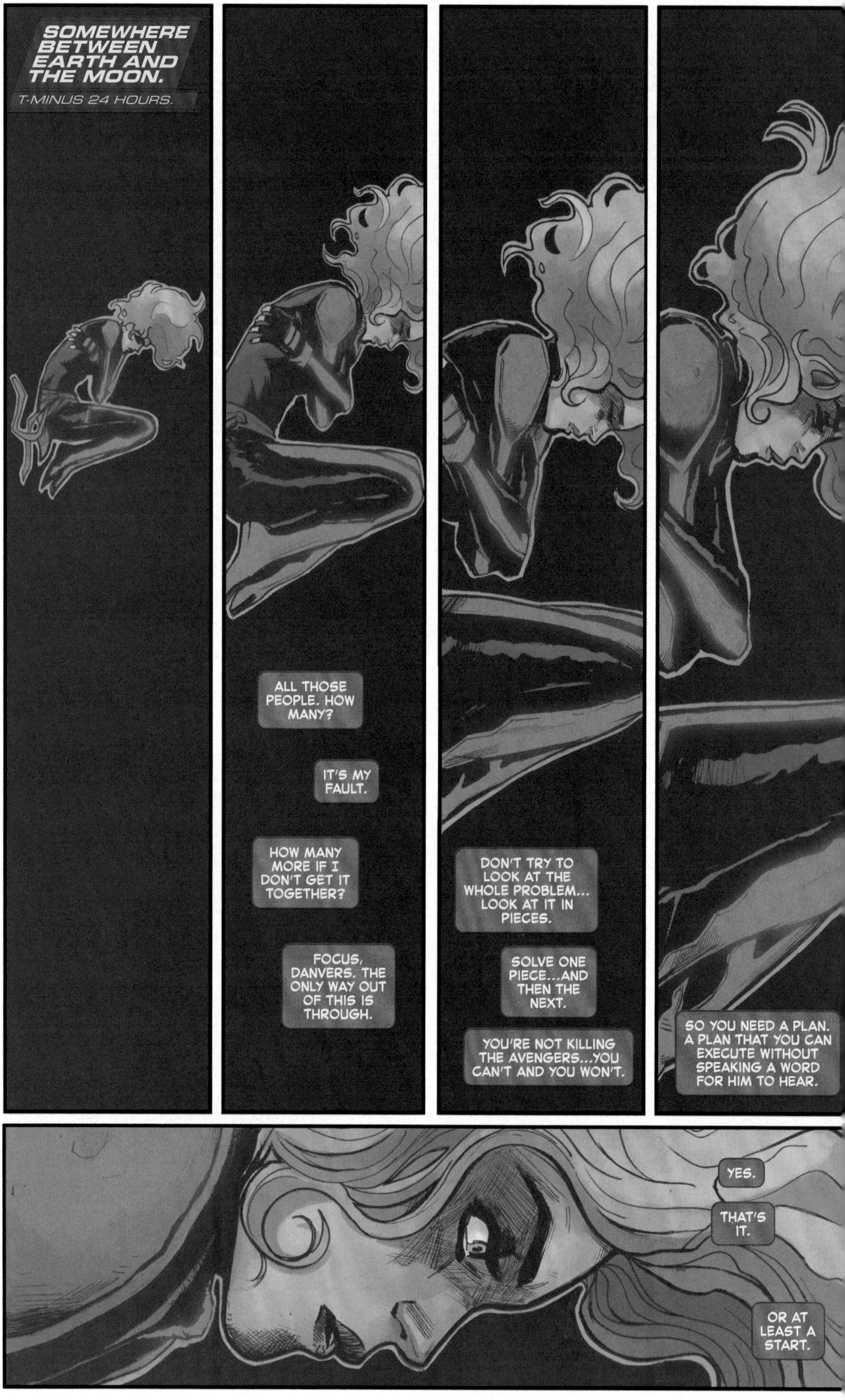
SOMEWHERE BETWEEN EARTH AND THE MOON.
T-MINUS 24 HOURS.
ALL THOSE PEOPLE. HOW MANY?
IT'S MY FAULT.
HOW MANY MORE IF I DON'T GET IT TOGETHER?
FOCUS, DANVERS. THE ONLY WAY OUT OF THIS IS THROUGH.
DON'T TRY TO LOOK AT THE WHOLE PROBLEM... LOOK AT IT IN PIECES.
SOLVE ONE PIECE...AND THEN THE NEXT.
YOU'RE NOT KILLING THE AVENGERS...YOU CAN'T AND YOU WON'T.
SO YOU NEED A PLAN. A PLAN THAT YOU CAN EXECUTE WITHOUT SPEAKING A WORD FOR HIM TO HEAR.
YES.
THAT'S IT.
OR AT LEAST A START.

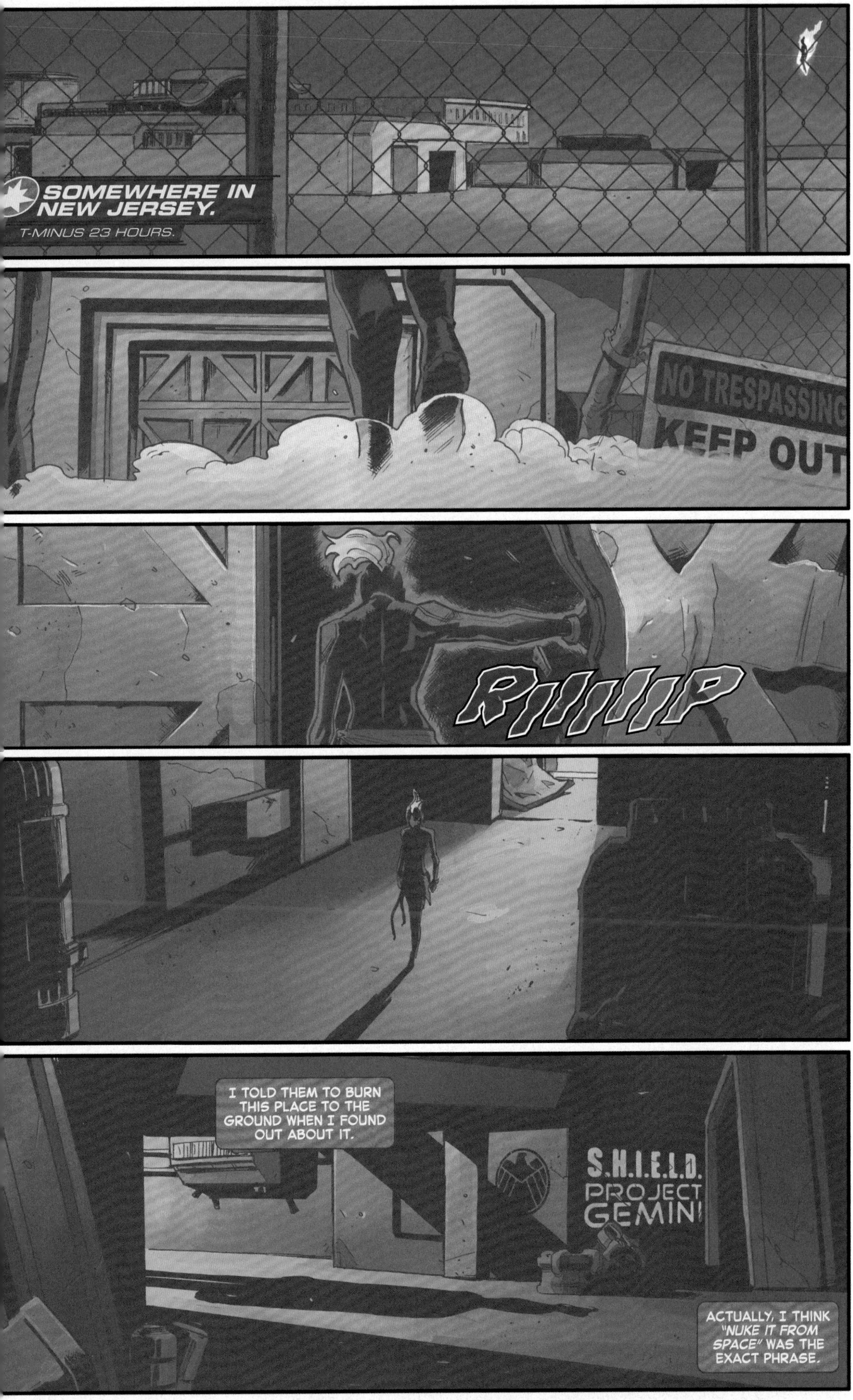
SOMEWHERE IN NEW JERSEY.
T-MINUS 23 HOURS.
NO TRESPASSING
KEEP OUT
RIIIIIP
I TOLD THEM TO BURN THIS PLACE TO THE GROUND WHEN I FOUND OUT ABOUT IT.
S.H.I.E.L.D.
PROJECT GEMINI
ACTUALLY, I THINK "NUKE IT FROM SPACE" WAS THE EXACT PHRASE.

WHAT A SURPRISE TO FIND THAT THEY DID THE COMPLETE OPPOSITE.
BUT IF THIS VERY BAD IDEA SOMEONE ONCE HAD CAN END UP SOLVING A VERY BAD PROBLEM I NOW HAVE...THEN I PROMISE NOT TO PERSONALLY HURL THAT PERSON WITH BAD IDEAS INTO THE SUN.
BECAUSE WHOEVER CAME UP WITH THE IDEA OF *CLONING THE AVENGERS* DEFINITELY DESERVES A FIERY SUN DEATH...
...UNLESS IT CAN SAVE THE WORLD.

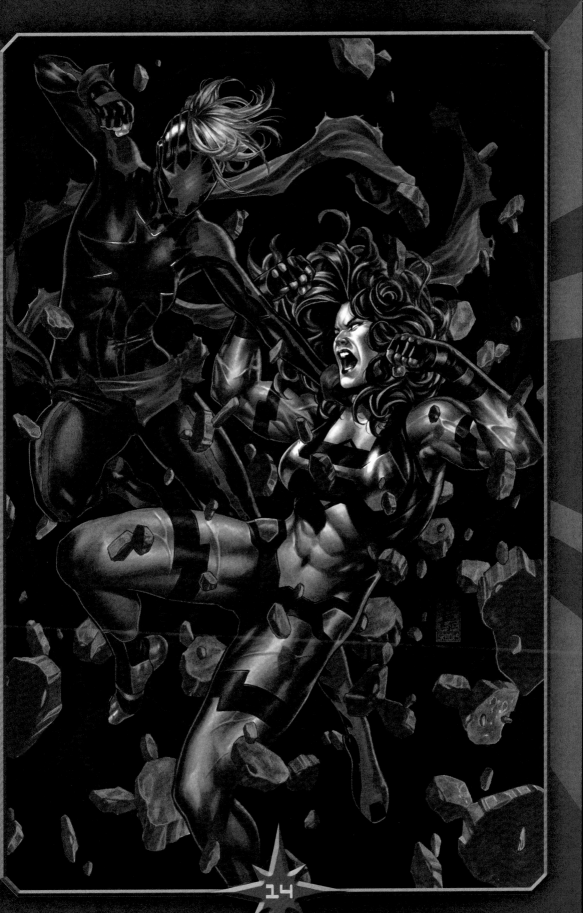

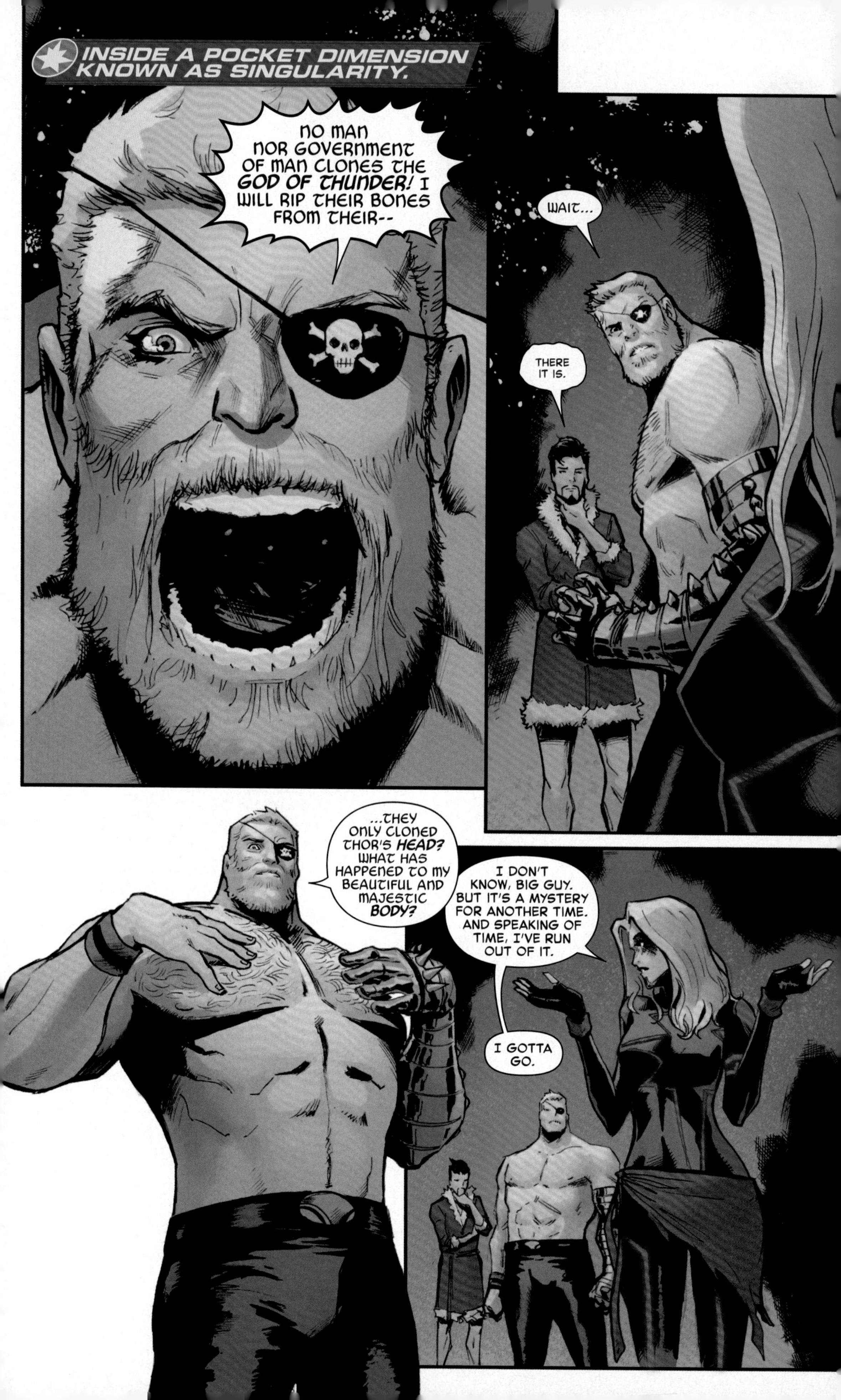
INSIDE A POCKET DIMENSION KNOWN AS SINGULARITY.
NO MAN NOR GOVERNMENT OF MAN CLONES THE GOD OF THUNDER! I WILL RIP THEIR BONES FROM THEIR--
WAIT...
THERE IT IS.
...THEY ONLY CLONED THOR'S HEAD? WHAT HAS HAPPENED TO MY BEAUTIFUL AND MAJESTIC BODY?
I DON'T KNOW, BIG GUY. BUT IT'S A MYSTERY FOR ANOTHER TIME. AND SPEAKING OF TIME, I'VE RUN OUT OF IT.
I GOTTA GO.

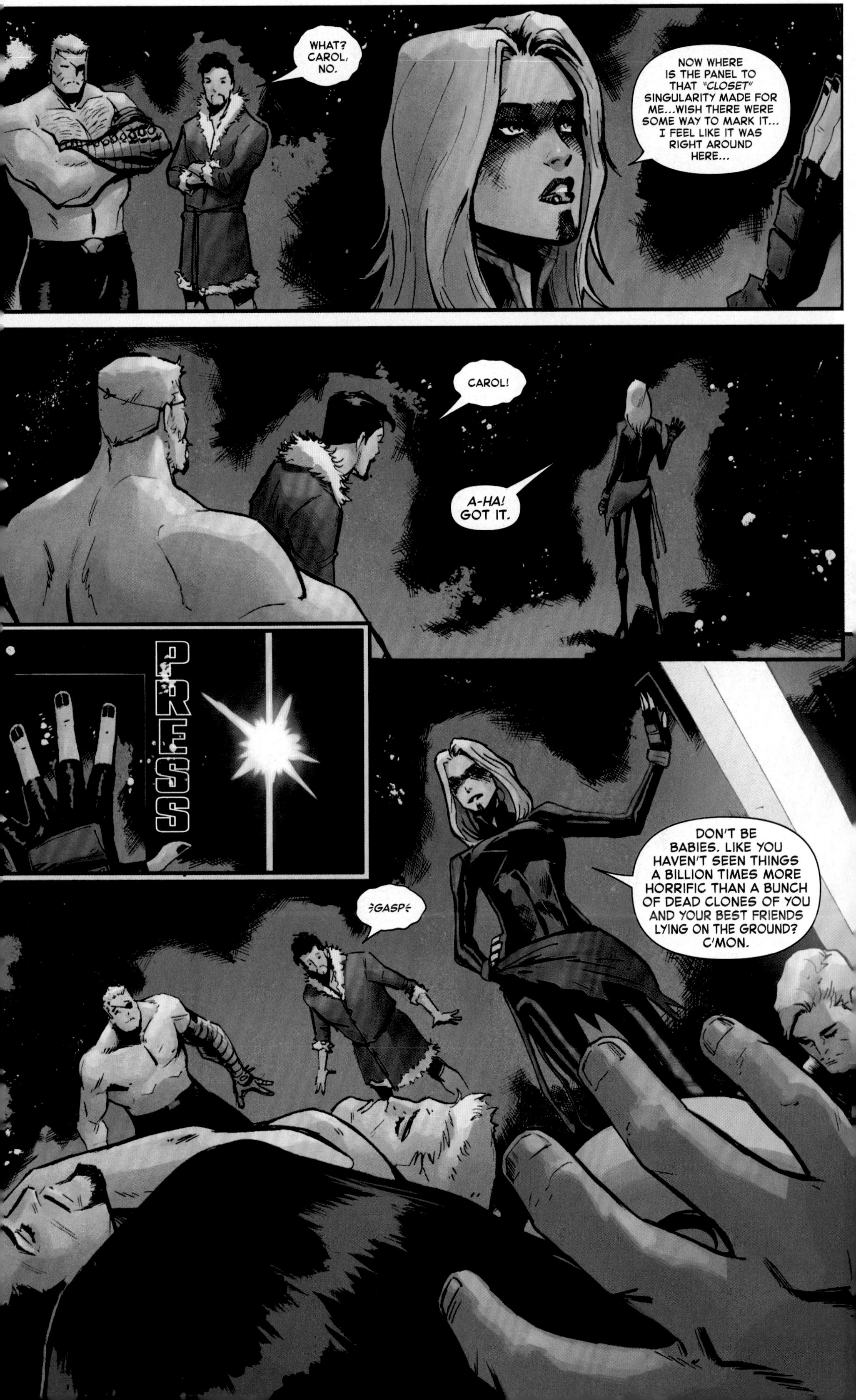

WHAT? CAROL, NO.
NOW WHERE IS THE PANEL TO THAT "CLOSET" SINGULARITY MADE FOR ME...WISH THERE WERE SOME WAY TO MARK IT... I FEEL LIKE IT WAS RIGHT AROUND HERE...
CAROL!
A-HA! GOT IT.
PRESS
DON'T BE BABIES. LIKE YOU HAVEN'T SEEN THINGS A BILLION TIMES MORE HORRIFIC THAN A BUNCH OF DEAD CLONES OF YOU AND YOUR BEST FRIENDS LYING ON THE GROUND? C'MON.
GASP

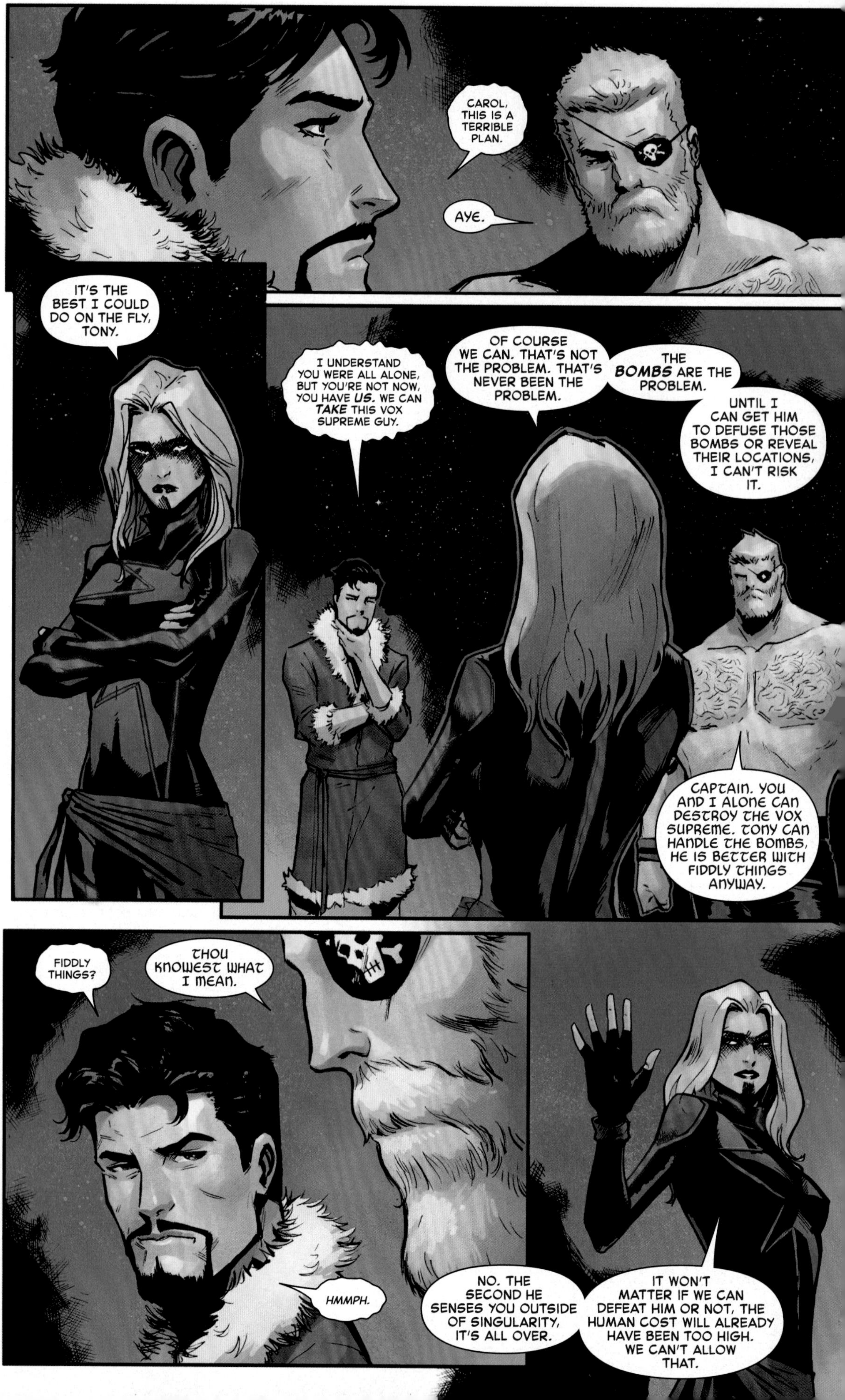
CAROL, THIS IS A TERRIBLE PLAN.
AYE.
IT'S THE BEST I COULD DO ON THE FLY, TONY.
I UNDERSTAND YOU WERE ALL ALONE, BUT YOU'RE NOT NOW, YOU HAVE US. WE CAN TAKE THIS VOX SUPREME GUY.
OF COURSE WE CAN. THAT'S NOT THE PROBLEM. THAT'S NEVER BEEN THE PROBLEM.
THE BOMBS ARE THE PROBLEM.
UNTIL I CAN GET HIM TO DEFUSE THOSE BOMBS OR REVEAL THEIR LOCATIONS, I CAN'T RISK IT.
CAPTAIN. YOU AND I ALONE CAN DESTROY THE VOX SUPREME. TONY CAN HANDLE THE BOMBS, HE IS BETTER WITH FIDDLY THINGS ANYWAY.
FIDDLY THINGS?
THOU KNOWEST WHAT I MEAN.
HMMPH.
NO. THE SECOND HE SENSES YOU OUTSIDE OF SINGULARITY, IT'S ALL OVER.
IT WON'T MATTER IF WE CAN DEFEAT HIM OR NOT, THE HUMAN COST WILL ALREADY HAVE BEEN TOO HIGH. WE CAN'T ALLOW THAT.

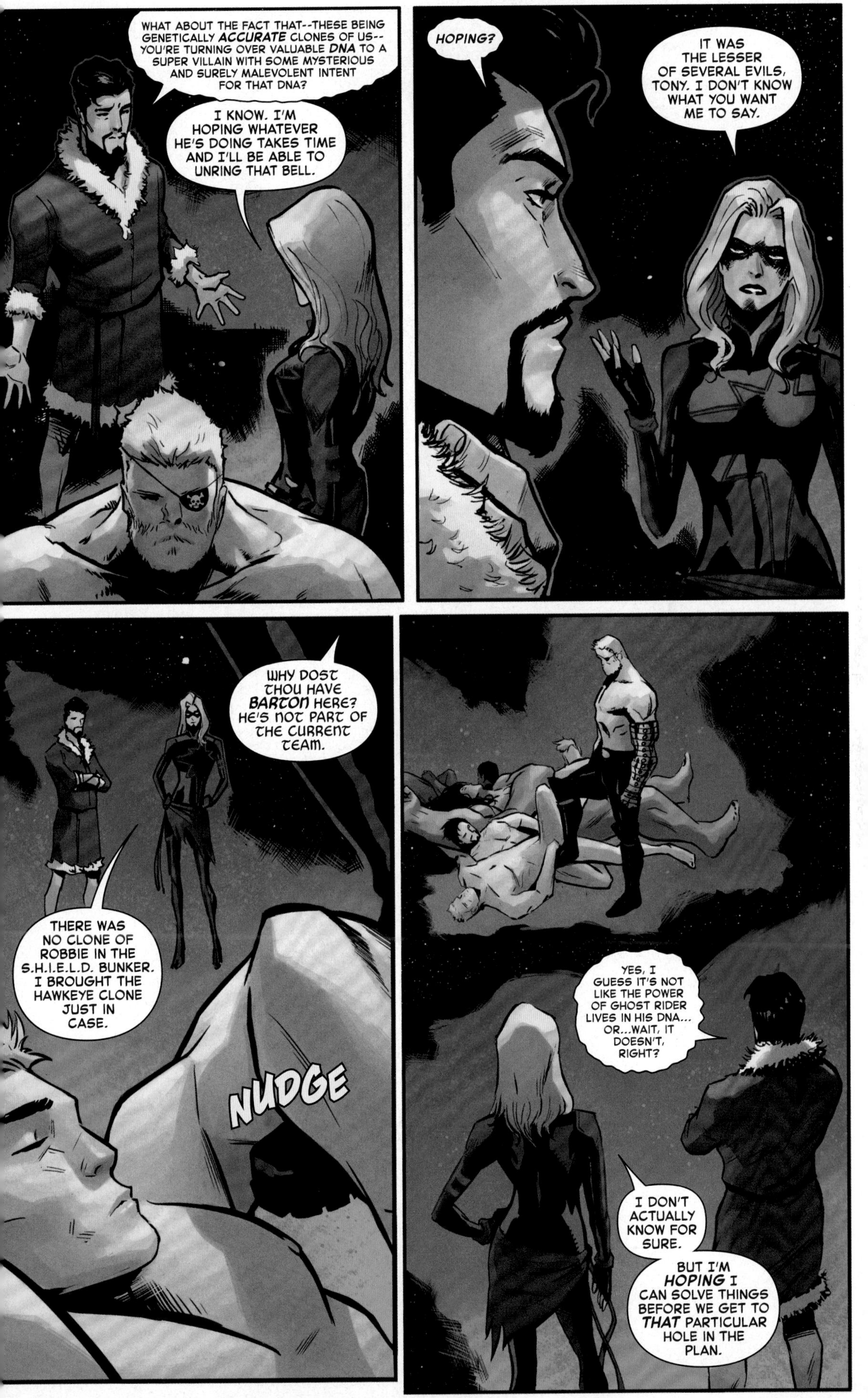
WHAT ABOUT THE FACT THAT--THESE BEING GENETICALLY ACCURATE CLONES OF US--YOU'RE TURNING OVER VALUABLE DNA TO A SUPER VILLAIN WITH SOME MYSTERIOUS AND SURELY MALEVOLENT INTENT FOR THAT DNA?
I KNOW. I'M HOPING WHATEVER HE'S DOING TAKES TIME AND I'LL BE ABLE TO UNRING THAT BELL.
HOPING?
IT WAS THE LESSER OF SEVERAL EVILS, TONY. I DON'T KNOW WHAT YOU WANT ME TO SAY.
WHY DOST THOU HAVE BARTON HERE? HE'S NOT PART OF THE CURRENT TEAM.
THERE WAS NO CLONE OF ROBBIE IN THE S.H.I.E.L.D. BUNKER. I BROUGHT THE HAWKEYE CLONE JUST IN CASE.
NUDGE
YES, I GUESS IT'S NOT LIKE THE POWER OF GHOST RIDER LIVES IN HIS DNA... OR...WAIT, IT DOESN'T, RIGHT?
I DON'T ACTUALLY KNOW FOR SURE.
BUT I'M HOPING I CAN SOLVE THINGS BEFORE WE GET TO THAT PARTICULAR HOLE IN THE PLAN.

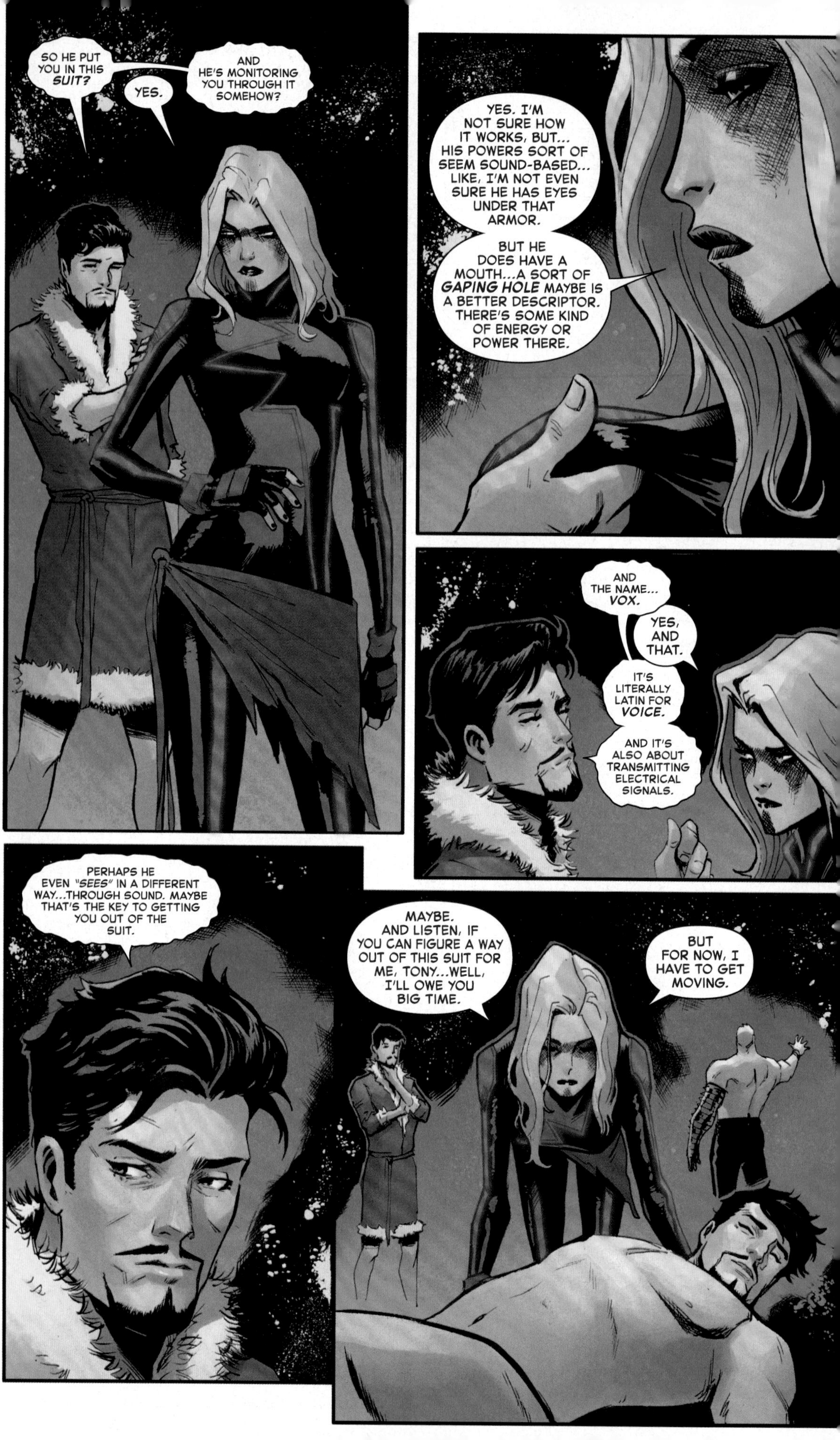
SO HE PUT YOU IN THIS *SUIT?*
YES.
AND HE'S MONITORING YOU THROUGH IT SOMEHOW?
YES. I'M NOT SURE HOW IT WORKS, BUT... HIS POWERS SORT OF SEEM SOUND-BASED... LIKE, I'M NOT EVEN SURE HE HAS EYES UNDER THAT ARMOR.
BUT HE DOES HAVE A MOUTH...A SORT OF *GAPING HOLE* MAYBE IS A BETTER DESCRIPTOR. THERE'S SOME KIND OF ENERGY OR POWER THERE.
AND THE NAME... *VOX.*
YES, AND THAT.
IT'S LITERALLY LATIN FOR *VOICE.*
AND IT'S ALSO ABOUT TRANSMITTING ELECTRICAL SIGNALS.
PERHAPS HE EVEN *"SEES"* IN A DIFFERENT WAY...THROUGH SOUND. MAYBE THAT'S THE KEY TO GETTING YOU OUT OF THE SUIT.
MAYBE. AND LISTEN, IF YOU CAN FIGURE A WAY OUT OF THIS SUIT FOR ME, TONY...WELL, I'LL OWE YOU BIG TIME.
BUT FOR NOW, I HAVE TO GET MOVING.

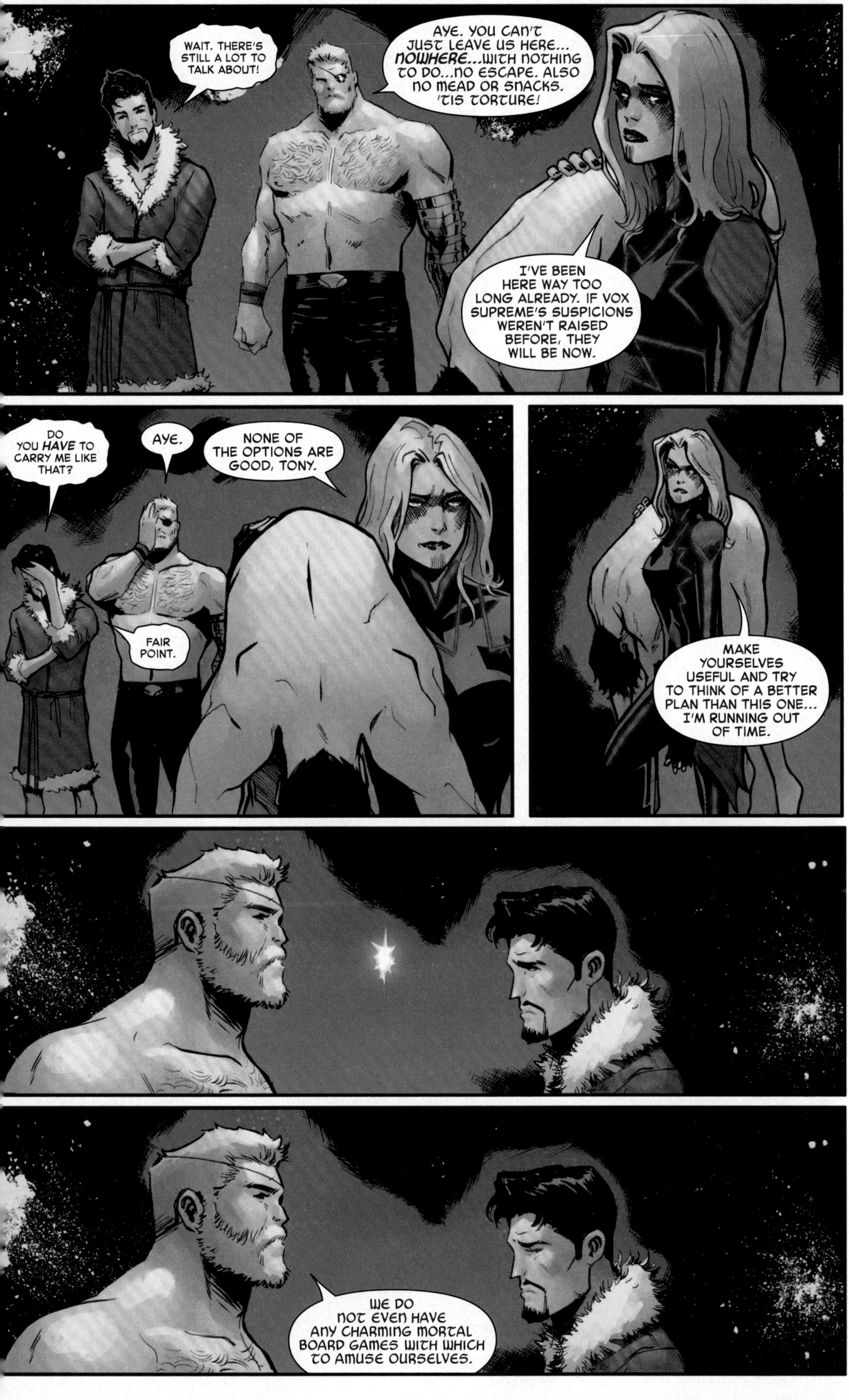

WAIT. THERE'S STILL A LOT TO TALK ABOUT!
AYE. YOU CAN'T JUST LEAVE US HERE... *NOWHERE*...WITH NOTHING TO DO...NO ESCAPE. ALSO NO MEAD OR SNACKS. 'TIS TORTURE!
I'VE BEEN HERE WAY TOO LONG ALREADY. IF VOX SUPREME'S SUSPICIONS WEREN'T RAISED BEFORE, THEY WILL BE NOW.
DO YOU *HAVE* TO CARRY ME LIKE THAT?
AYE.
NONE OF THE OPTIONS ARE GOOD, TONY.
FAIR POINT.
MAKE YOURSELVES USEFUL AND TRY TO THINK OF A BETTER PLAN THAN THIS ONE... I'M RUNNING OUT OF TIME.
WE DO NOT EVEN HAVE ANY CHARMING MORTAL BOARD GAMES WITH WHICH TO AMUSE OURSELVES.

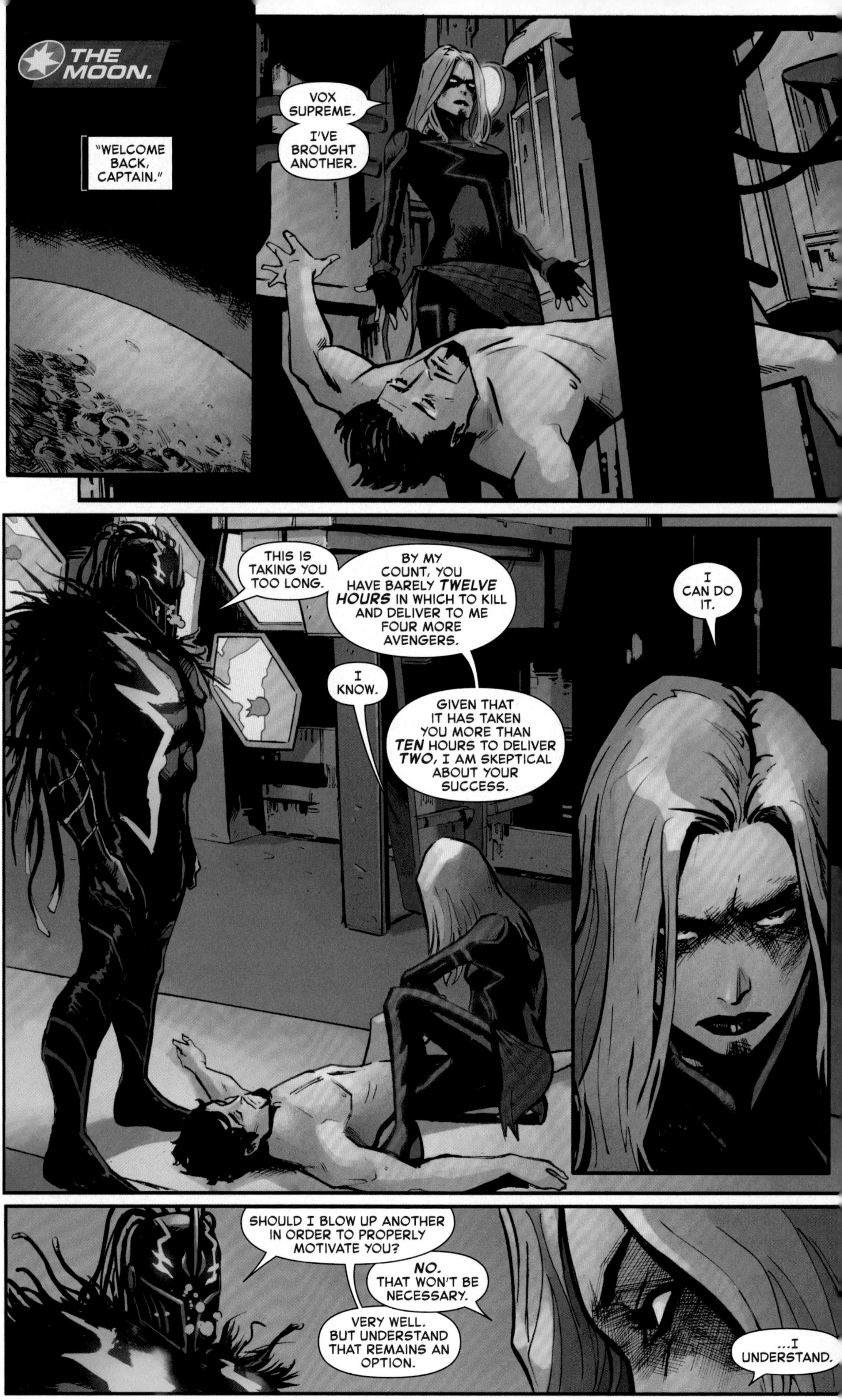
THE MOON.
"WELCOME BACK, CAPTAIN."
VOX SUPREME.
I'VE BROUGHT ANOTHER.
THIS IS TAKING YOU TOO LONG.
BY MY COUNT, YOU HAVE BARELY TWELVE HOURS IN WHICH TO KILL AND DELIVER TO ME FOUR MORE AVENGERS.
I KNOW.
GIVEN THAT IT HAS TAKEN YOU MORE THAN TEN HOURS TO DELIVER TWO, I AM SKEPTICAL ABOUT YOUR SUCCESS.
I CAN DO IT.
SHOULD I BLOW UP ANOTHER IN ORDER TO PROPERLY MOTIVATE YOU?
NO. THAT WON'T BE NECESSARY.
VERY WELL. BUT UNDERSTAND THAT REMAINS AN OPTION.
...I UNDERSTAND.

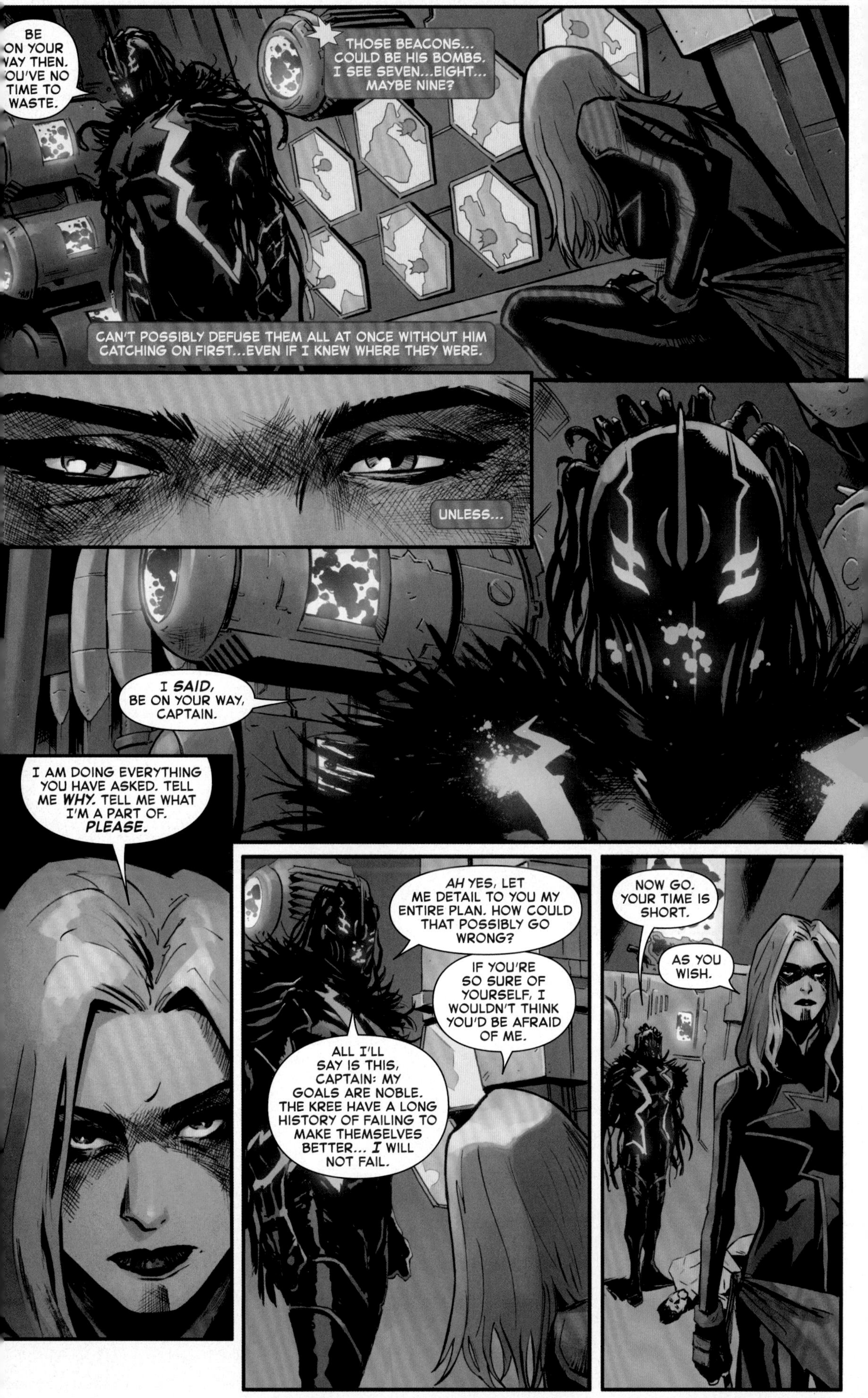
BE ON YOUR WAY THEN. YOU'VE NO TIME TO WASTE.
THOSE BEACONS... COULD BE HIS BOMBS. I SEE SEVEN...EIGHT... MAYBE NINE?
CAN'T POSSIBLY DEFUSE THEM ALL AT ONCE WITHOUT HIM CATCHING ON FIRST...EVEN IF I KNEW WHERE THEY WERE.
UNLESS...
I SAID, BE ON YOUR WAY, CAPTAIN.
I AM DOING EVERYTHING YOU HAVE ASKED. TELL ME WHY. TELL ME WHAT I'M A PART OF. PLEASE.
AH YES, LET ME DETAIL TO YOU MY ENTIRE PLAN. HOW COULD THAT POSSIBLY GO WRONG?
IF YOU'RE SO SURE OF YOURSELF, I WOULDN'T THINK YOU'D BE AFRAID OF ME.
ALL I'LL SAY IS THIS, CAPTAIN: MY GOALS ARE NOBLE. THE KREE HAVE A LONG HISTORY OF FAILING TO MAKE THEMSELVES BETTER... I WILL NOT FAIL.
NOW GO. YOUR TIME IS SHORT.
AS YOU WISH.

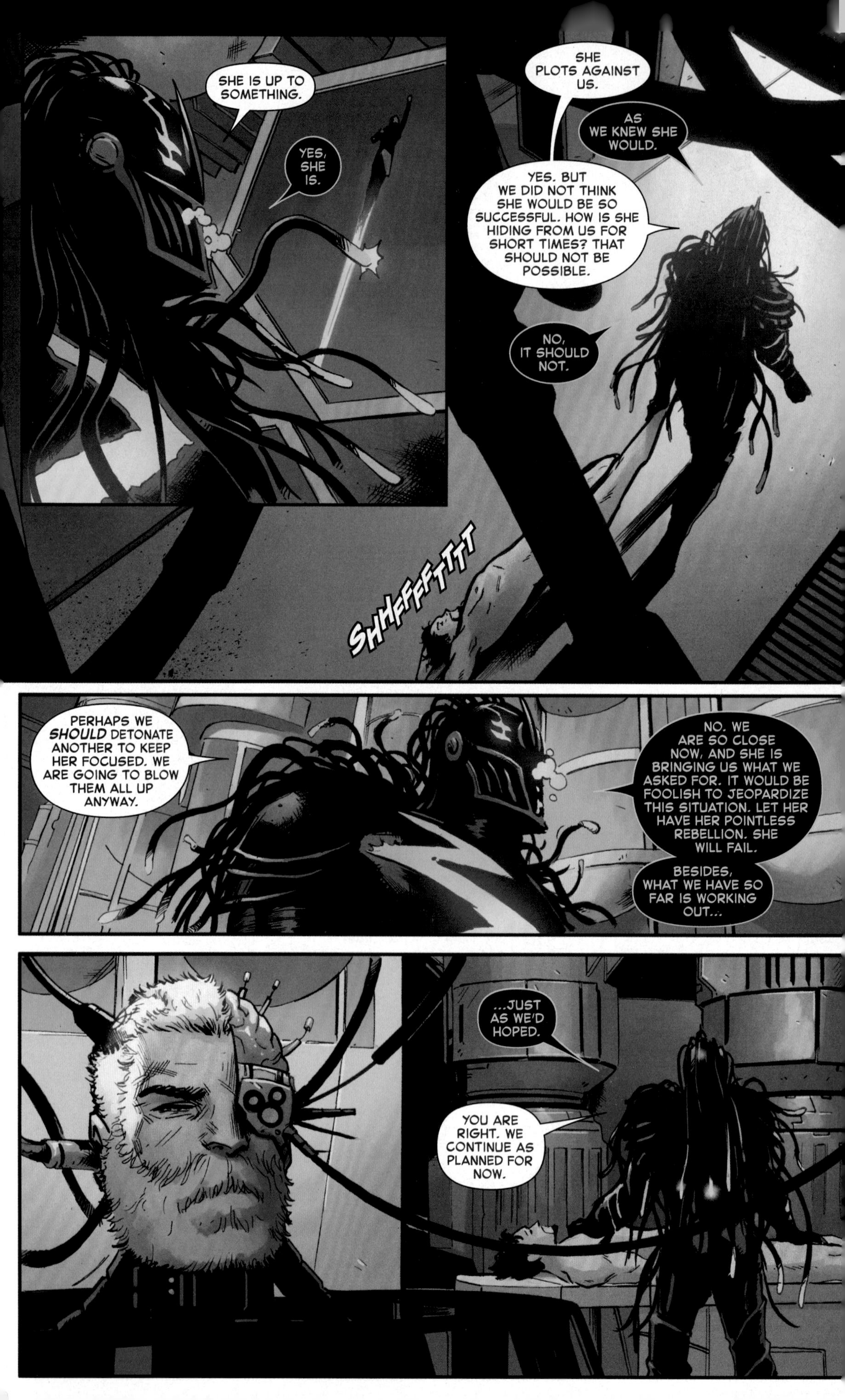
SHE IS UP TO SOMETHING.
YES, SHE IS.
SHE PLOTS AGAINST US.
AS WE KNEW SHE WOULD.
YES. BUT WE DID NOT THINK SHE WOULD BE SO SUCCESSFUL. HOW IS SHE HIDING FROM US FOR SHORT TIMES? THAT SHOULD NOT BE POSSIBLE.
NO, IT SHOULD NOT.
SHHFFFTTTT
PERHAPS WE SHOULD DETONATE ANOTHER TO KEEP HER FOCUSED. WE ARE GOING TO BLOW THEM ALL UP ANYWAY.
NO. WE ARE SO CLOSE NOW, AND SHE IS BRINGING US WHAT WE ASKED FOR. IT WOULD BE FOOLISH TO JEOPARDIZE THIS SITUATION. LET HER HAVE HER POINTLESS REBELLION. SHE WILL FAIL.
BESIDES, WHAT WE HAVE SO FAR IS WORKING OUT...
...JUST AS WE'D HOPED.
YOU ARE RIGHT. WE CONTINUE AS PLANNED FOR NOW.

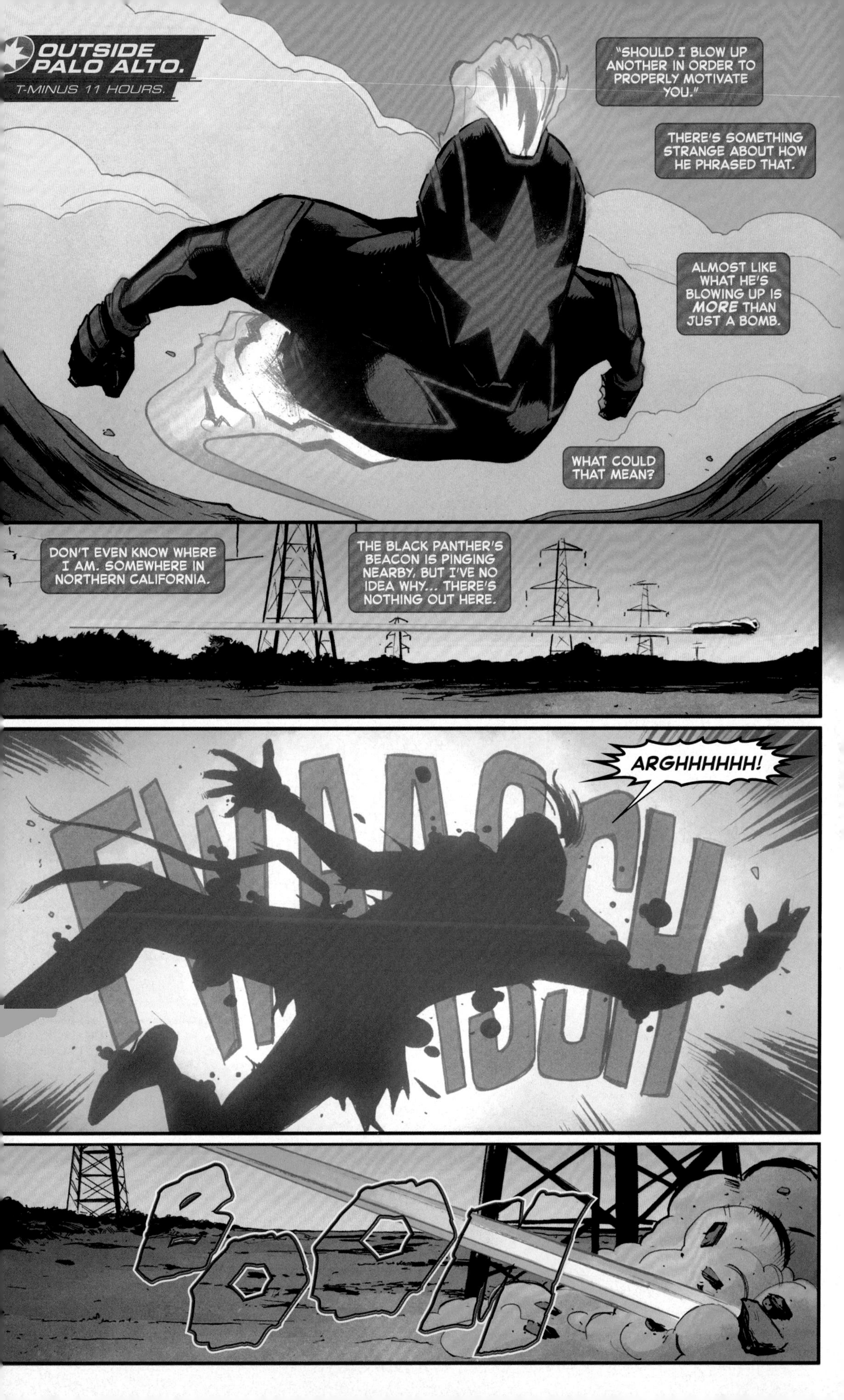
OUTSIDE PALO ALTO.
T-MINUS 11 HOURS.
"SHOULD I BLOW UP ANOTHER IN ORDER TO PROPERLY MOTIVATE YOU."
THERE'S SOMETHING STRANGE ABOUT HOW HE PHRASED THAT.
ALMOST LIKE WHAT HE'S BLOWING UP IS *MORE* THAN JUST A BOMB.
WHAT COULD THAT MEAN?
DON'T EVEN KNOW WHERE I AM. SOMEWHERE IN NORTHERN CALIFORNIA.
THE BLACK PANTHER'S BEACON IS PINGING NEARBY, BUT I'VE NO IDEA WHY... THERE'S NOTHING OUT HERE.
ARGHHHHHH!

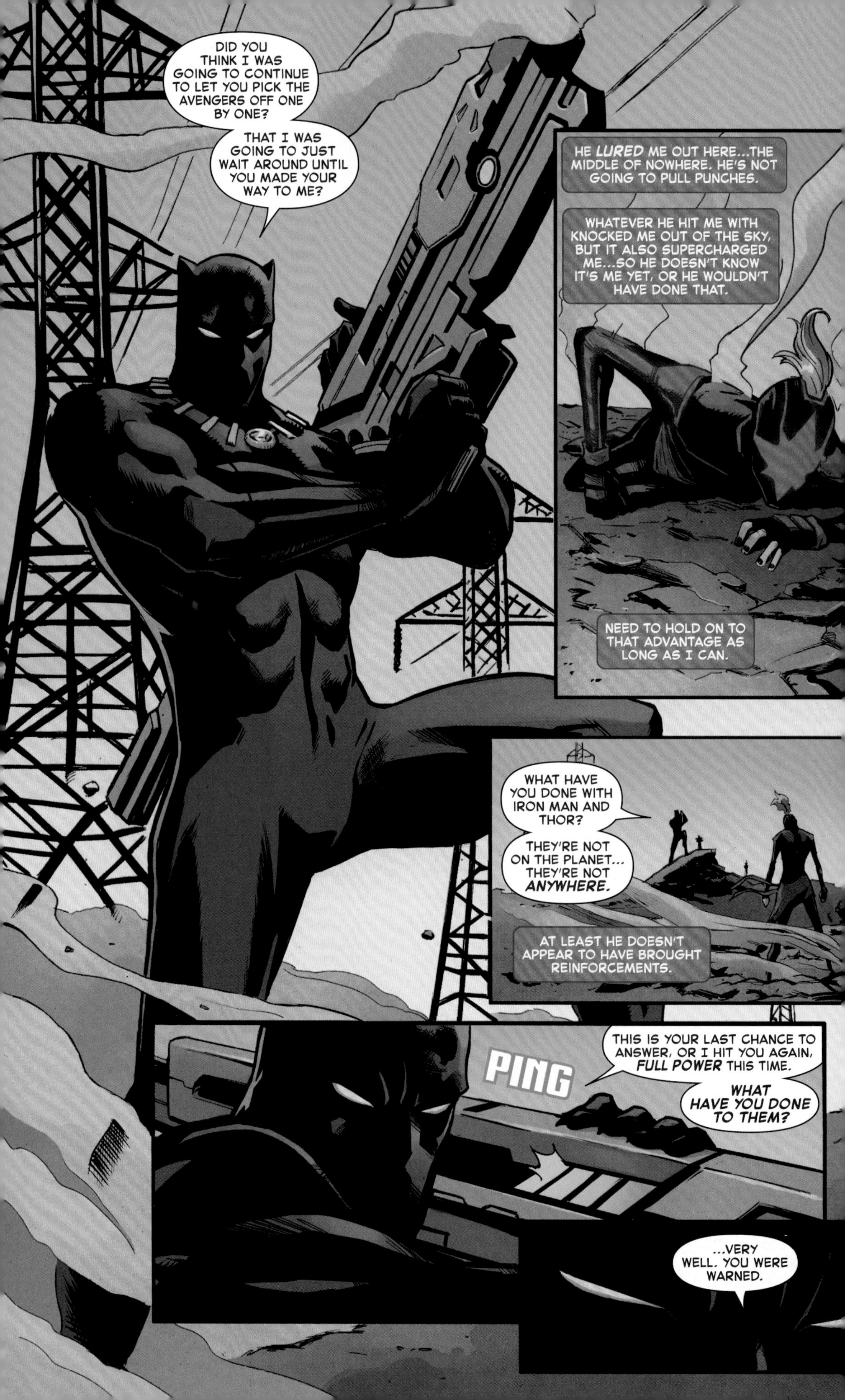
DID YOU THINK I WAS GOING TO CONTINUE TO LET YOU PICK THE AVENGERS OFF ONE BY ONE?
THAT I WAS GOING TO JUST WAIT AROUND UNTIL YOU MADE YOUR WAY TO ME?
HE LURED ME OUT HERE...THE MIDDLE OF NOWHERE. HE'S NOT GOING TO PULL PUNCHES.
WHATEVER HE HIT ME WITH KNOCKED ME OUT OF THE SKY, BUT IT ALSO SUPERCHARGED ME...SO HE DOESN'T KNOW IT'S ME YET, OR HE WOULDN'T HAVE DONE THAT.
NEED TO HOLD ON TO THAT ADVANTAGE AS LONG AS I CAN.
WHAT HAVE YOU DONE WITH IRON MAN AND THOR?
THEY'RE NOT ON THE PLANET... THEY'RE NOT ANYWHERE.
AT LEAST HE DOESN'T APPEAR TO HAVE BROUGHT REINFORCEMENTS.
PING
THIS IS YOUR LAST CHANCE TO ANSWER, OR I HIT YOU AGAIN, FULL POWER THIS TIME.
WHAT HAVE YOU DONE TO THEM?
...VERY WELL. YOU WERE WARNED.

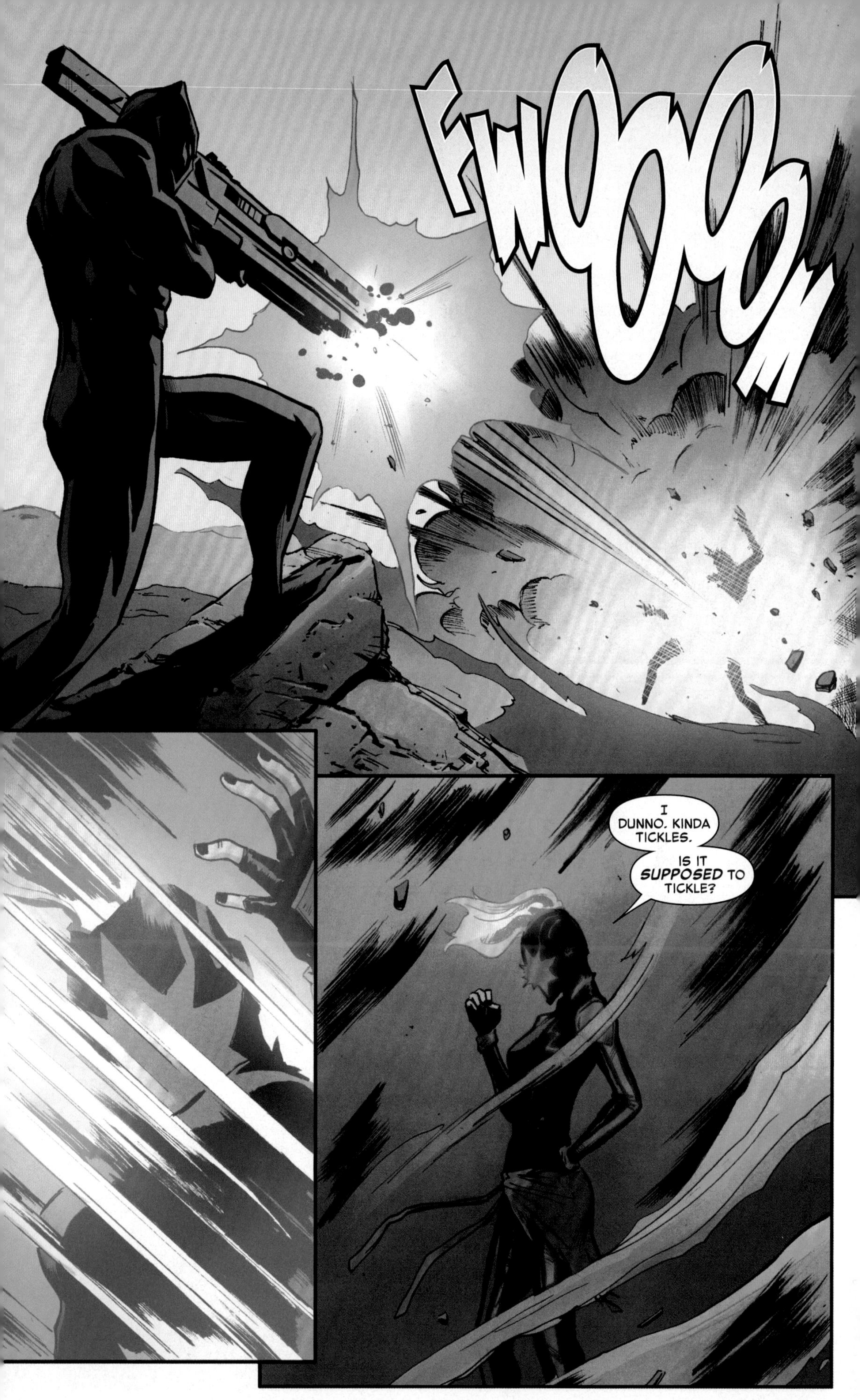
FWOOOOM
I DUNNO. KINDA TICKLES.
IS IT *SUPPOSED* TO TICKLE?

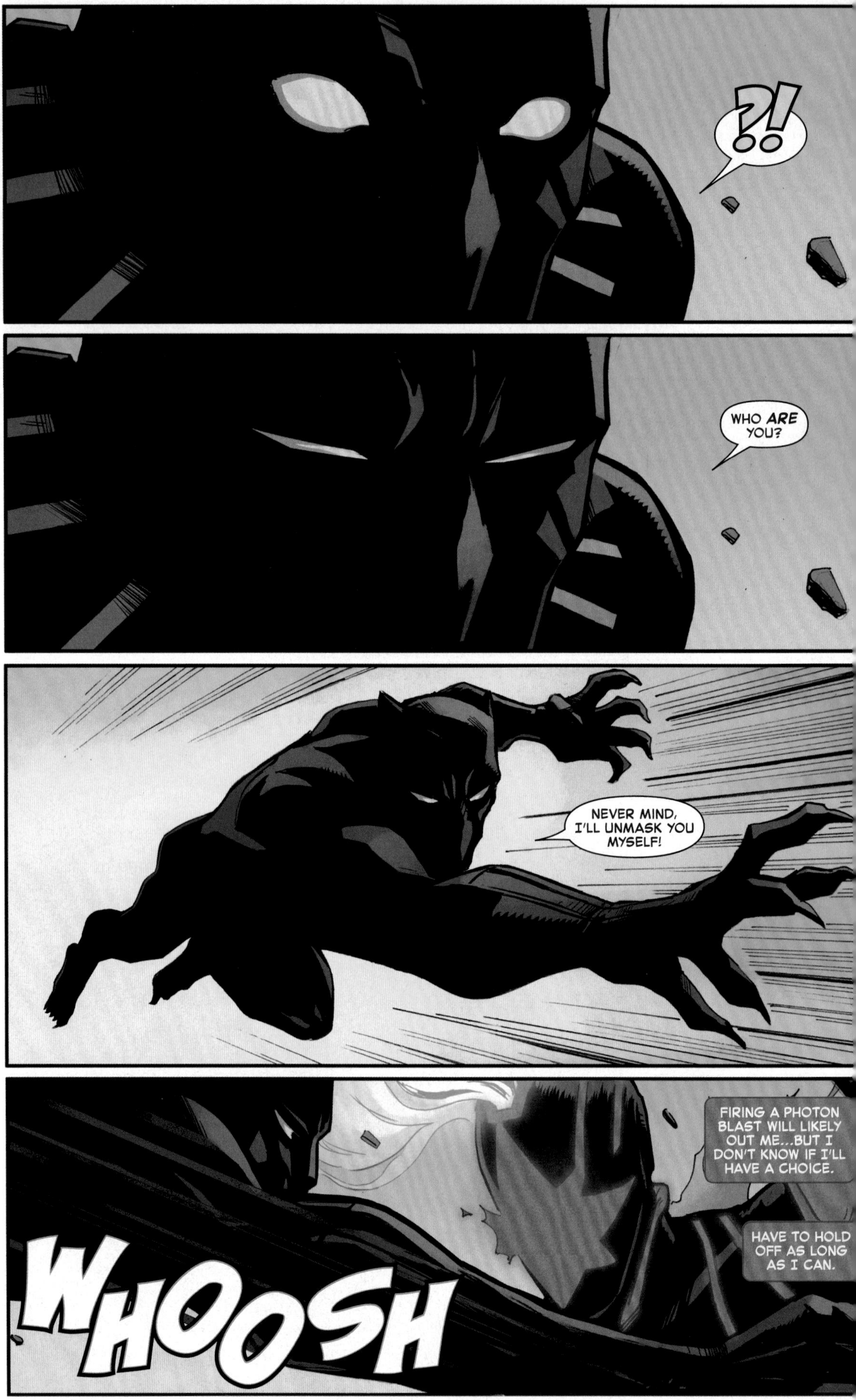
?!
WHO ARE YOU?
NEVER MIND, I'LL UNMASK YOU MYSELF!
FIRING A PHOTON BLAST WILL LIKELY OUT ME...BUT I DON'T KNOW IF I'LL HAVE A CHOICE.
HAVE TO HOLD OFF AS LONG AS I CAN.
WHOOSH

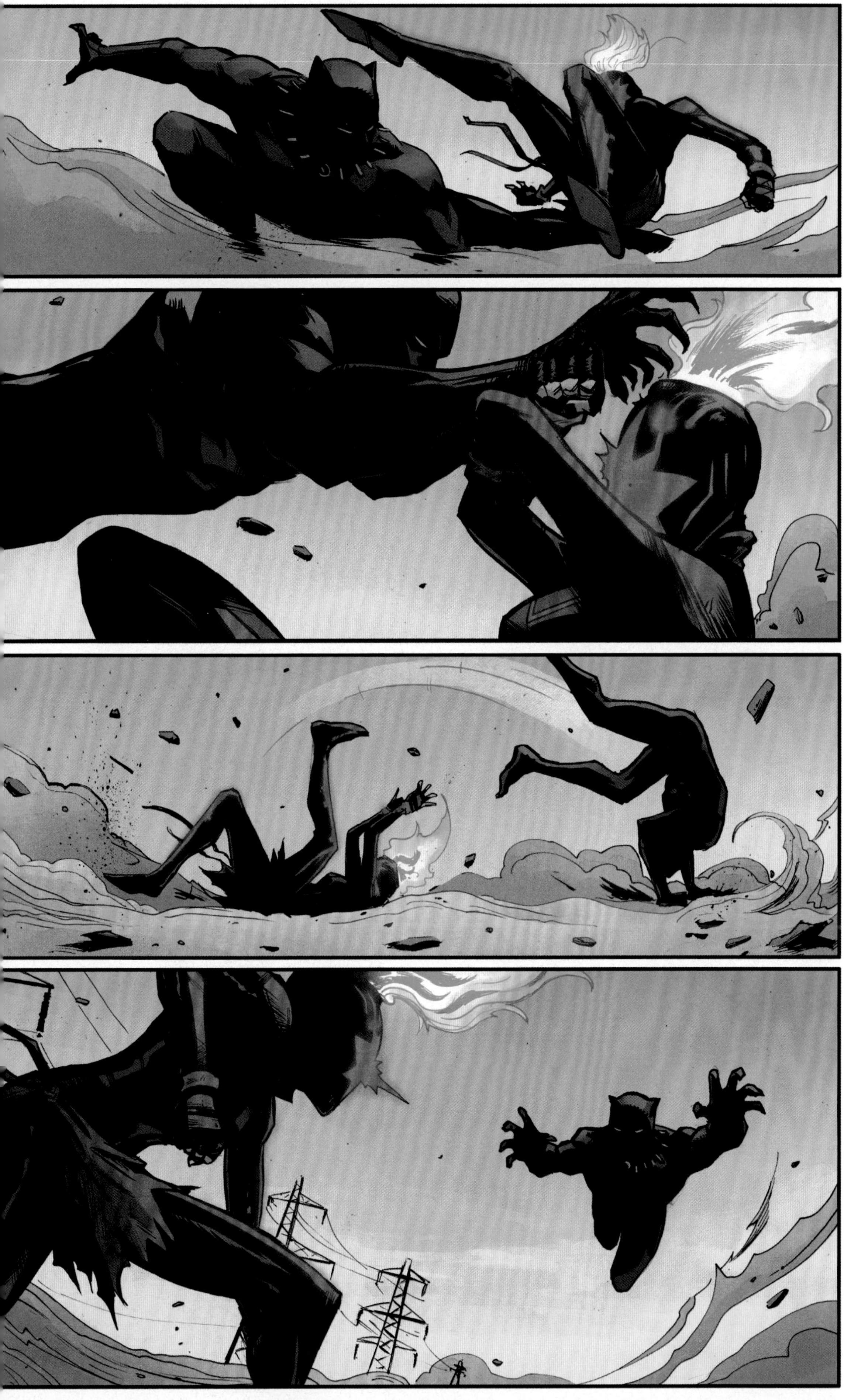

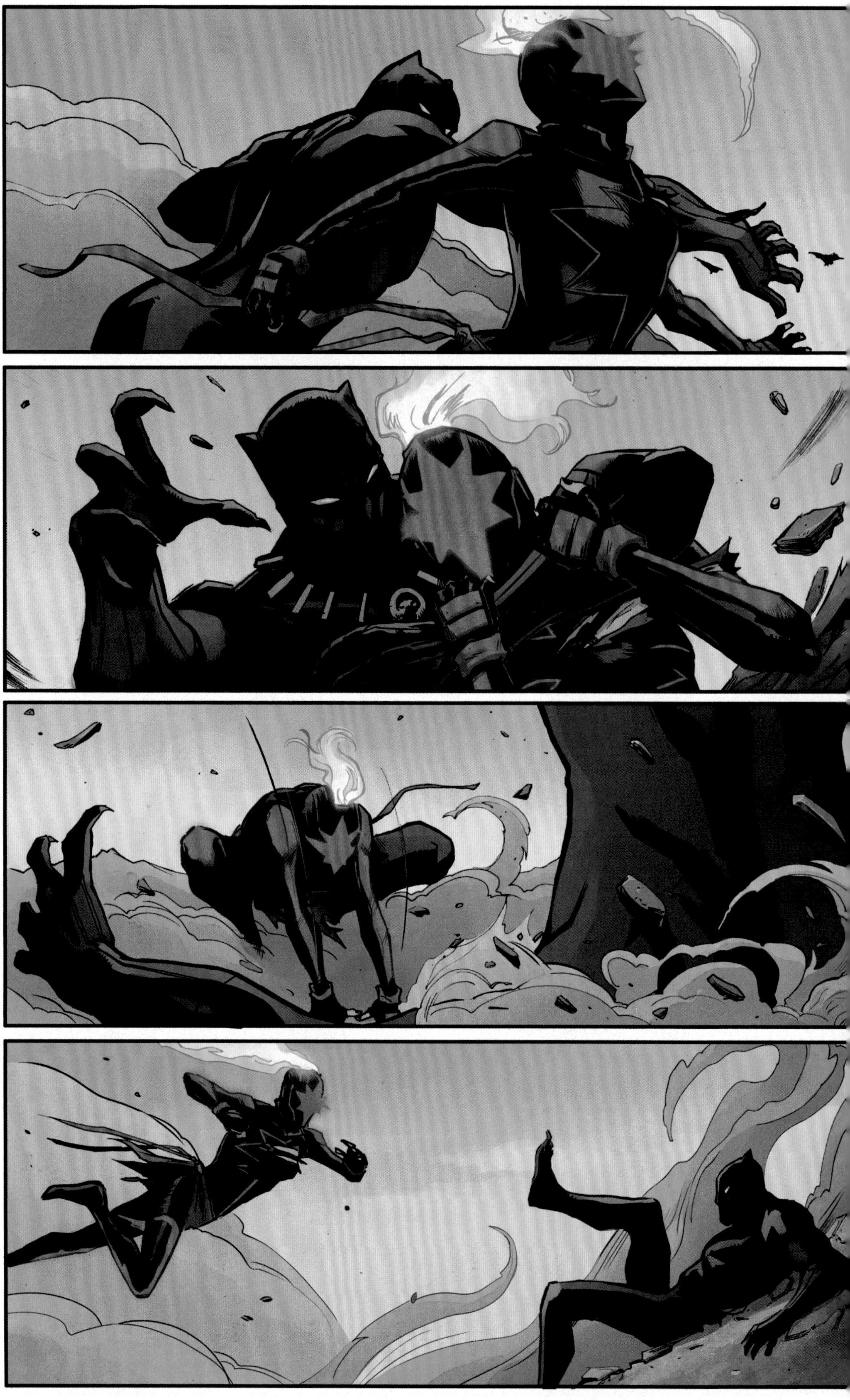

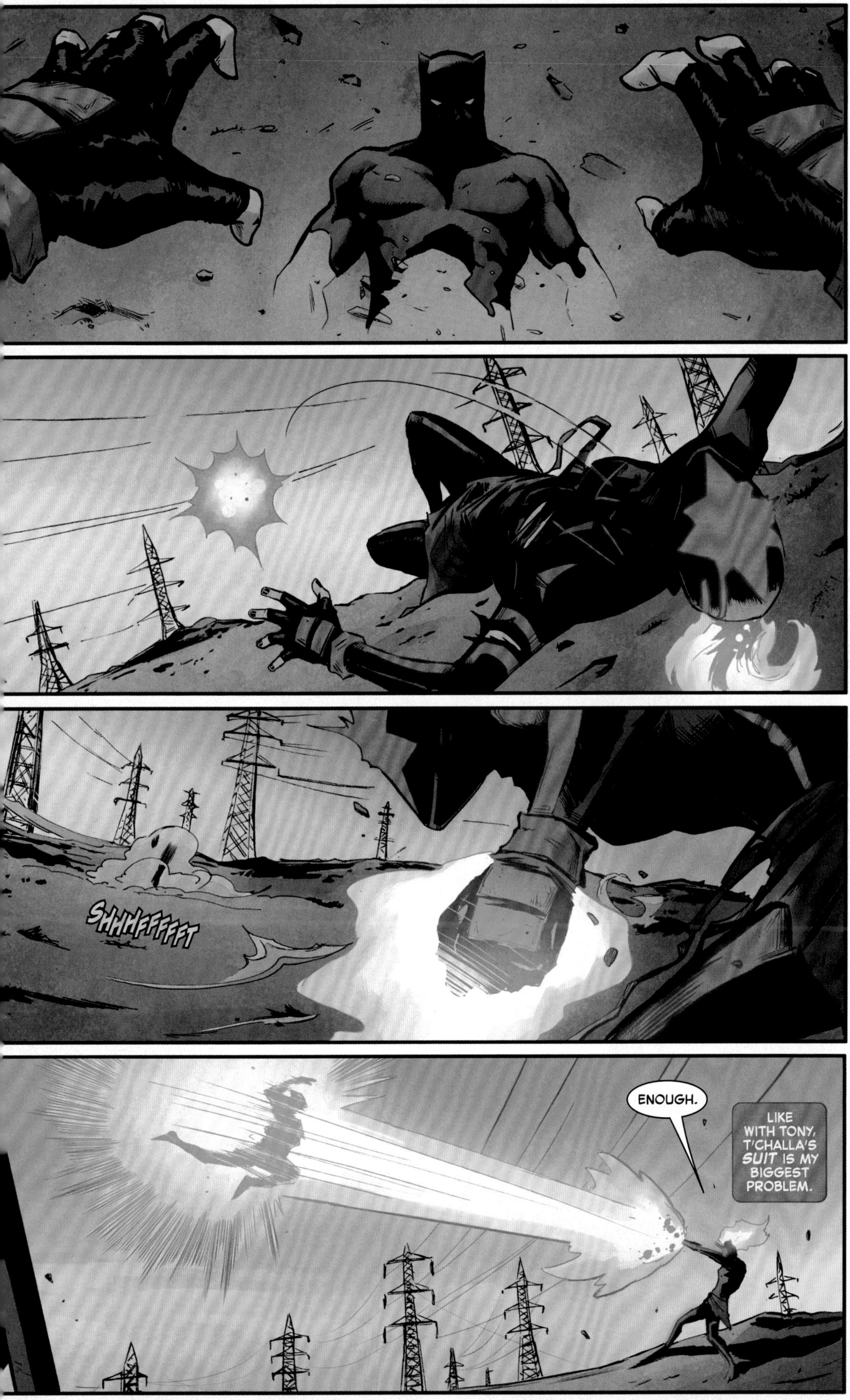
SHHHFFFFFT
ENOUGH.
LIKE WITH TONY, T'CHALLA'S SUIT IS MY BIGGEST PROBLEM.

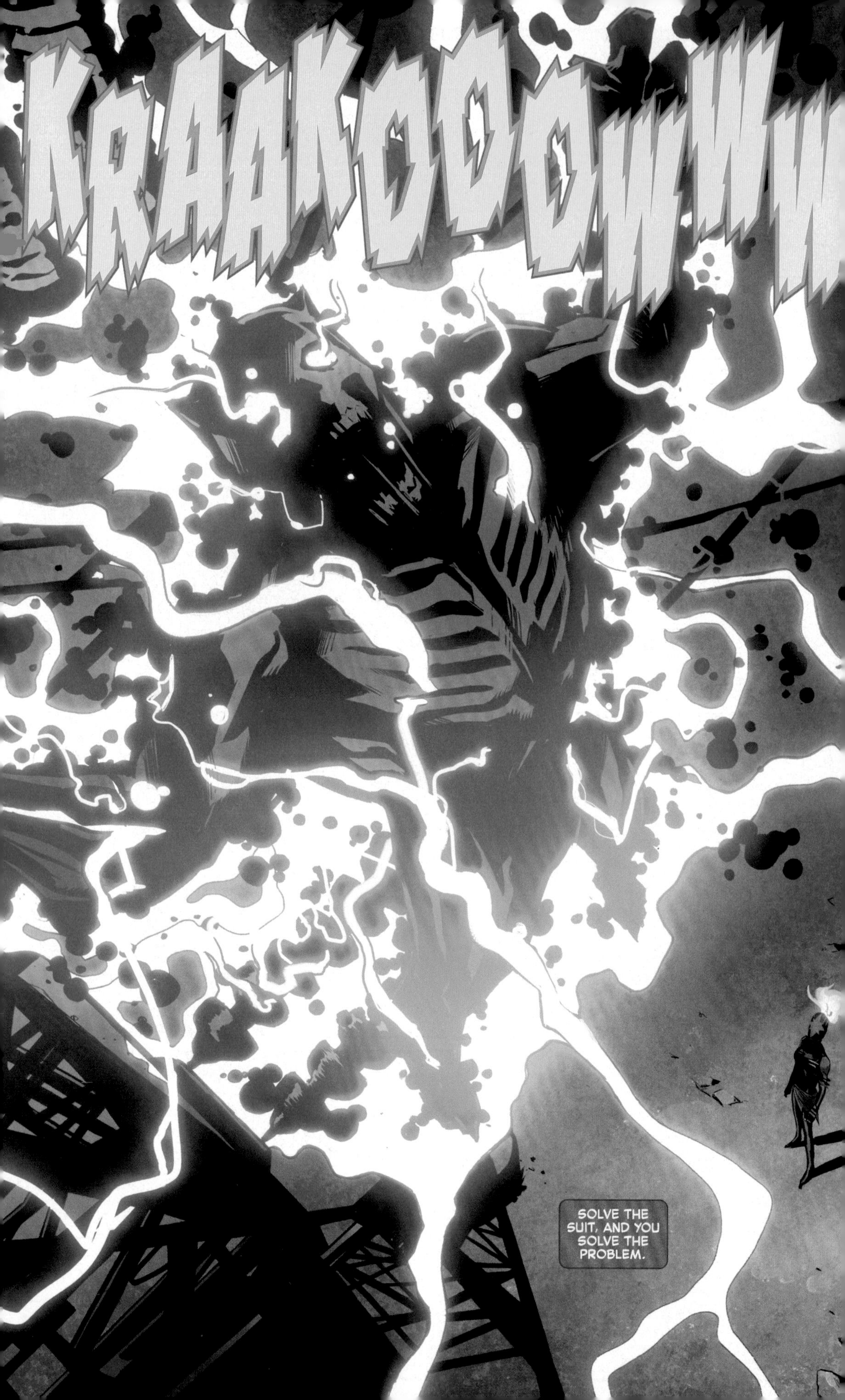
KRAAKOOOWWW
SOLVE THE SUIT, AND YOU SOLVE THE PROBLEM.

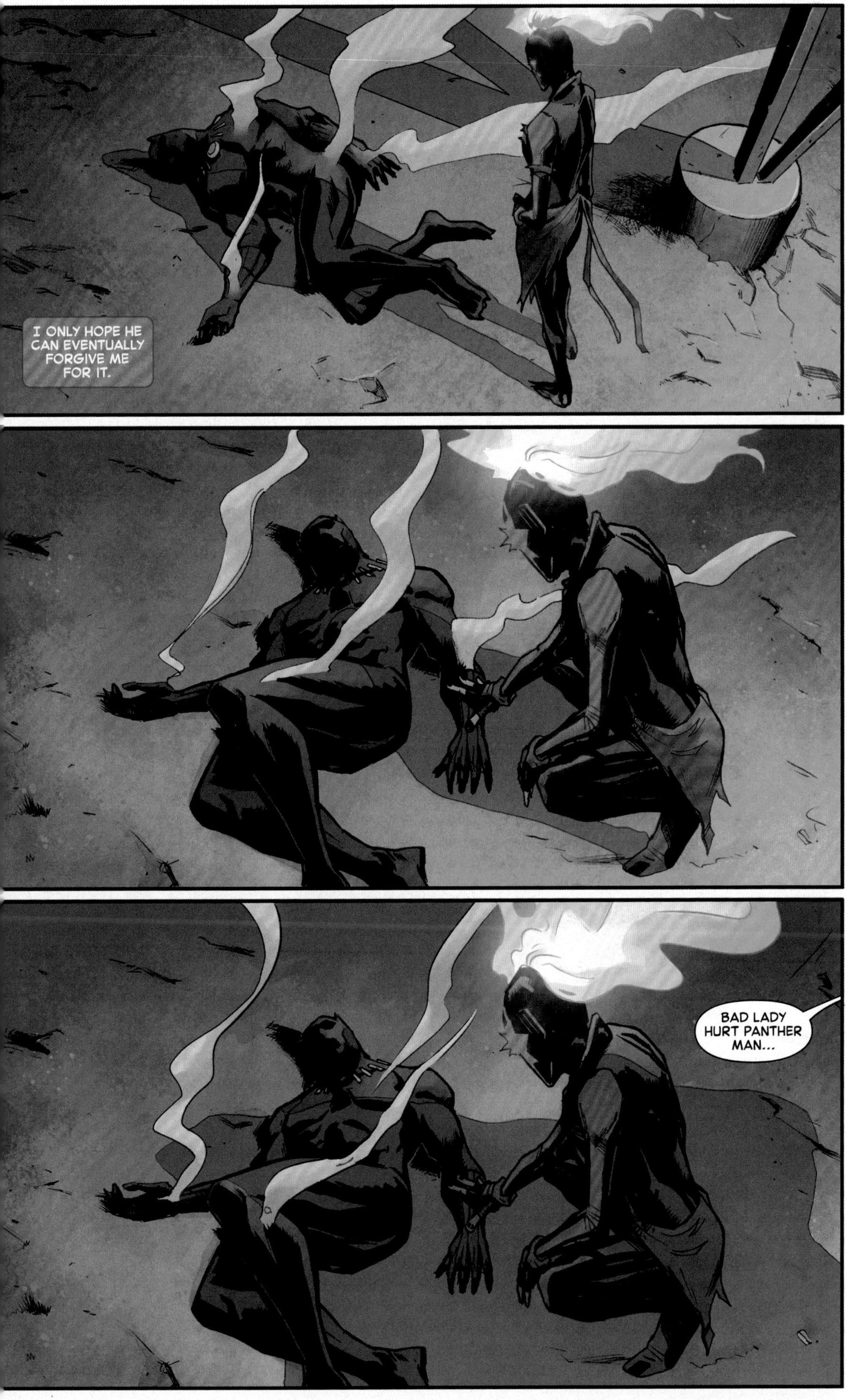
I ONLY HOPE HE CAN EVENTUALLY FORGIVE ME FOR IT.
BAD LADY HURT PANTHER MAN...

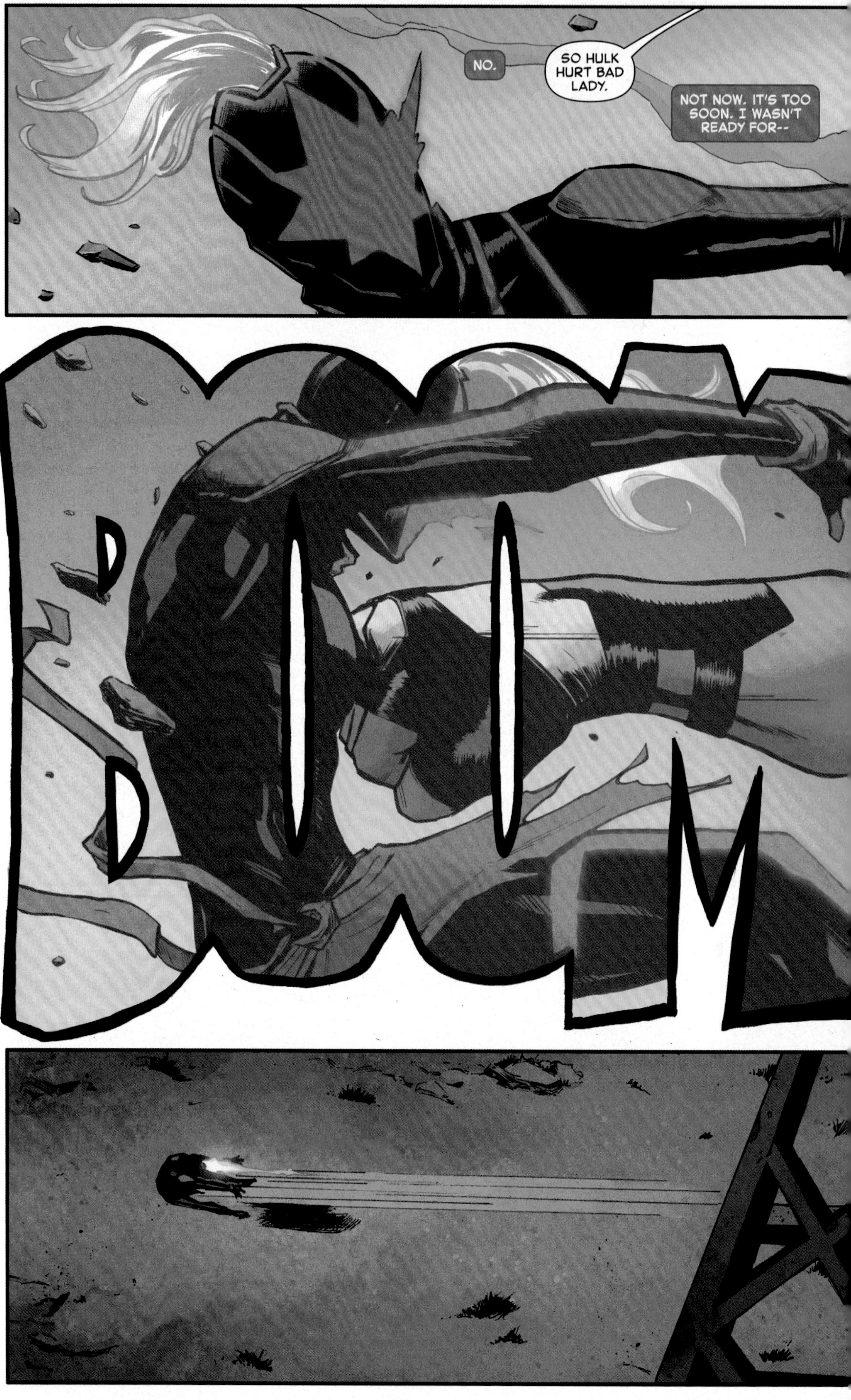
SO HULK HURT BAD LADY.
NO.
NOT NOW. IT'S TOO SOON. I WASN'T READY FOR--
DOOM

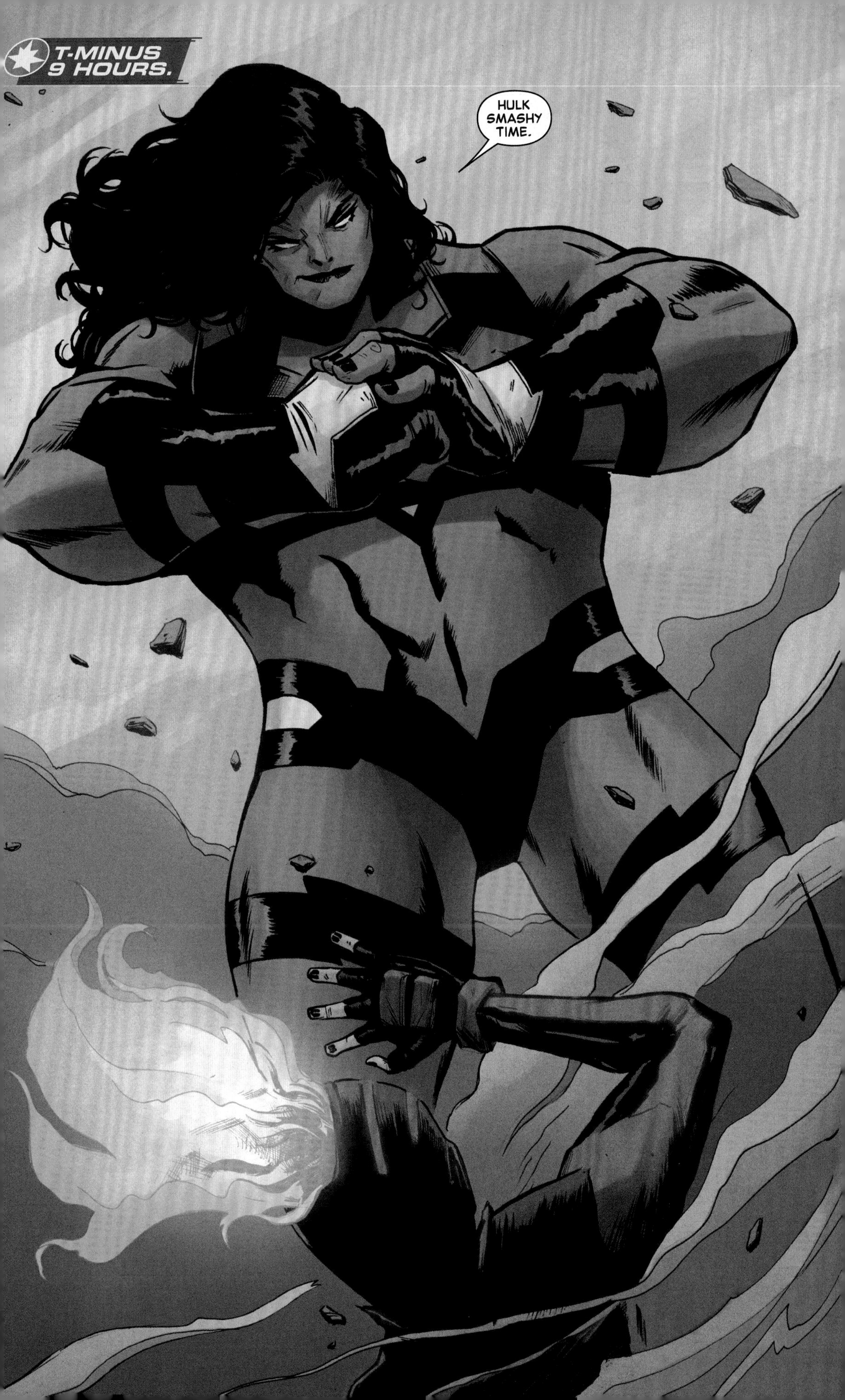
T-MINUS 9 HOURS.
HULK SMASHY TIME.

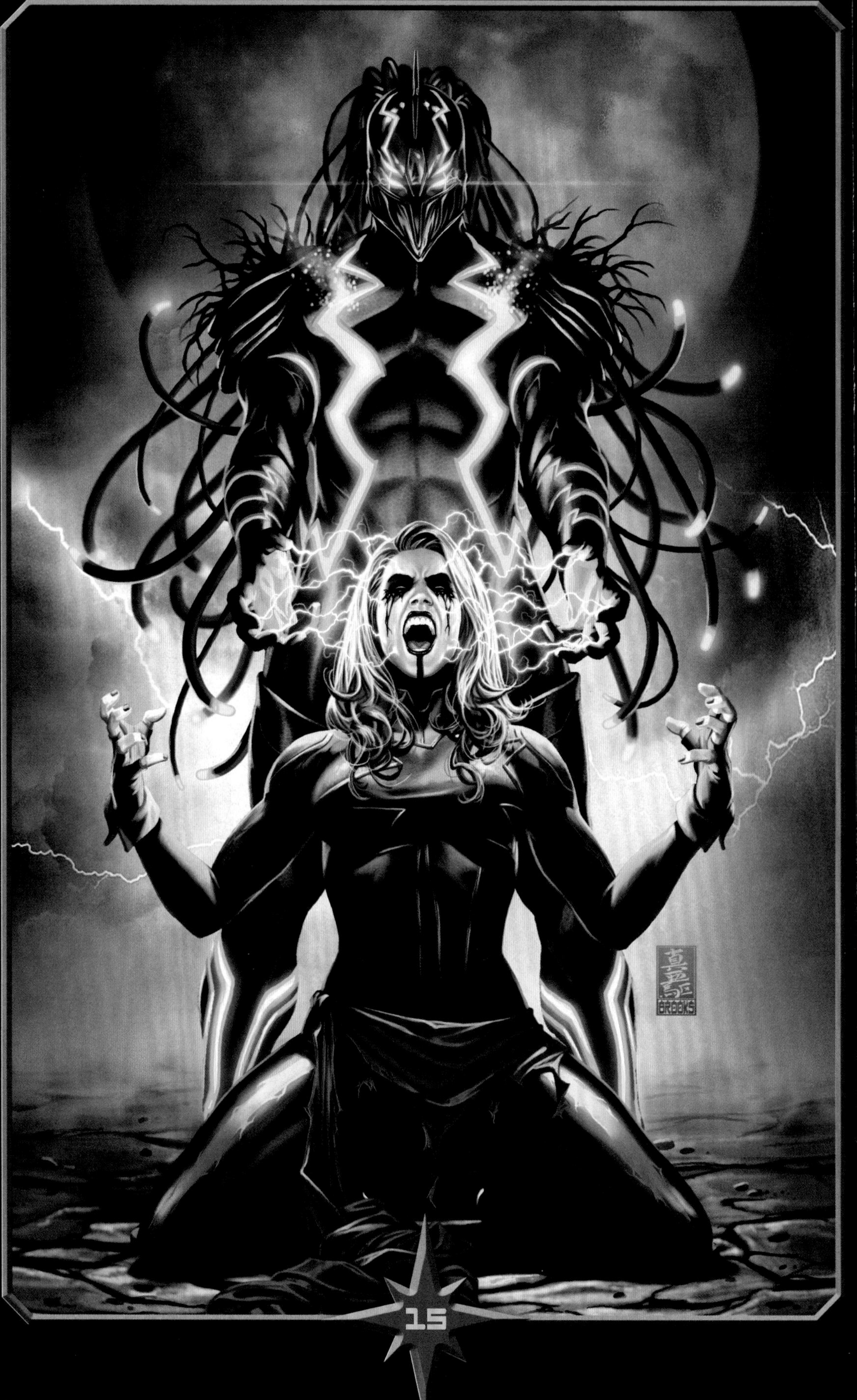
BROOKS
15

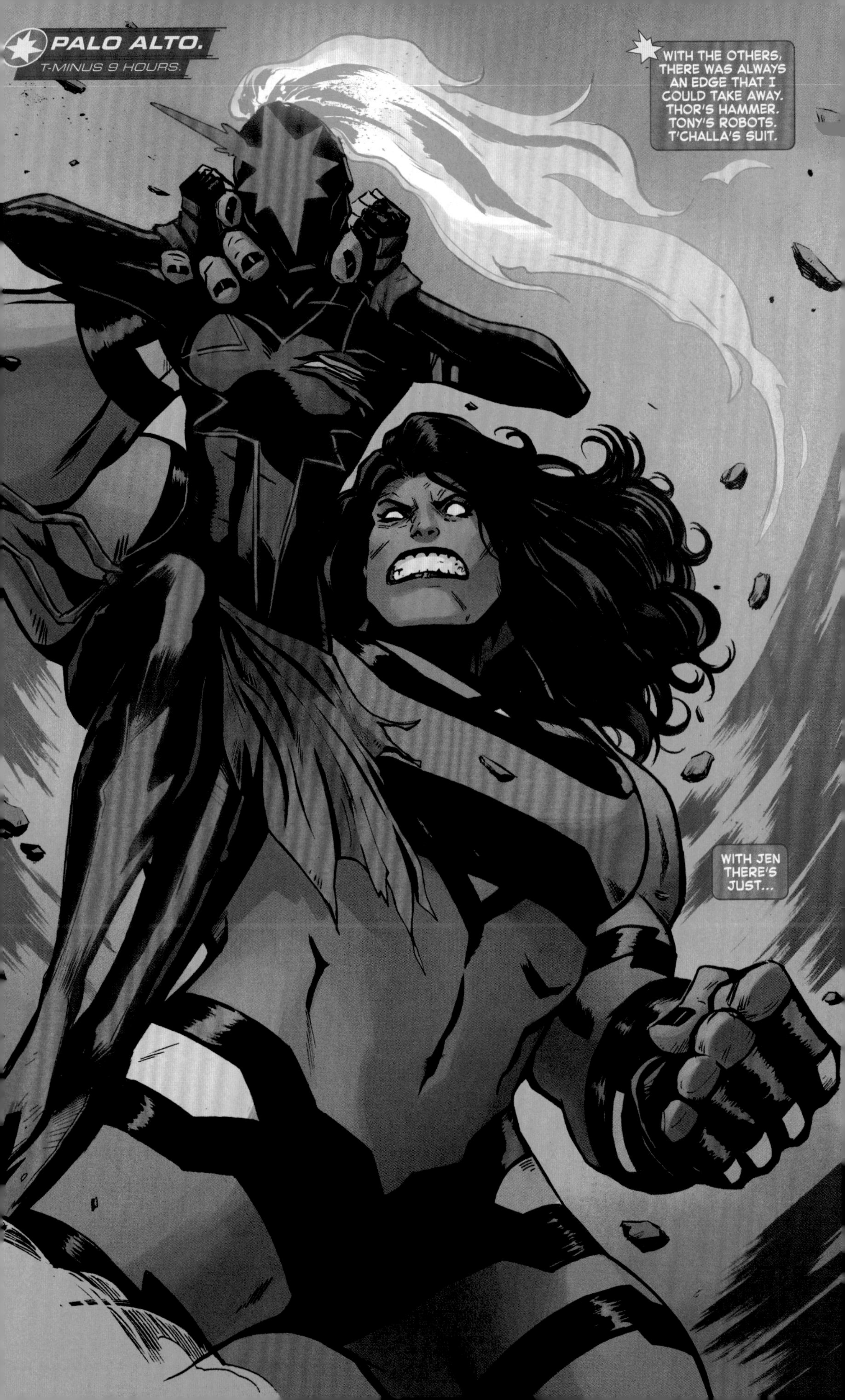
PALO ALTO.
T-MINUS 9 HOURS.
WITH THE OTHERS, THERE WAS ALWAYS AN EDGE THAT I COULD TAKE AWAY. THOR'S HAMMER. TONY'S ROBOTS. T'CHALLA'S SUIT.
WITH JEN THERE'S JUST...

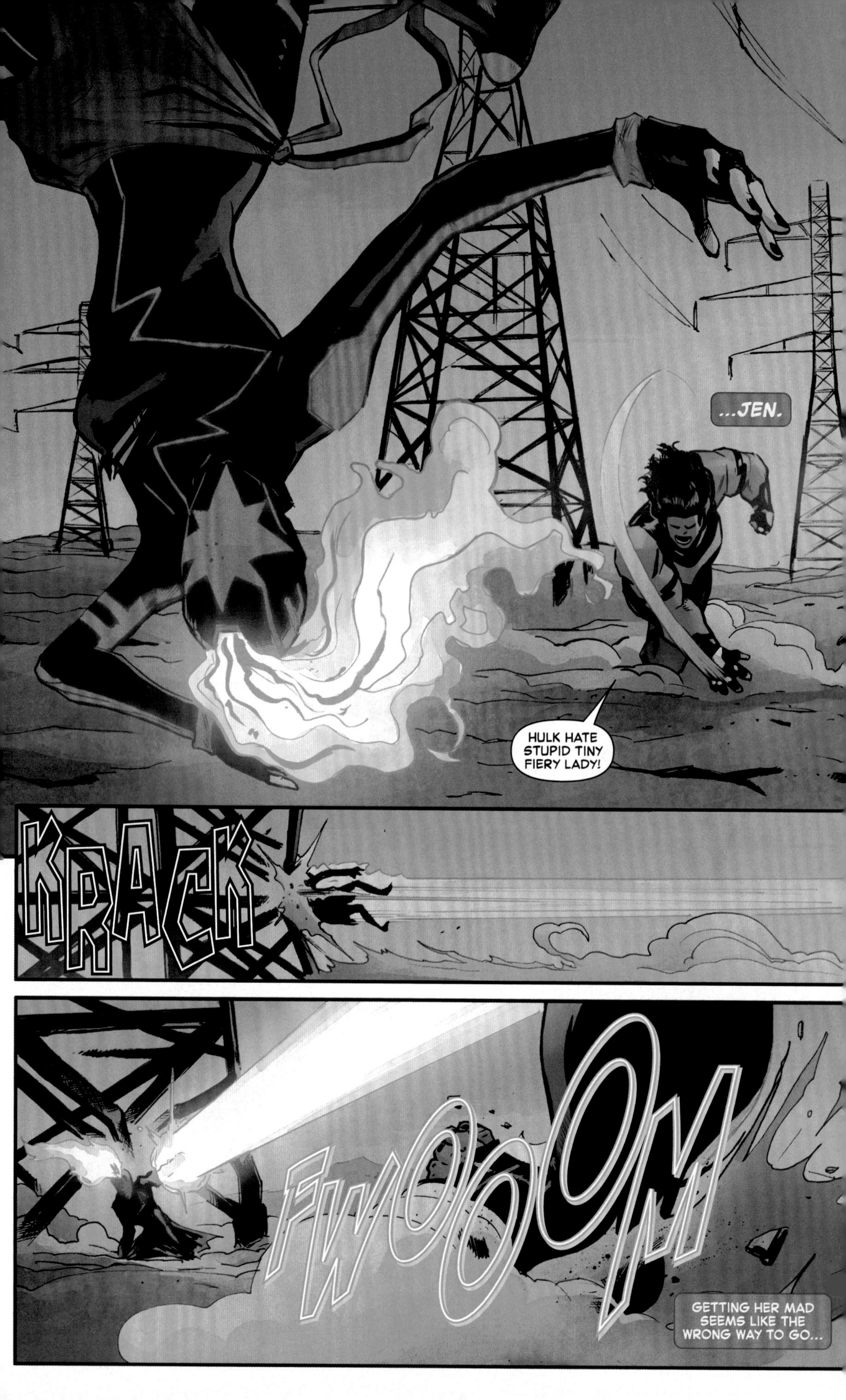
...JEN.
HULK HATE STUPID TINY FIERY LADY!
KRACK
FWOOOOM
GETTING HER MAD SEEMS LIKE THE WRONG WAY TO GO...

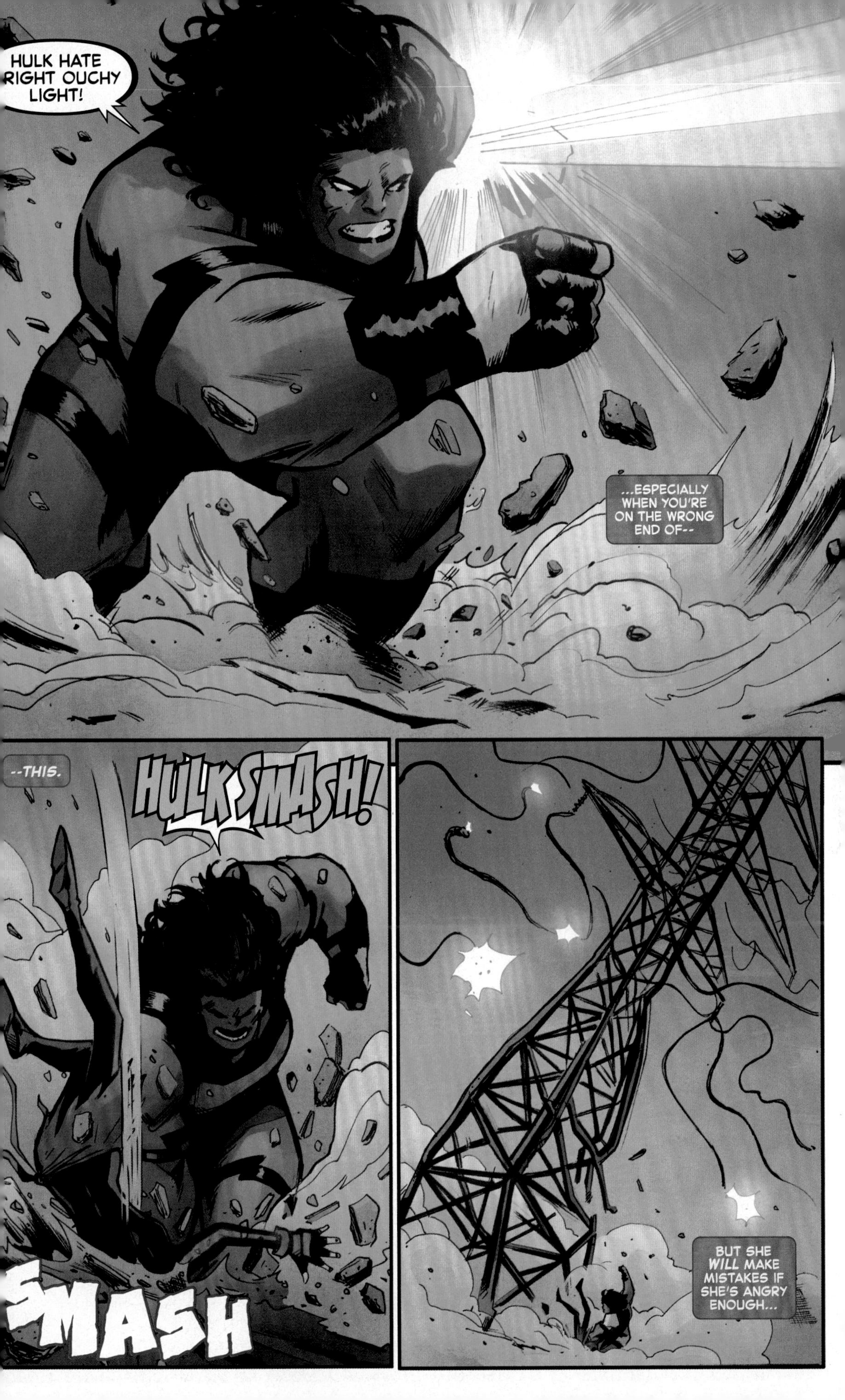
HULK HATE RIGHT OUCHY LIGHT!
...ESPECIALLY WHEN YOU'RE ON THE WRONG END OF--
--THIS.
HULK SMASH!
SMASH
BUT SHE WILL MAKE MISTAKES IF SHE'S ANGRY ENOUGH...

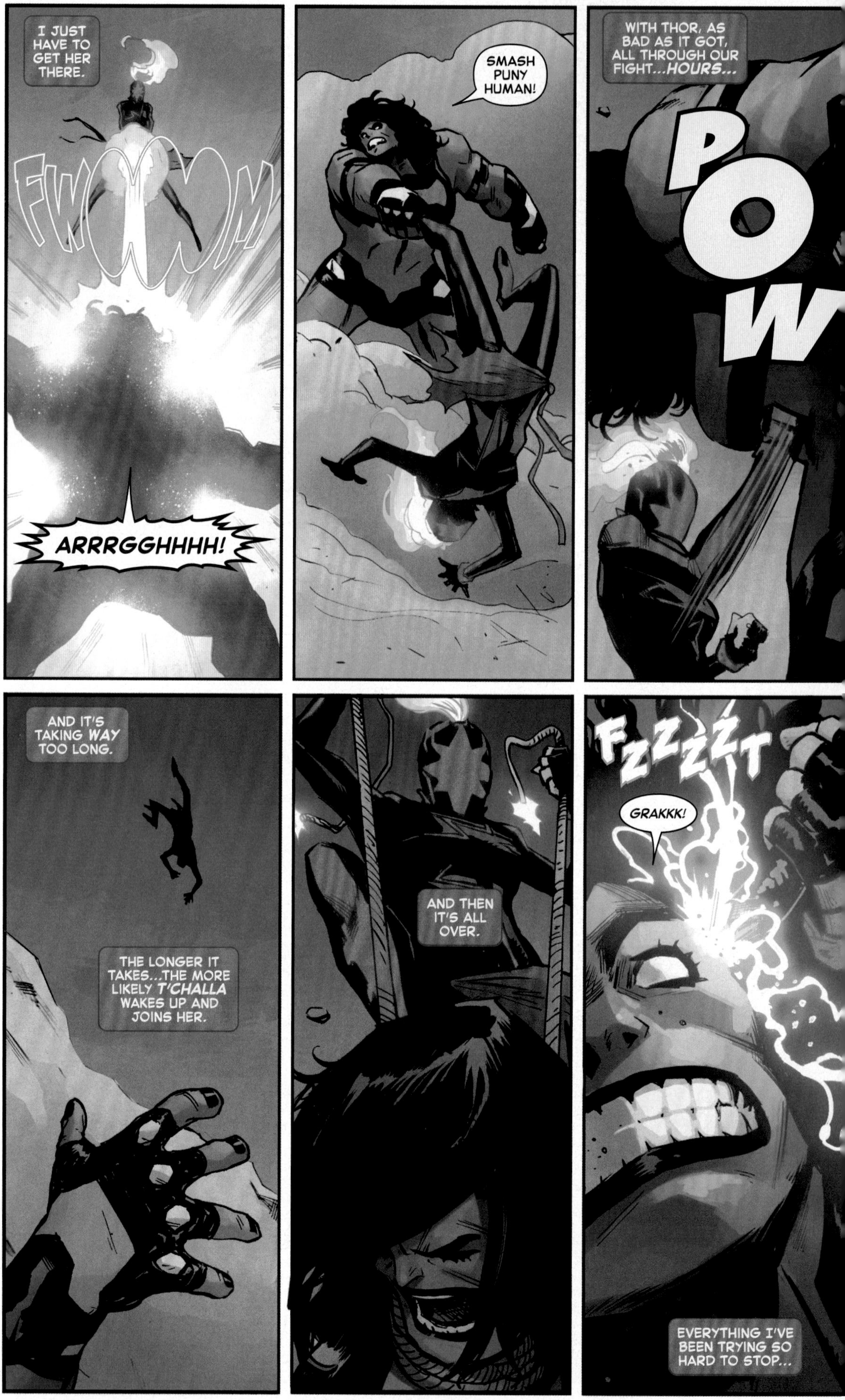
I JUST HAVE TO GET HER THERE.
FWOOOM
ARRRGGHHHH!
SMASH PUNY HUMAN!
WITH THOR, AS BAD AS IT GOT, ALL THROUGH OUR FIGHT...HOURS...
POW
AND IT'S TAKING WAY TOO LONG.
THE LONGER IT TAKES...THE MORE LIKELY T'CHALLA WAKES UP AND JOINS HER.
AND THEN IT'S ALL OVER.
FZZZZT
GRAKKK!
EVERYTHING I'VE BEEN TRYING SO HARD TO STOP...

AGH!

...HE KEPT CHARGING ME WITH ENERGY.

CRUSH!

IT WAS ENOUGH TO TAKE HIM OUT WHEN I HAD THE OPENING.

FWOOMM

GRAAAH!

WHAMMO

THAT'S NOT HAPPENING HERE.

ALL THOSE BOMBS...

ALL THOSE PEOPLE.

OH MY GOD. PEOPLE. VOX SUPREME PUT HIS BOMBS IN THE ACTUAL KREE REFUGEES THEMSELVES!

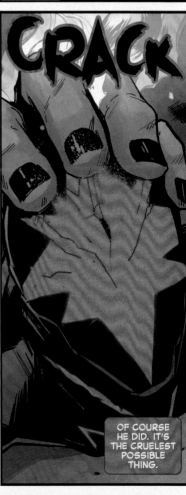

CRACK

OF COURSE HE DID. IT'S THE CRUELEST POSSIBLE THING.

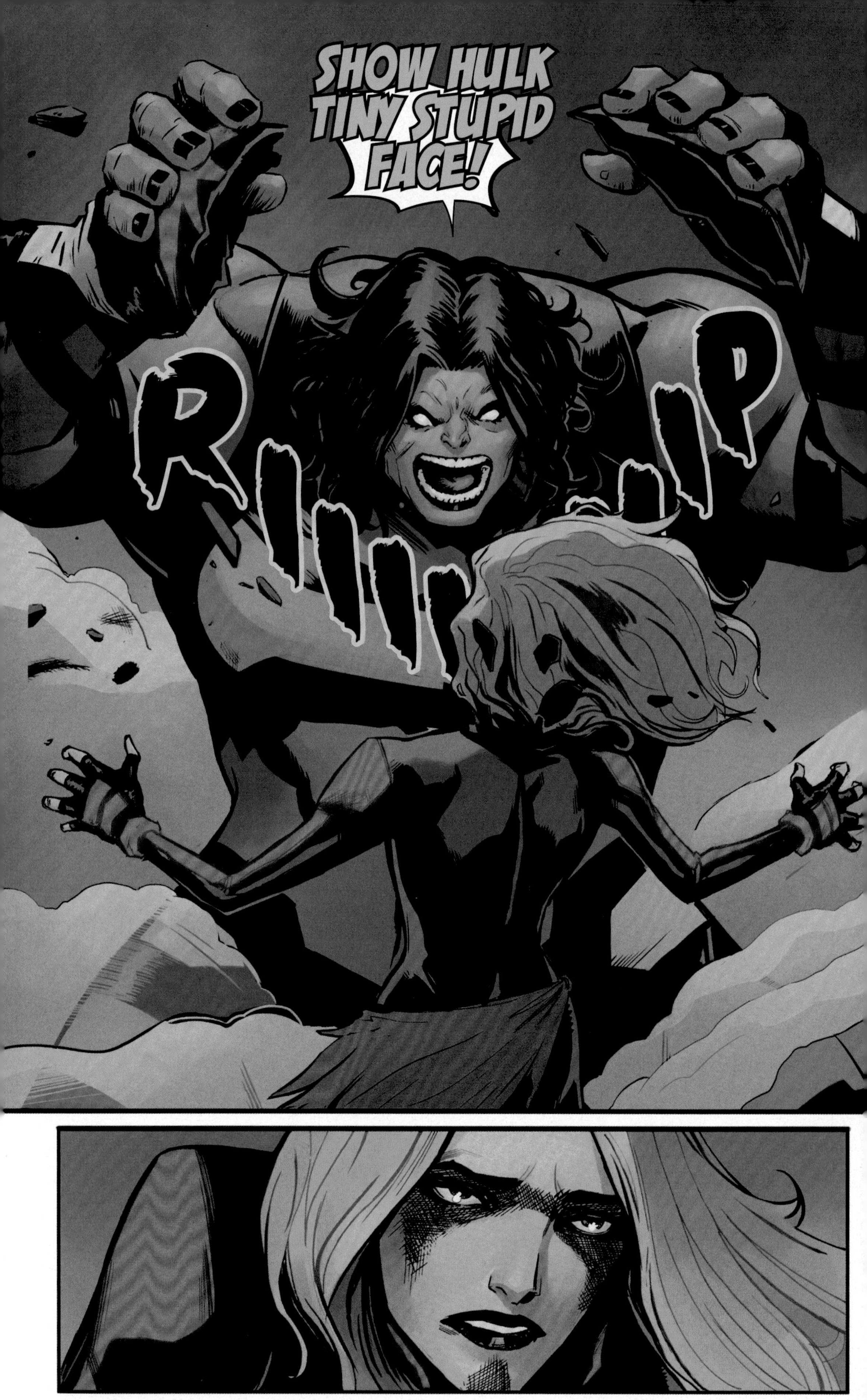
SHOW HULK TINY STUPID FACE!
RIIIIIIP

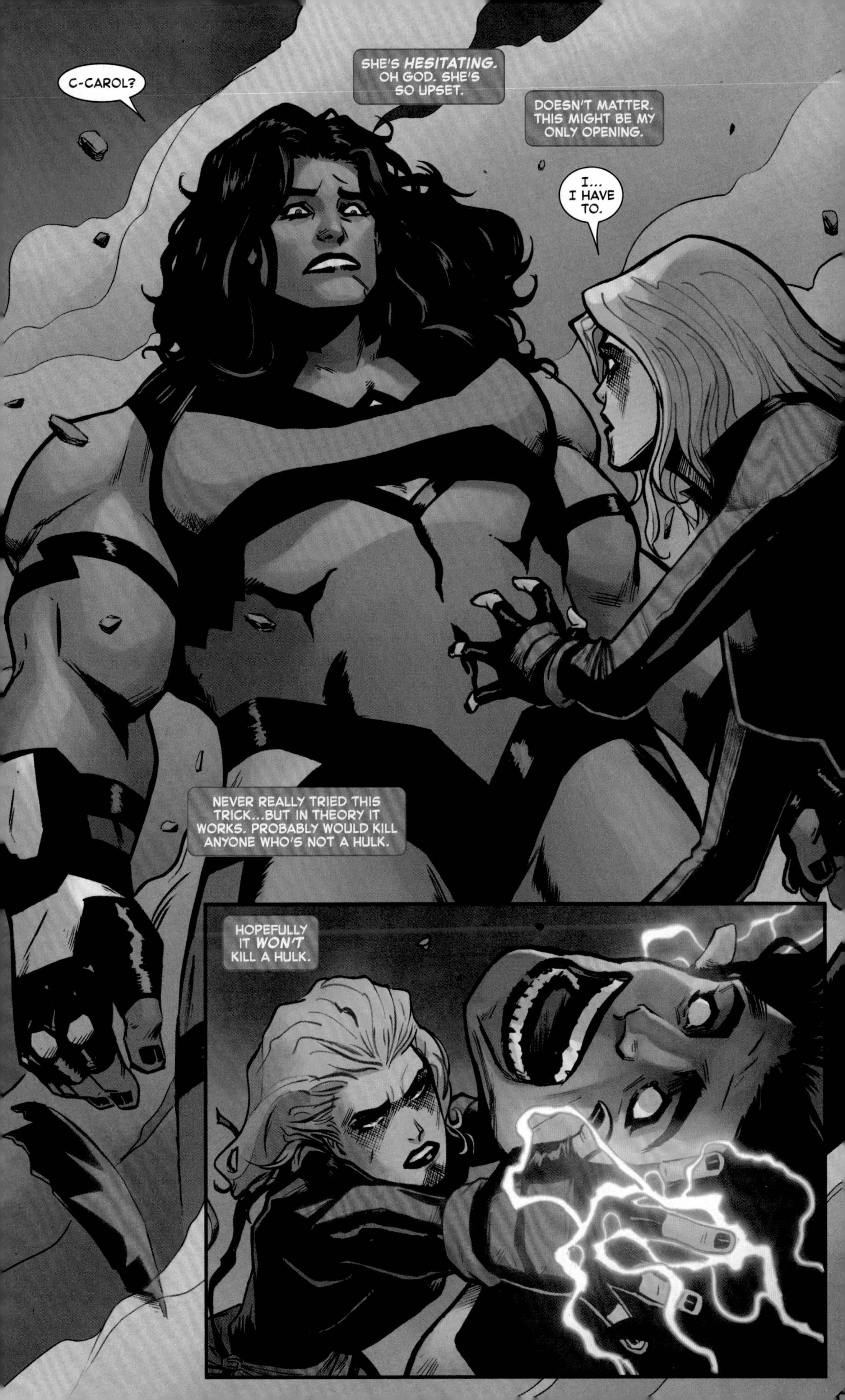
C-CAROL?
SHE'S HESITATING. OH GOD. SHE'S SO UPSET.
DOESN'T MATTER. THIS MIGHT BE MY ONLY OPENING.
I... I HAVE TO.
NEVER REALLY TRIED THIS TRICK...BUT IN THEORY IT WORKS. PROBABLY WOULD KILL ANYONE WHO'S NOT A HULK.
HOPEFULLY IT WON'T KILL A HULK.

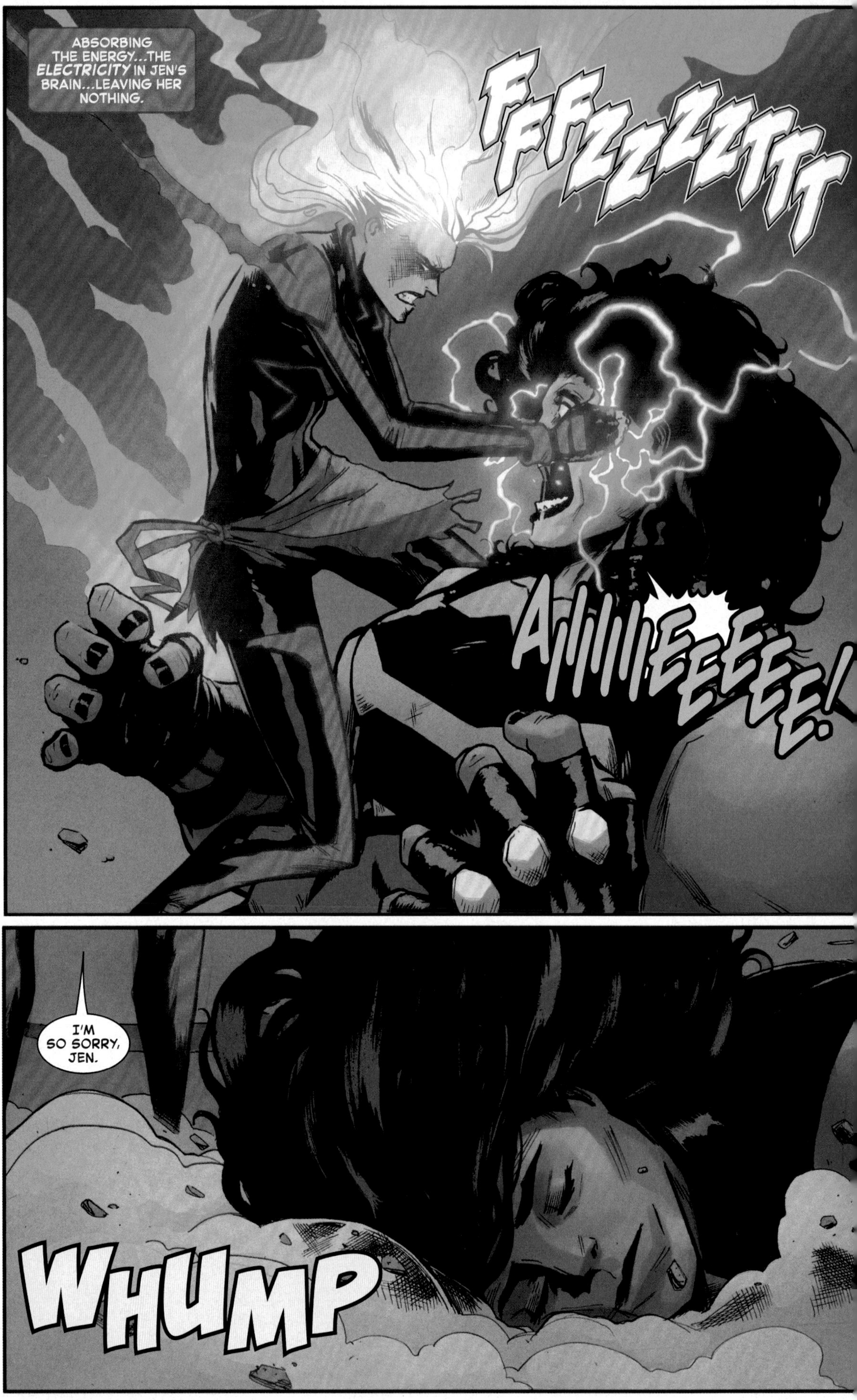
ABSORBING THE ENERGY...THE ELECTRICITY IN JEN'S BRAIN...LEAVING HER NOTHING.
FFFZZZZZTTTT
AIIIIIIEEEEEE!
I'M SO SORRY, JEN.
WHUMP

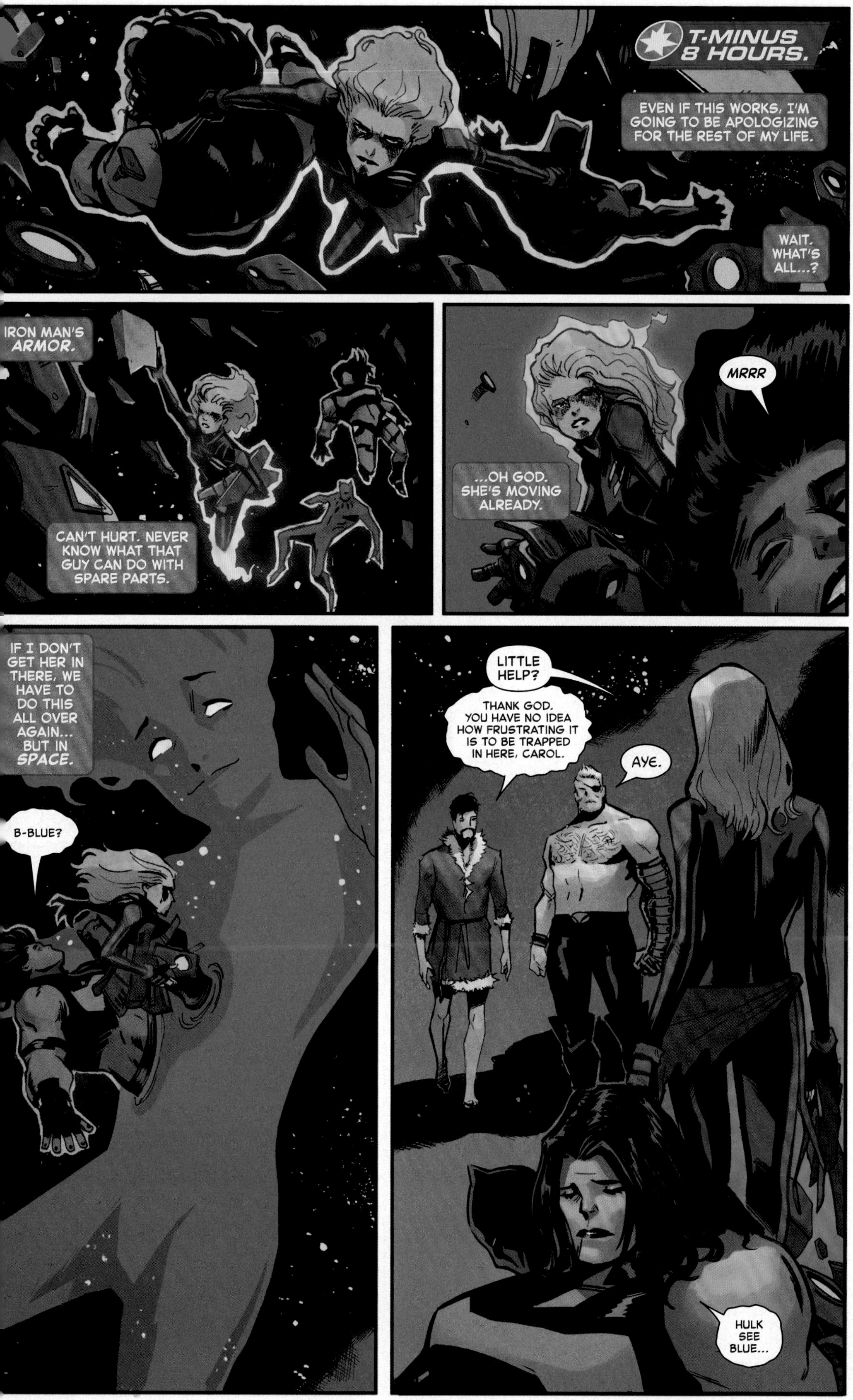
T-MINUS 8 HOURS.
EVEN IF THIS WORKS, I'M GOING TO BE APOLOGIZING FOR THE REST OF MY LIFE.
WAIT. WHAT'S ALL...?
IRON MAN'S ARMOR.
CAN'T HURT. NEVER KNOW WHAT THAT GUY CAN DO WITH SPARE PARTS.
MRRR
...OH GOD. SHE'S MOVING ALREADY.
IF I DON'T GET HER IN THERE, WE HAVE TO DO THIS ALL OVER AGAIN... BUT IN SPACE.
B-BLUE?
LITTLE HELP?
THANK GOD. YOU HAVE NO IDEA HOW FRUSTRATING IT IS TO BE TRAPPED IN HERE, CAROL.
AYE.
HULK SEE BLUE...

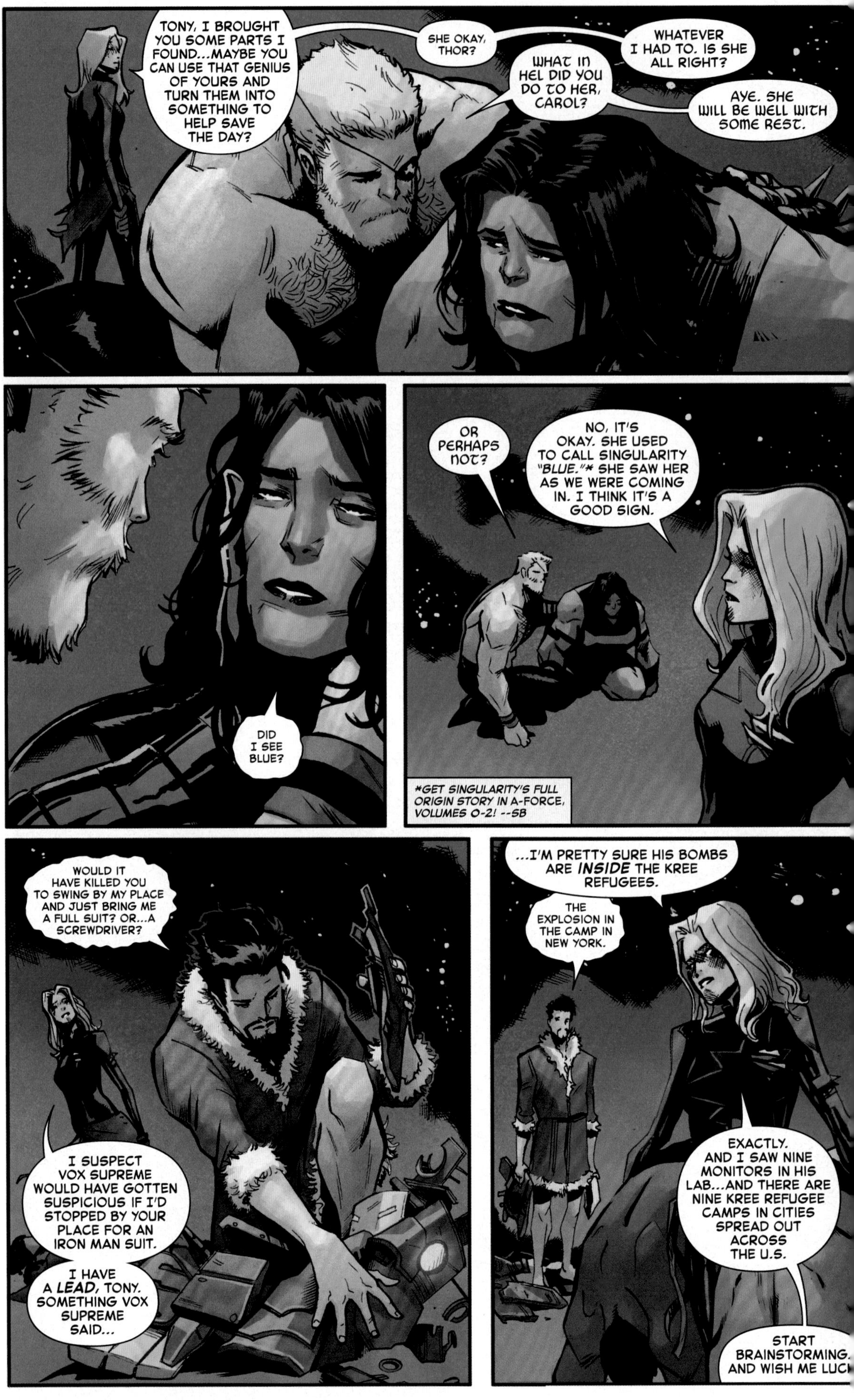

TONY, I BROUGHT YOU SOME PARTS I FOUND...MAYBE YOU CAN USE THAT GENIUS OF YOURS AND TURN THEM INTO SOMETHING TO HELP SAVE THE DAY?
SHE OKAY, THOR?
WHAT IN HEL DID YOU DO TO HER, CAROL?
WHATEVER I HAD TO. IS SHE ALL RIGHT?
AYE. SHE WILL BE WELL WITH SOME REST.
DID I SEE BLUE?
OR PERHAPS NOT?
NO, IT'S OKAY. SHE USED TO CALL SINGULARITY "BLUE."* SHE SAW HER AS WE WERE COMING IN. I THINK IT'S A GOOD SIGN.
*GET SINGULARITY'S FULL ORIGIN STORY IN A-FORCE, VOLUMES 0-2! --SB
WOULD IT HAVE KILLED YOU TO SWING BY MY PLACE AND JUST BRING ME A FULL SUIT? OR...A SCREWDRIVER?
I SUSPECT VOX SUPREME WOULD HAVE GOTTEN SUSPICIOUS IF I'D STOPPED BY YOUR PLACE FOR AN IRON MAN SUIT.
I HAVE A LEAD, TONY. SOMETHING VOX SUPREME SAID...
...I'M PRETTY SURE HIS BOMBS ARE INSIDE THE KREE REFUGEES.
THE EXPLOSION IN THE CAMP IN NEW YORK.
EXACTLY. AND I SAW NINE MONITORS IN HIS LAB...AND THERE ARE NINE KREE REFUGEE CAMPS IN CITIES SPREAD OUT ACROSS THE U.S.
START BRAINSTORMING. AND WISH ME LUCK

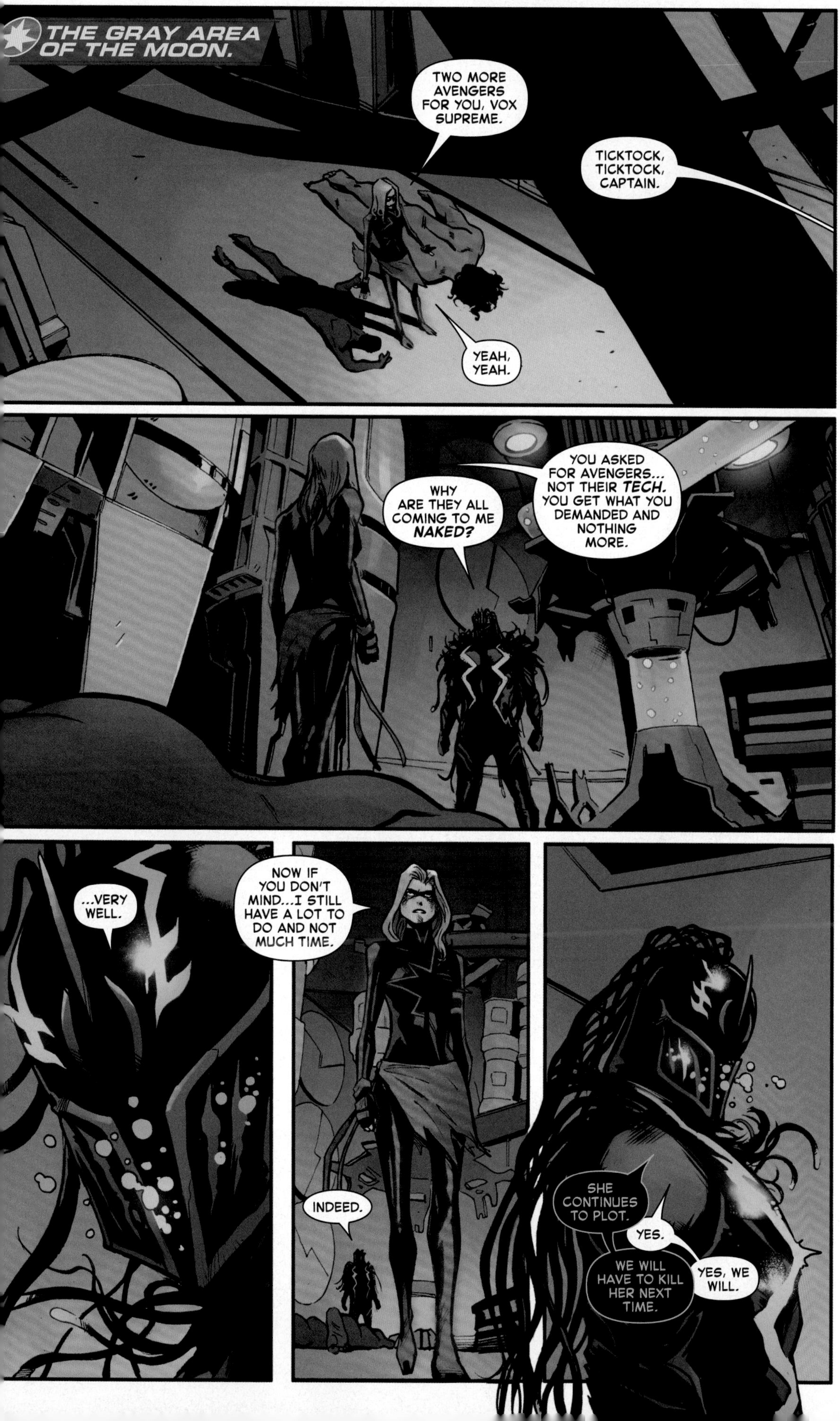
THE GRAY AREA OF THE MOON.
TWO MORE AVENGERS FOR YOU, VOX SUPREME.
TICKTOCK, TICKTOCK, CAPTAIN.
YEAH, YEAH.
WHY ARE THEY ALL COMING TO ME *NAKED?*
YOU ASKED FOR AVENGERS... NOT THEIR *TECH.* YOU GET WHAT YOU DEMANDED AND NOTHING MORE.
...VERY WELL.
NOW IF YOU DON'T MIND...I STILL HAVE A LOT TO DO AND NOT MUCH TIME.
INDEED.
SHE CONTINUES TO PLOT.
YES.
WE WILL HAVE TO KILL HER NEXT TIME.
YES, WE WILL.

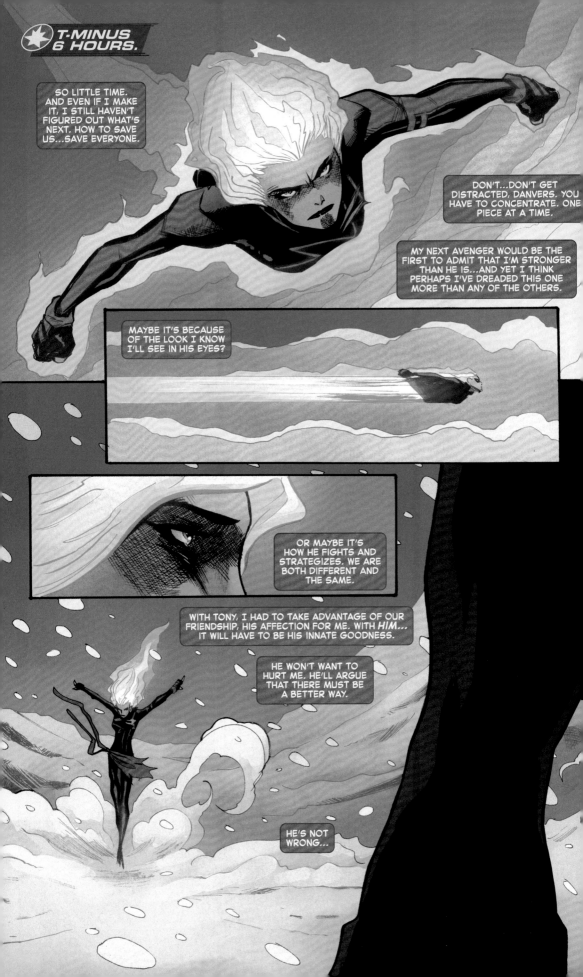

SO LITTLE TIME. AND EVEN IF I MAKE IT, I STILL HAVEN'T FIGURED OUT WHAT'S NEXT. HOW TO SAVE US...SAVE EVERYONE.

DON'T...DON'T GET DISTRACTED, DANVERS. YOU HAVE TO CONCENTRATE. ONE PIECE AT A TIME.

MY NEXT AVENGER WOULD BE THE FIRST TO ADMIT THAT I'M STRONGER THAN HE IS...AND YET I THINK PERHAPS I'VE DREADED THIS ONE MORE THAN ANY OF THE OTHERS.

MAYBE IT'S BECAUSE OF THE LOOK I KNOW I'LL SEE IN HIS EYES?

OR MAYBE IT'S HOW HE FIGHTS AND STRATEGIZES. WE ARE BOTH DIFFERENT AND THE SAME.

WITH TONY, I HAD TO TAKE ADVANTAGE OF OUR FRIENDSHIP, HIS AFFECTION FOR ME. WITH *HIM*... IT WILL HAVE TO BE HIS INNATE GOODNESS.

HE WON'T WANT TO HURT ME. HE'LL ARGUE THAT THERE MUST BE A BETTER WAY.

HE'S NOT WRONG...

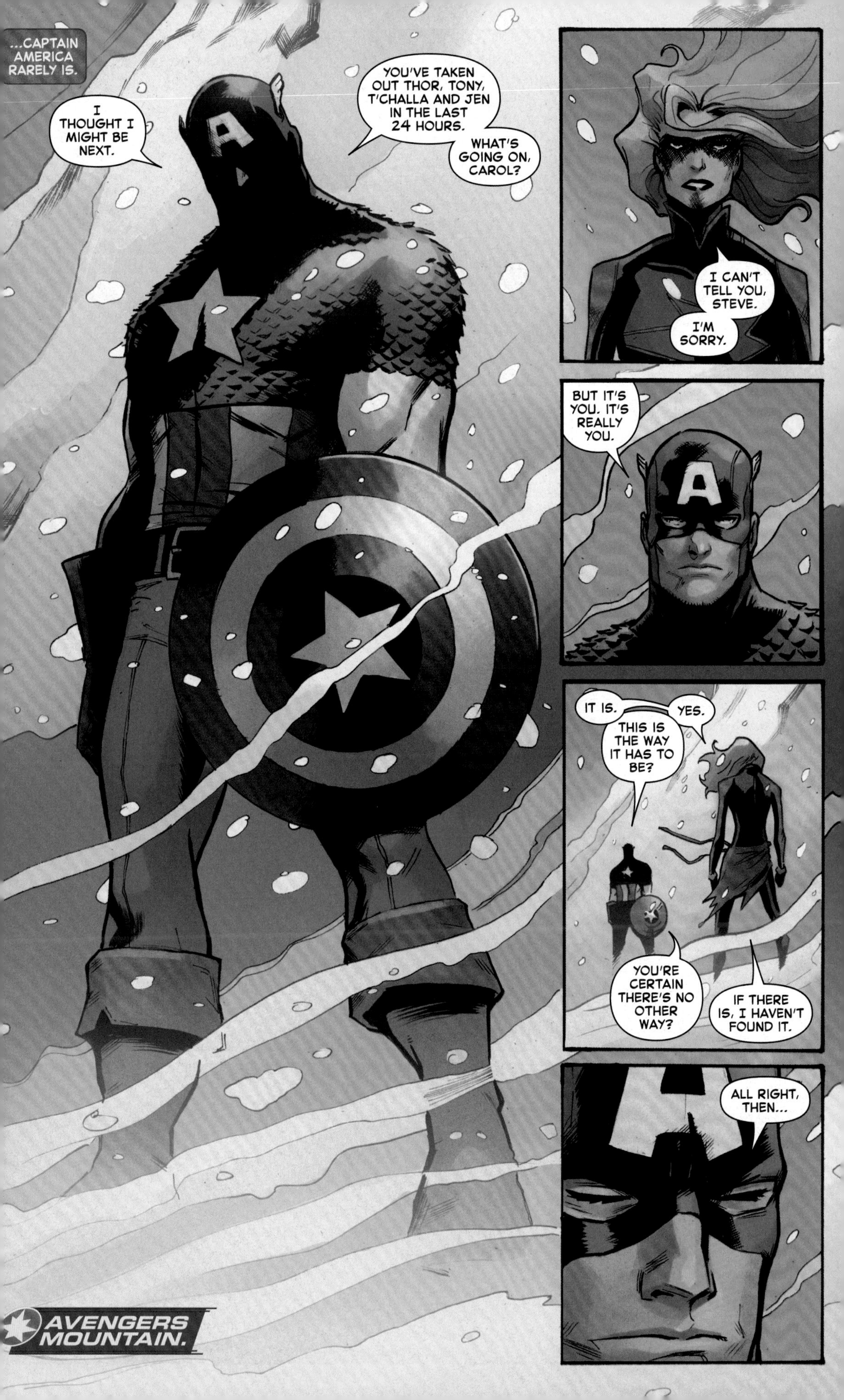

...CAPTAIN AMERICA RARELY IS.
I THOUGHT I MIGHT BE NEXT.
YOU'VE TAKEN OUT THOR, TONY, T'CHALLA AND JEN IN THE LAST 24 HOURS.
WHAT'S GOING ON, CAROL?
I CAN'T TELL YOU, STEVE.
I'M SORRY.
BUT IT'S YOU. IT'S REALLY YOU.
IT IS.
YES.
THIS IS THE WAY IT HAS TO BE?
YOU'RE CERTAIN THERE'S NO OTHER WAY?
IF THERE IS, I HAVEN'T FOUND IT.
ALL RIGHT, THEN...
AVENGERS MOUNTAIN.

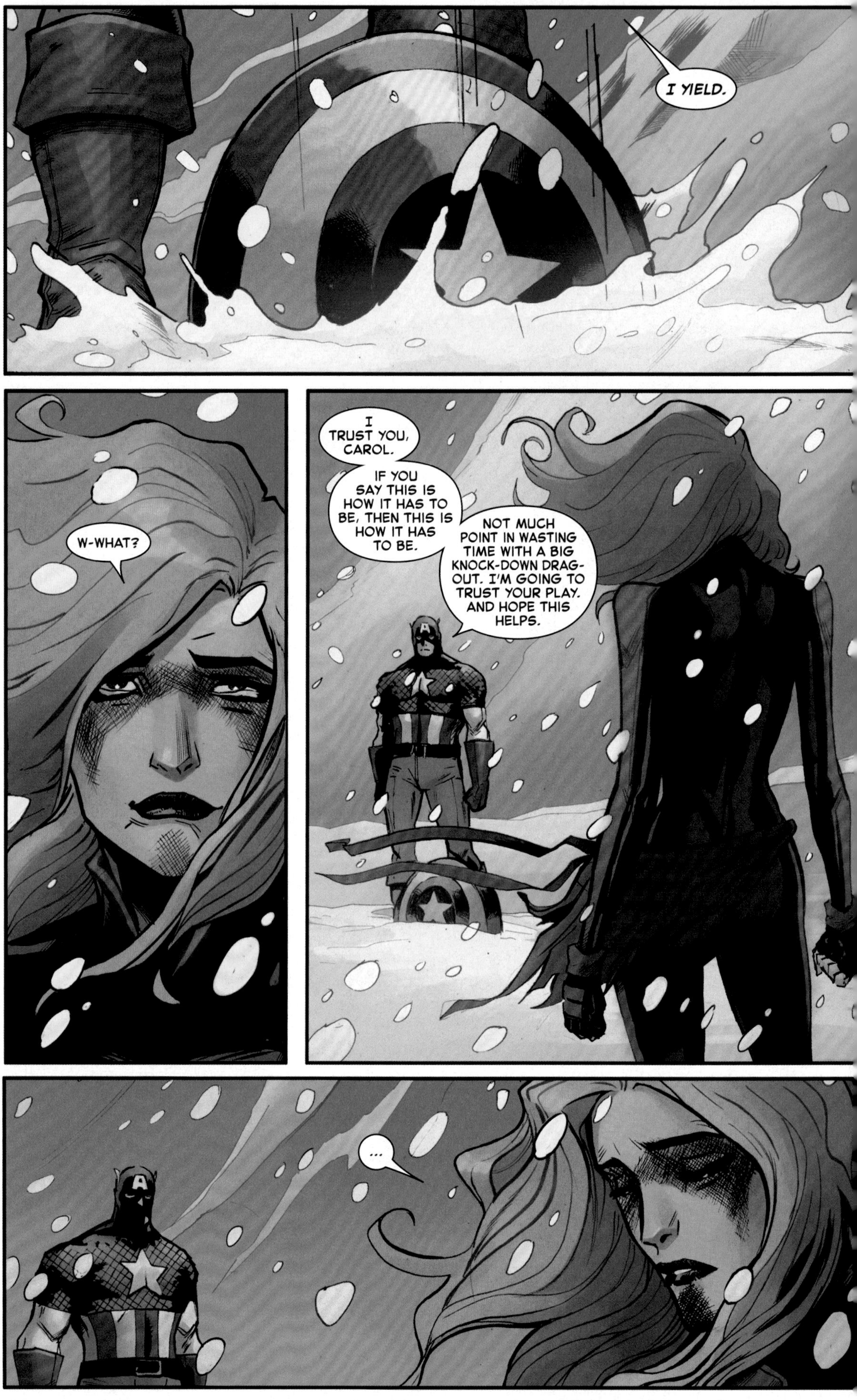
I YIELD.
W-WHAT?
I TRUST YOU, CAROL.
IF YOU SAY THIS IS HOW IT HAS TO BE, THEN THIS IS HOW IT HAS TO BE.
NOT MUCH POINT IN WASTING TIME WITH A BIG KNOCK-DOWN DRAG-OUT. I'M GOING TO TRUST YOUR PLAY. AND HOPE THIS HELPS.
...

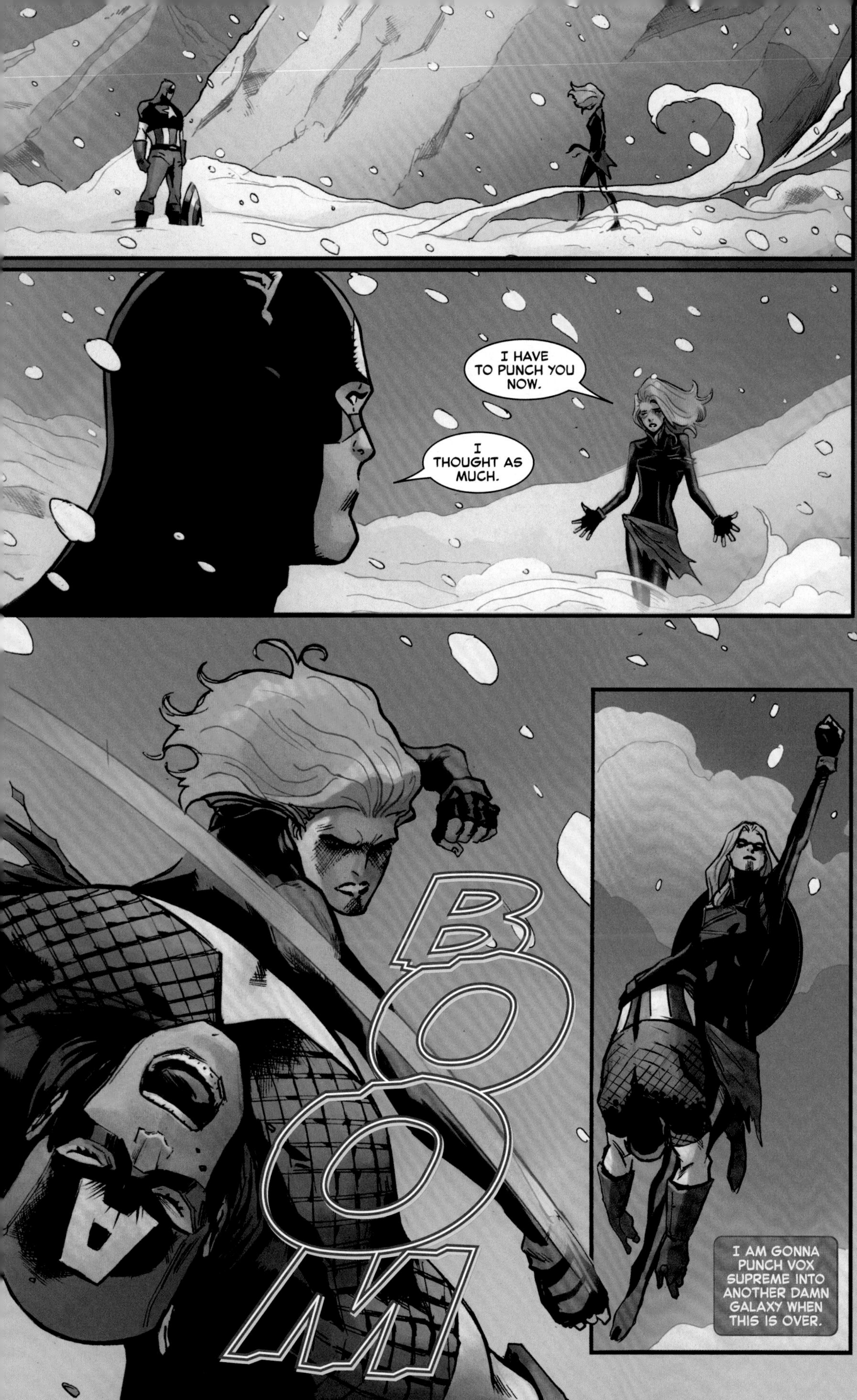
I HAVE TO PUNCH YOU NOW.
I THOUGHT AS MUCH.
BOOM
I AM GONNA PUNCH VOX SUPREME INTO ANOTHER DAMN GALAXY WHEN THIS IS OVER.

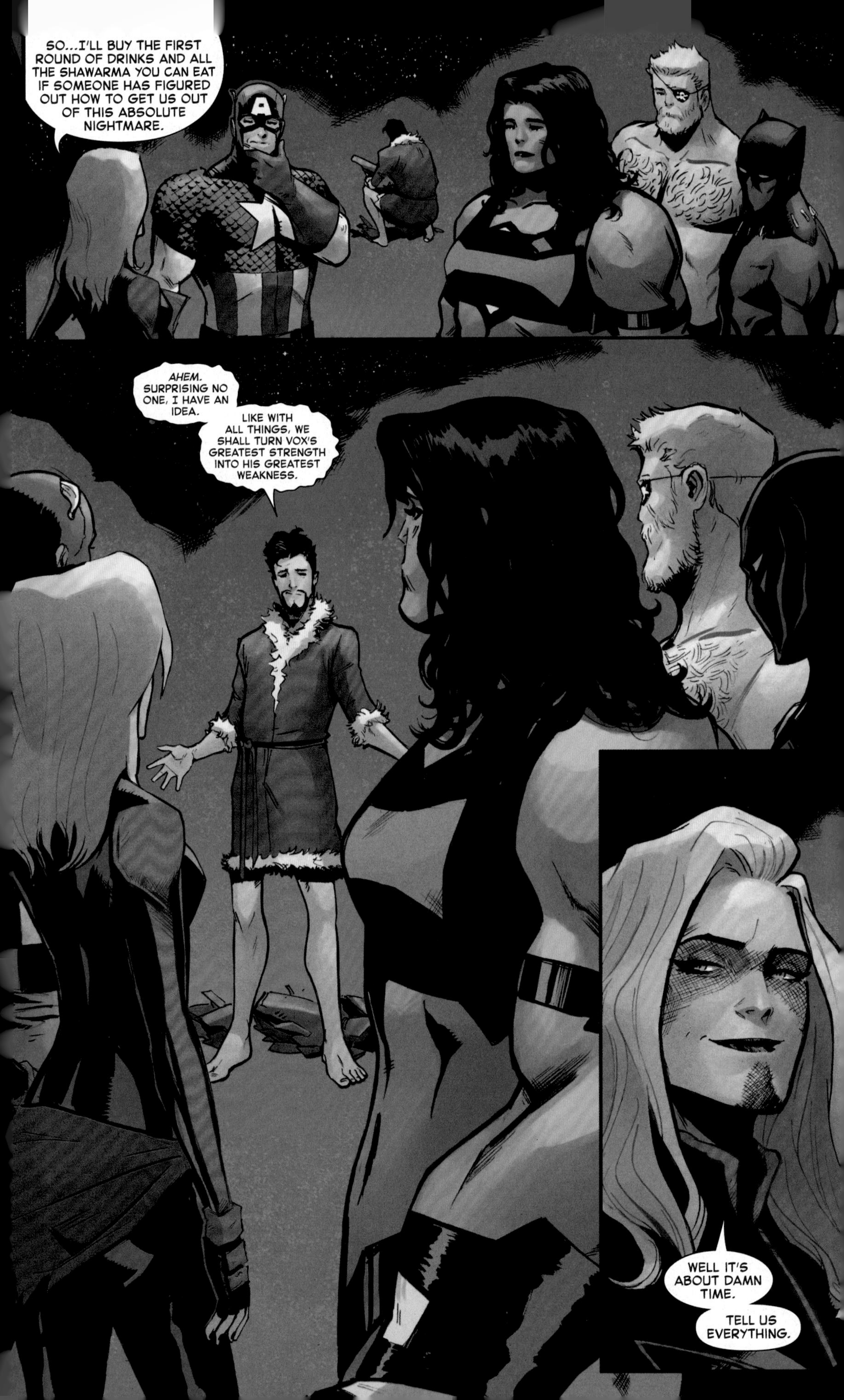
SO...I'LL BUY THE FIRST ROUND OF DRINKS AND ALL THE SHAWARMA YOU CAN EAT IF SOMEONE HAS FIGURED OUT HOW TO GET US OUT OF THIS ABSOLUTE NIGHTMARE.
AHEM. SURPRISING NO ONE, I HAVE AN IDEA.
LIKE WITH ALL THINGS, WE SHALL TURN VOX'S GREATEST STRENGTH INTO HIS GREATEST WEAKNESS.
WELL IT'S ABOUT DAMN TIME.
TELL US EVERYTHING.

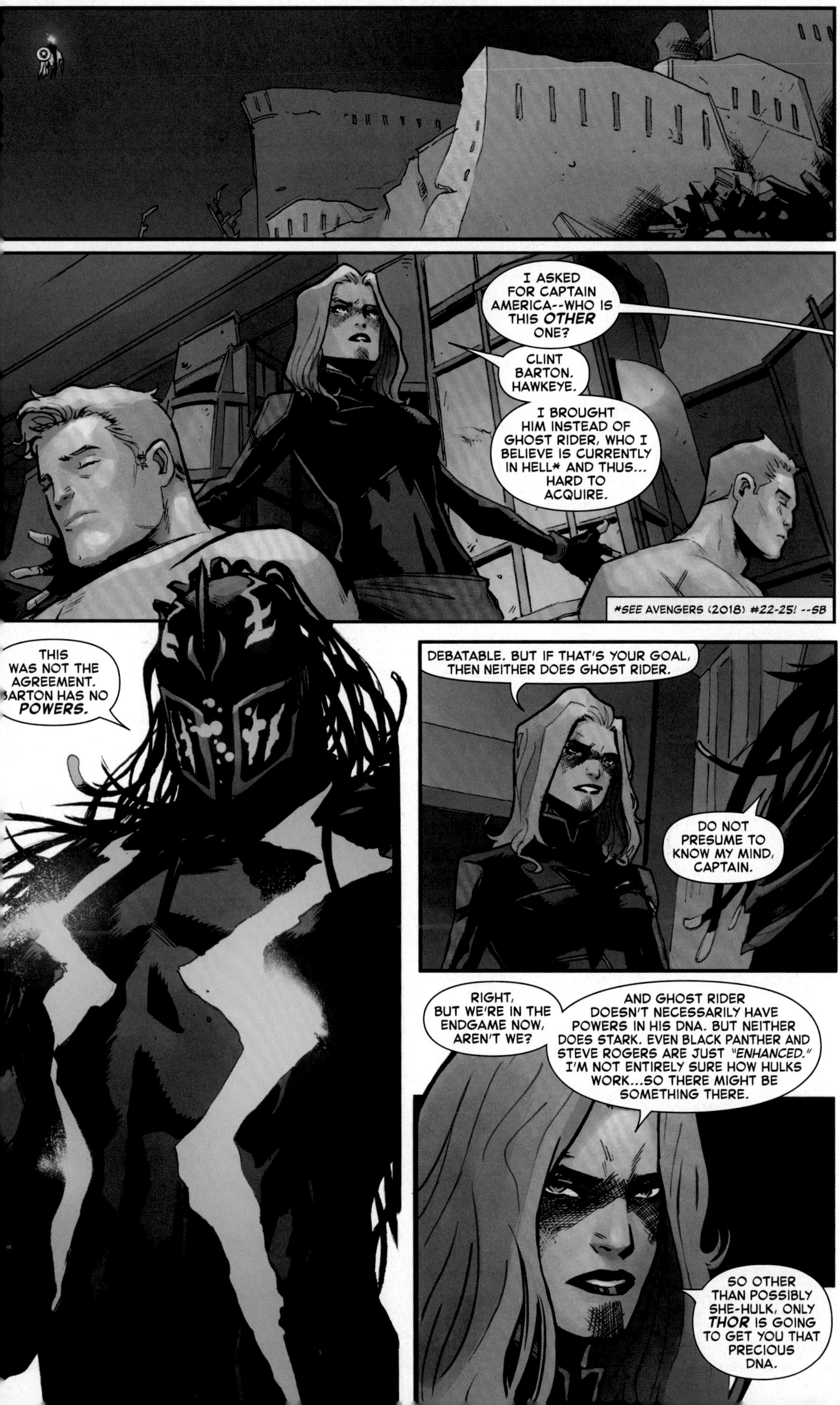
I ASKED FOR CAPTAIN AMERICA--WHO IS THIS *OTHER* ONE?
CLINT BARTON. HAWKEYE.
I BROUGHT HIM INSTEAD OF GHOST RIDER, WHO I BELIEVE IS CURRENTLY IN HELL* AND THUS... HARD TO ACQUIRE.
*SEE AVENGERS (2018) #22-25! --SB
THIS WAS NOT THE AGREEMENT. BARTON HAS NO *POWERS.*
DEBATABLE. BUT IF THAT'S YOUR GOAL, THEN NEITHER DOES GHOST RIDER.
DO NOT PRESUME TO KNOW MY MIND, CAPTAIN.
RIGHT, BUT WE'RE IN THE ENDGAME NOW, AREN'T WE?
AND GHOST RIDER DOESN'T NECESSARILY HAVE POWERS IN HIS DNA. BUT NEITHER DOES STARK. EVEN BLACK PANTHER AND STEVE ROGERS ARE JUST *"ENHANCED."* I'M NOT ENTIRELY SURE HOW HULKS WORK...SO THERE MIGHT BE SOMETHING THERE.
SO OTHER THAN POSSIBLY SHE-HULK, ONLY *THOR* IS GOING TO GET YOU THAT PRECIOUS DNA.

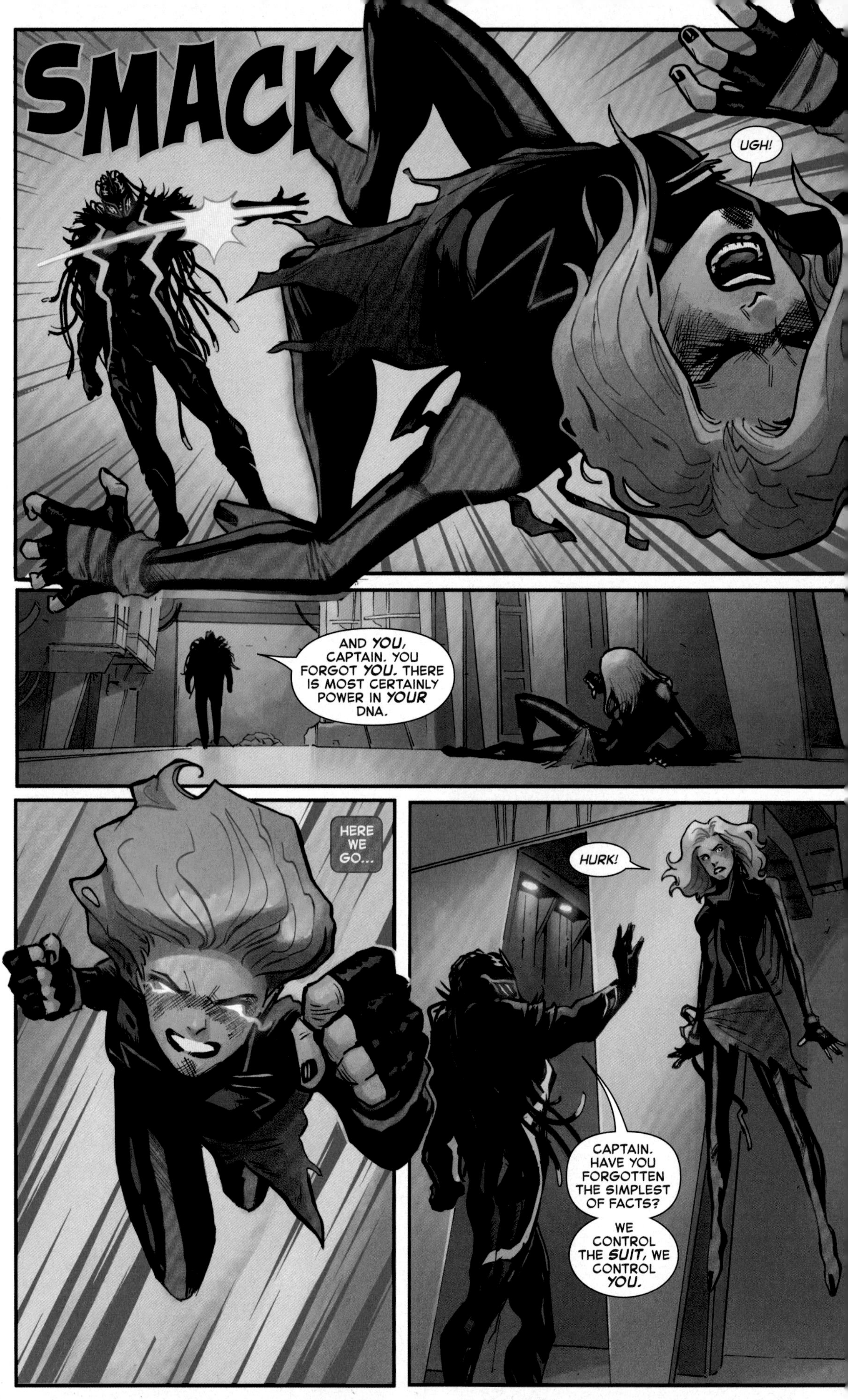
SMACK
UGH!
AND YOU, CAPTAIN. YOU FORGOT YOU. THERE IS MOST CERTAINLY POWER IN YOUR DNA.
HERE WE GO...
HURK!
CAPTAIN. HAVE YOU FORGOTTEN THE SIMPLEST OF FACTS?
WE CONTROL THE SUIT, WE CONTROL YOU.

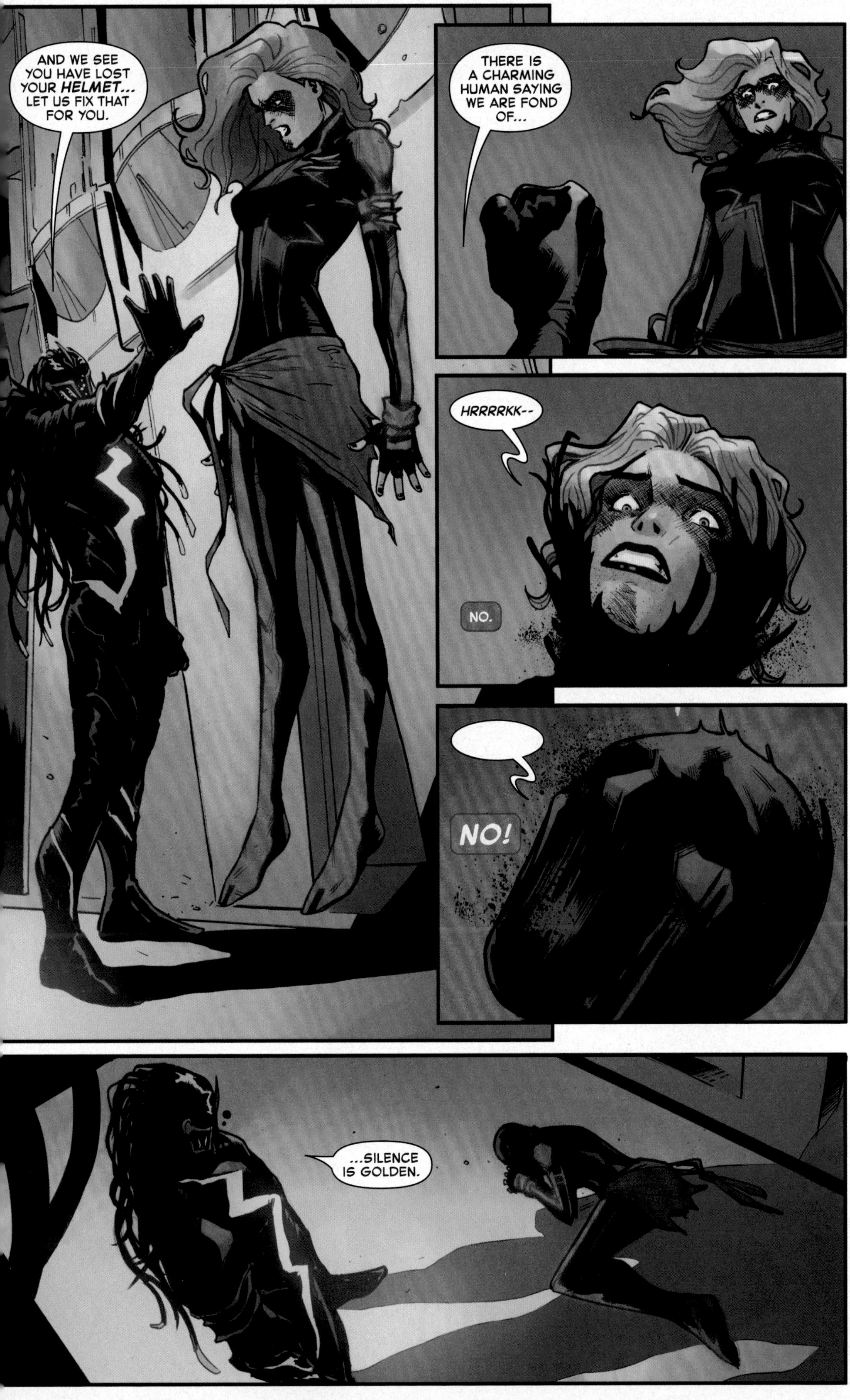
AND WE SEE YOU HAVE LOST YOUR HELMET... LET US FIX THAT FOR YOU.
THERE IS A CHARMING HUMAN SAYING WE ARE FOND OF...
HRRRRKK--
NO.
NO!
...SILENCE IS GOLDEN.

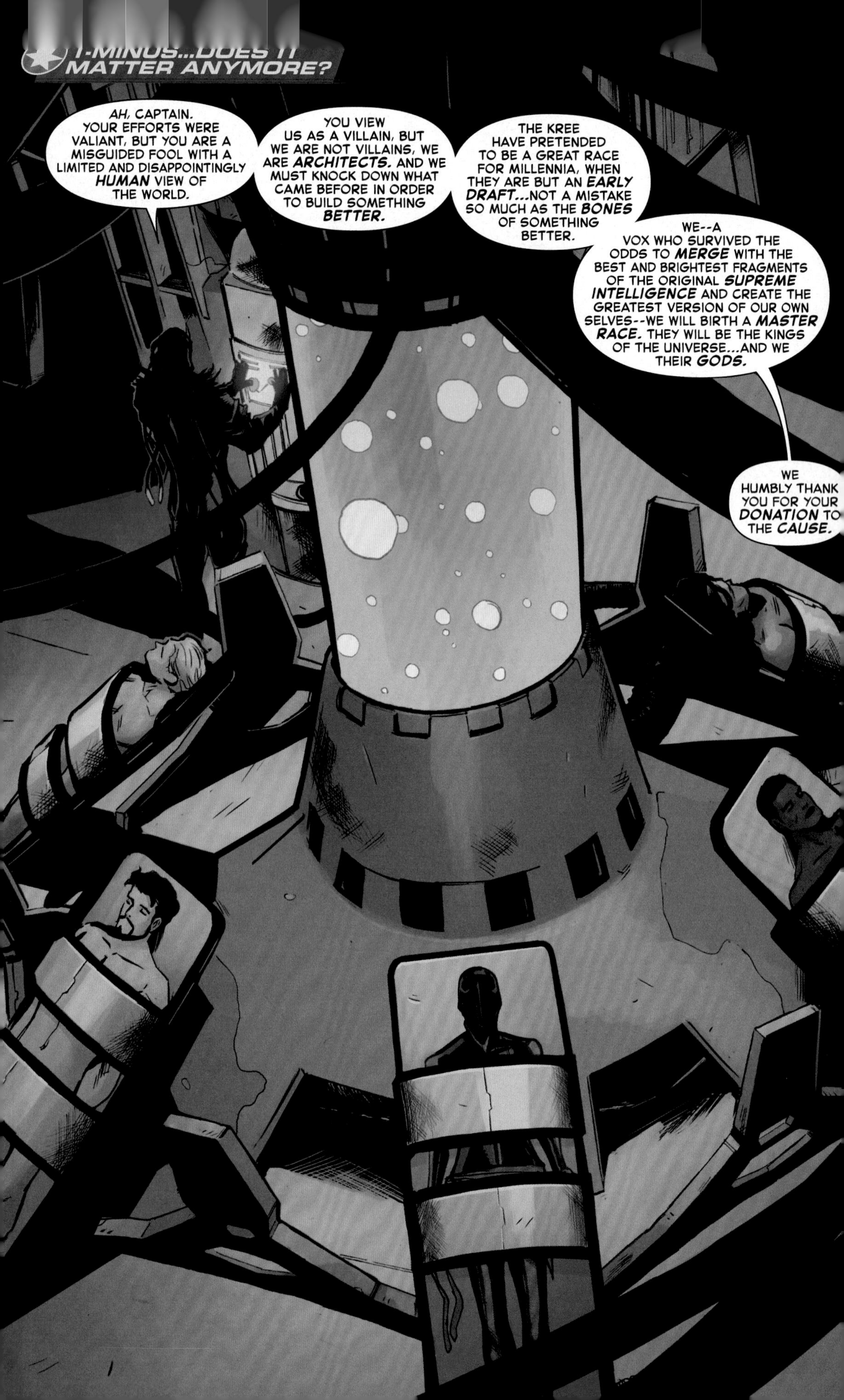
T-MINUS...DOES IT MATTER ANYMORE?
AH, CAPTAIN. YOUR EFFORTS WERE VALIANT, BUT YOU ARE A MISGUIDED FOOL WITH A LIMITED AND DISAPPOINTINGLY HUMAN VIEW OF THE WORLD.
YOU VIEW US AS A VILLAIN, BUT WE ARE NOT VILLAINS, WE ARE ARCHITECTS. AND WE MUST KNOCK DOWN WHAT CAME BEFORE IN ORDER TO BUILD SOMETHING BETTER.
THE KREE HAVE PRETENDED TO BE A GREAT RACE FOR MILLENNIA, WHEN THEY ARE BUT AN EARLY DRAFT...NOT A MISTAKE SO MUCH AS THE BONES OF SOMETHING BETTER.
WE--A VOX WHO SURVIVED THE ODDS TO MERGE WITH THE BEST AND BRIGHTEST FRAGMENTS OF THE ORIGINAL SUPREME INTELLIGENCE AND CREATE THE GREATEST VERSION OF OUR OWN SELVES--WE WILL BIRTH A MASTER RACE. THEY WILL BE THE KINGS OF THE UNIVERSE...AND WE THEIR GODS.
WE HUMBLY THANK YOU FOR YOUR DONATION TO THE CAUSE.

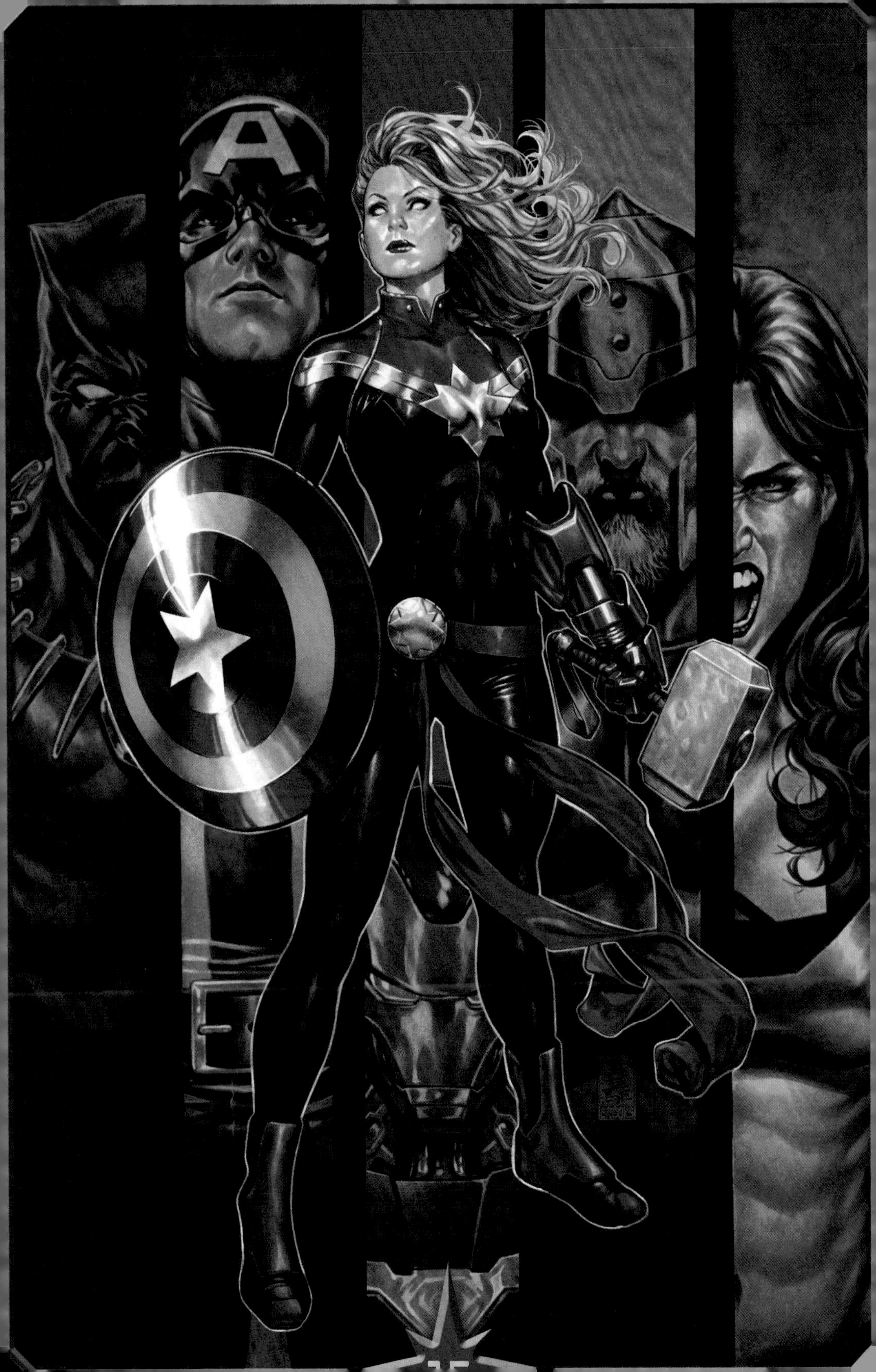

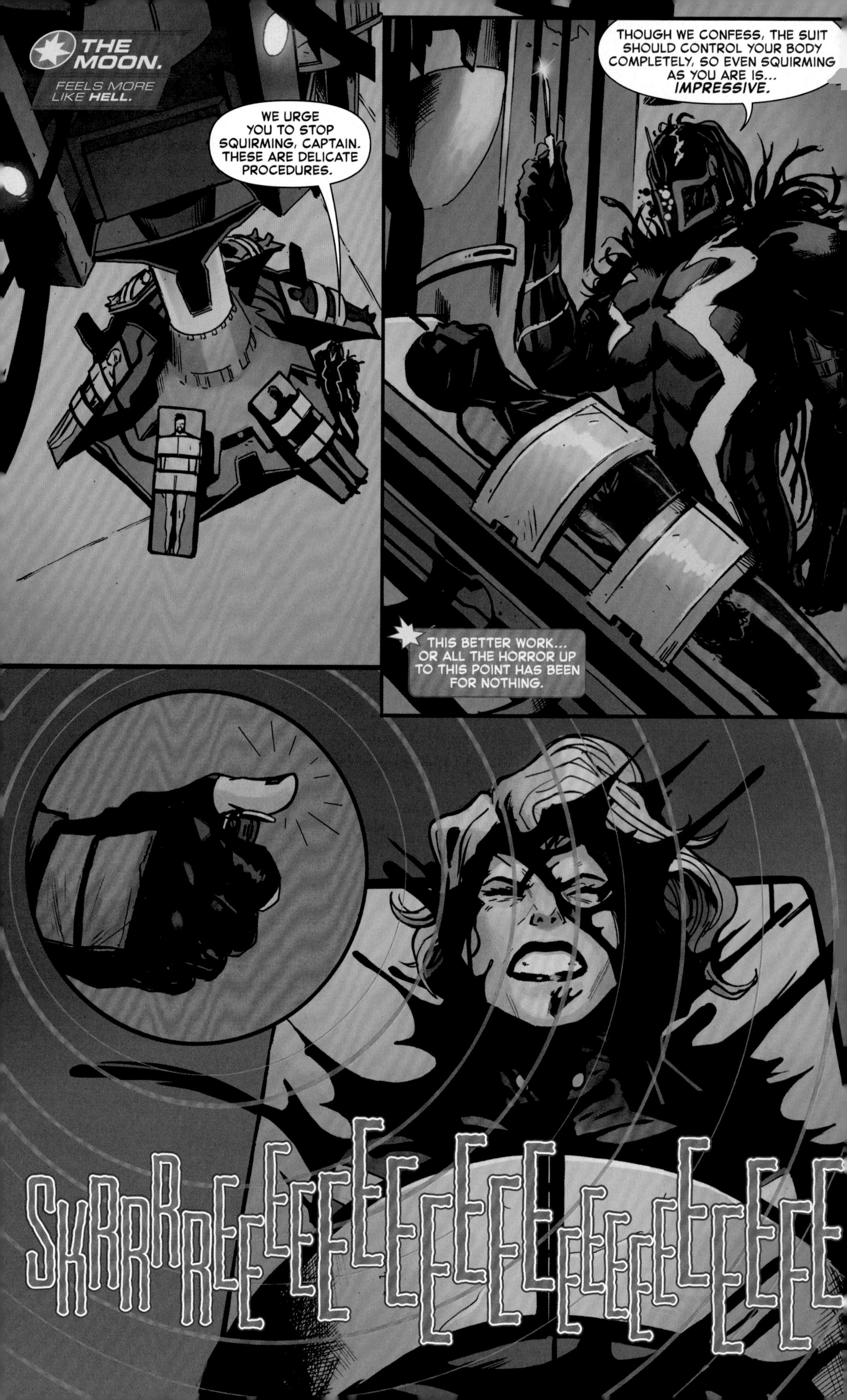
THE MOON.
FEELS MORE LIKE HELL.
WE URGE YOU TO STOP SQUIRMING, CAPTAIN. THESE ARE DELICATE PROCEDURES.
THOUGH WE CONFESS, THE SUIT SHOULD CONTROL YOUR BODY COMPLETELY, SO EVEN SQUIRMING AS YOU ARE IS... IMPRESSIVE.
THIS BETTER WORK... OR ALL THE HORROR UP TO THIS POINT HAS BEEN FOR NOTHING.
SKRRRREEEEEEEEEEEEEEEEEEEEE

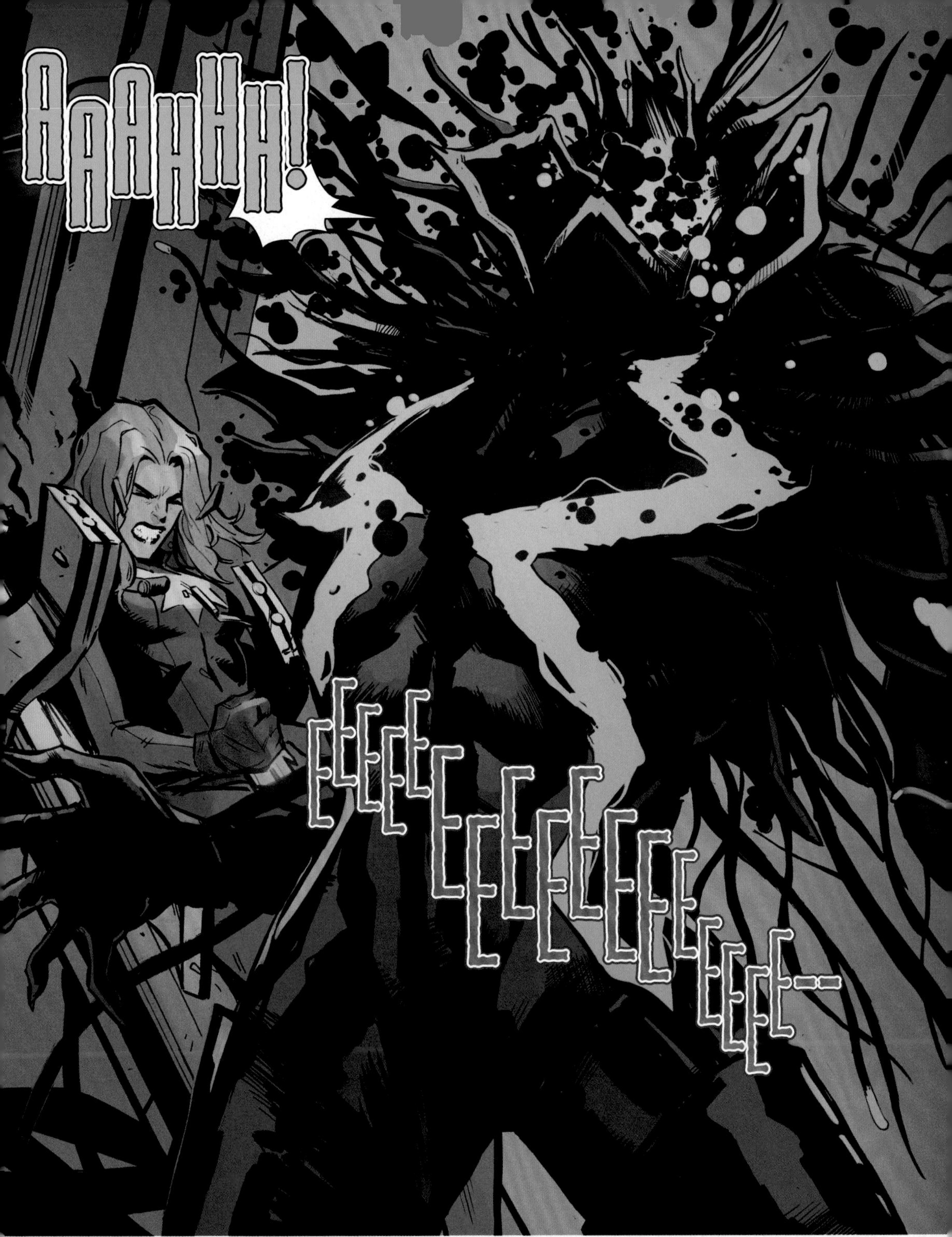
AAAHHH!
EEEEEEEEEEEEEEEEE--

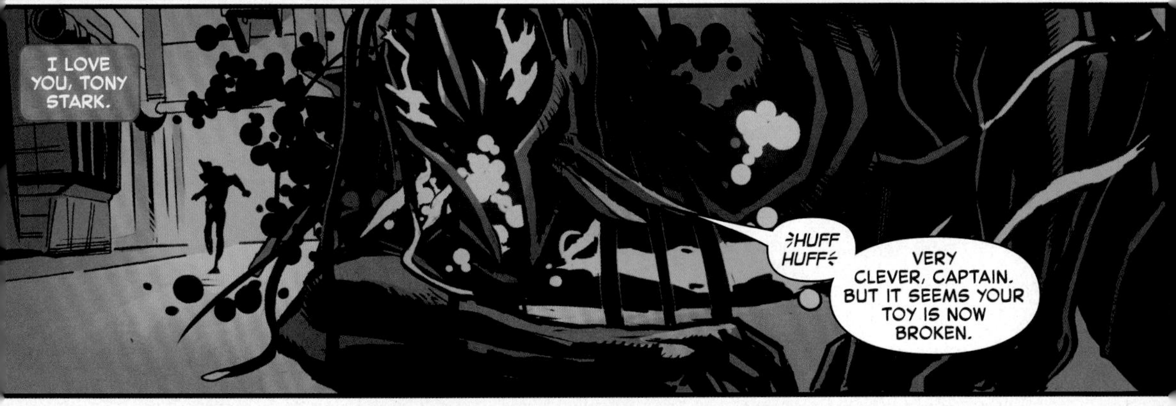
I LOVE YOU, TONY STARK.
HUFF HUFF
VERY CLEVER, CAPTAIN. BUT IT SEEMS YOUR TOY IS NOW BROKEN.

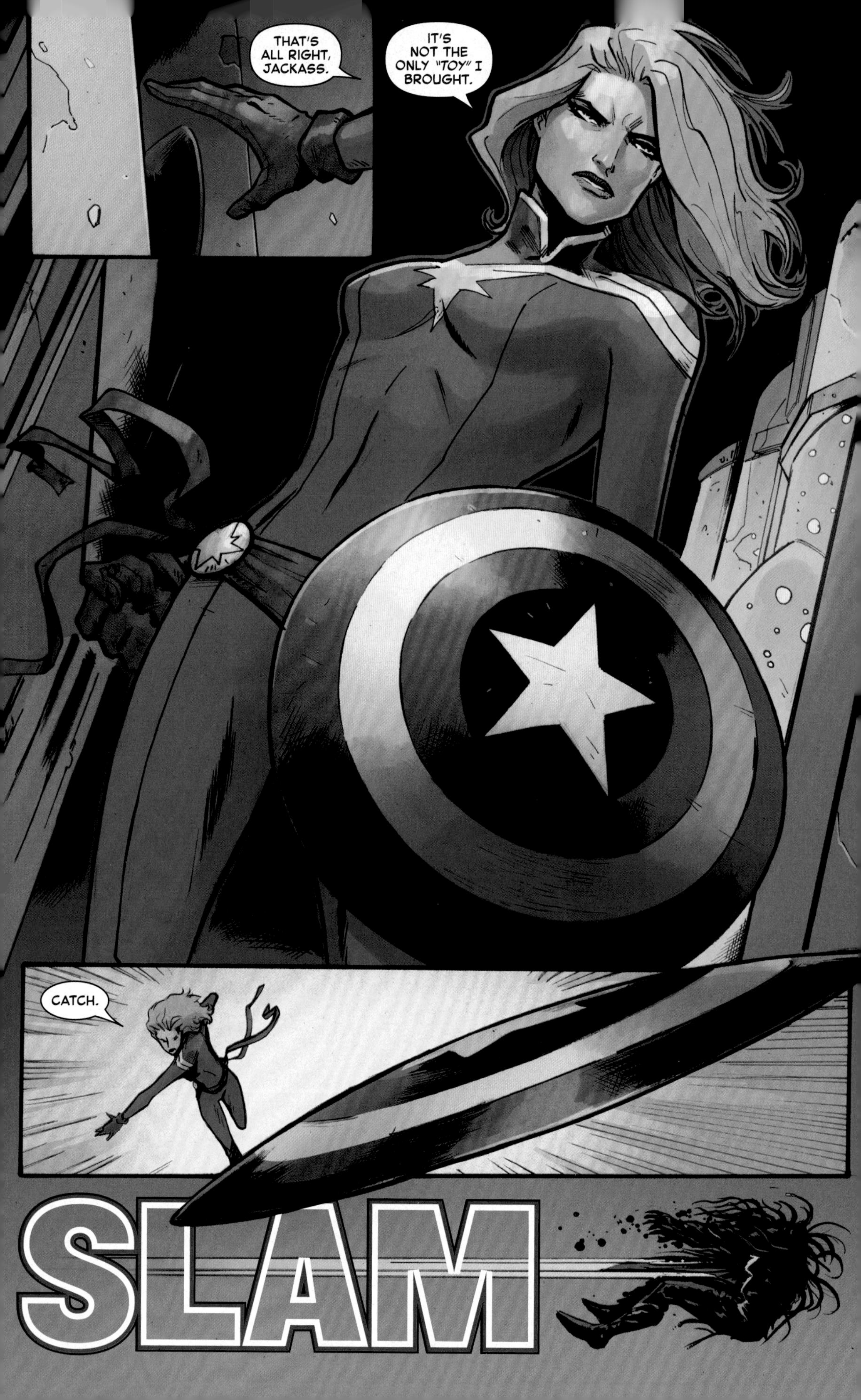
THAT'S ALL RIGHT, JACKASS.
IT'S NOT THE ONLY "TOY" I BROUGHT.
CATCH.
SLAM

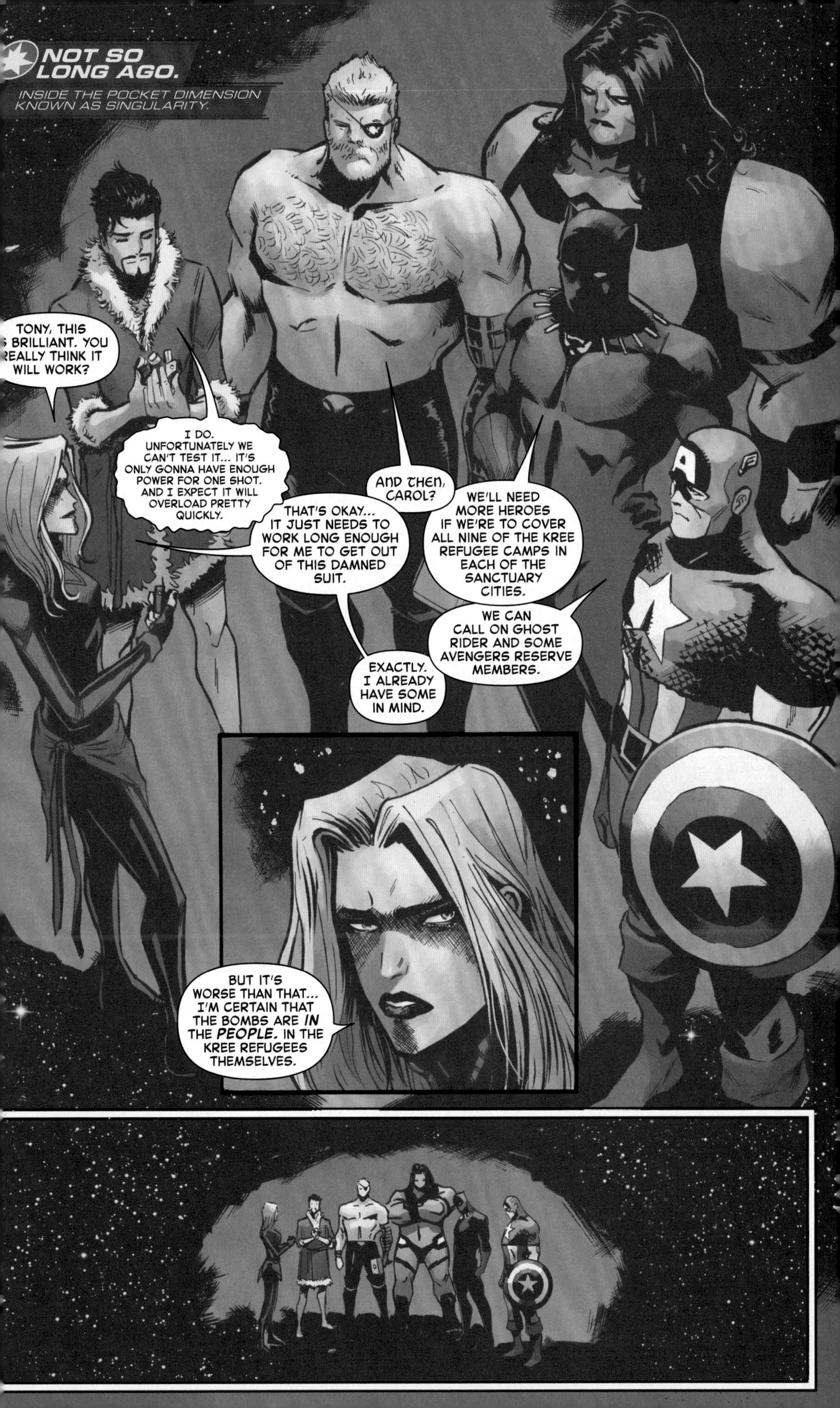
NOT SO LONG AGO.
INSIDE THE POCKET DIMENSION KNOWN AS SINGULARITY.
TONY, THIS IS BRILLIANT. YOU REALLY THINK IT WILL WORK?
I DO. UNFORTUNATELY WE CAN'T TEST IT... IT'S ONLY GONNA HAVE ENOUGH POWER FOR ONE SHOT. AND I EXPECT IT WILL OVERLOAD PRETTY QUICKLY.
THAT'S OKAY... IT JUST NEEDS TO WORK LONG ENOUGH FOR ME TO GET OUT OF THIS DAMNED SUIT.
AND THEN, CAROL?
WE'LL NEED MORE HEROES IF WE'RE TO COVER ALL NINE OF THE KREE REFUGEE CAMPS IN EACH OF THE SANCTUARY CITIES.
WE CAN CALL ON GHOST RIDER AND SOME AVENGERS RESERVE MEMBERS.
EXACTLY. I ALREADY HAVE SOME IN MIND.
BUT IT'S WORSE THAN THAT... I'M CERTAIN THAT THE BOMBS ARE *IN* THE *PEOPLE*. IN THE KREE REFUGEES THEMSELVES.

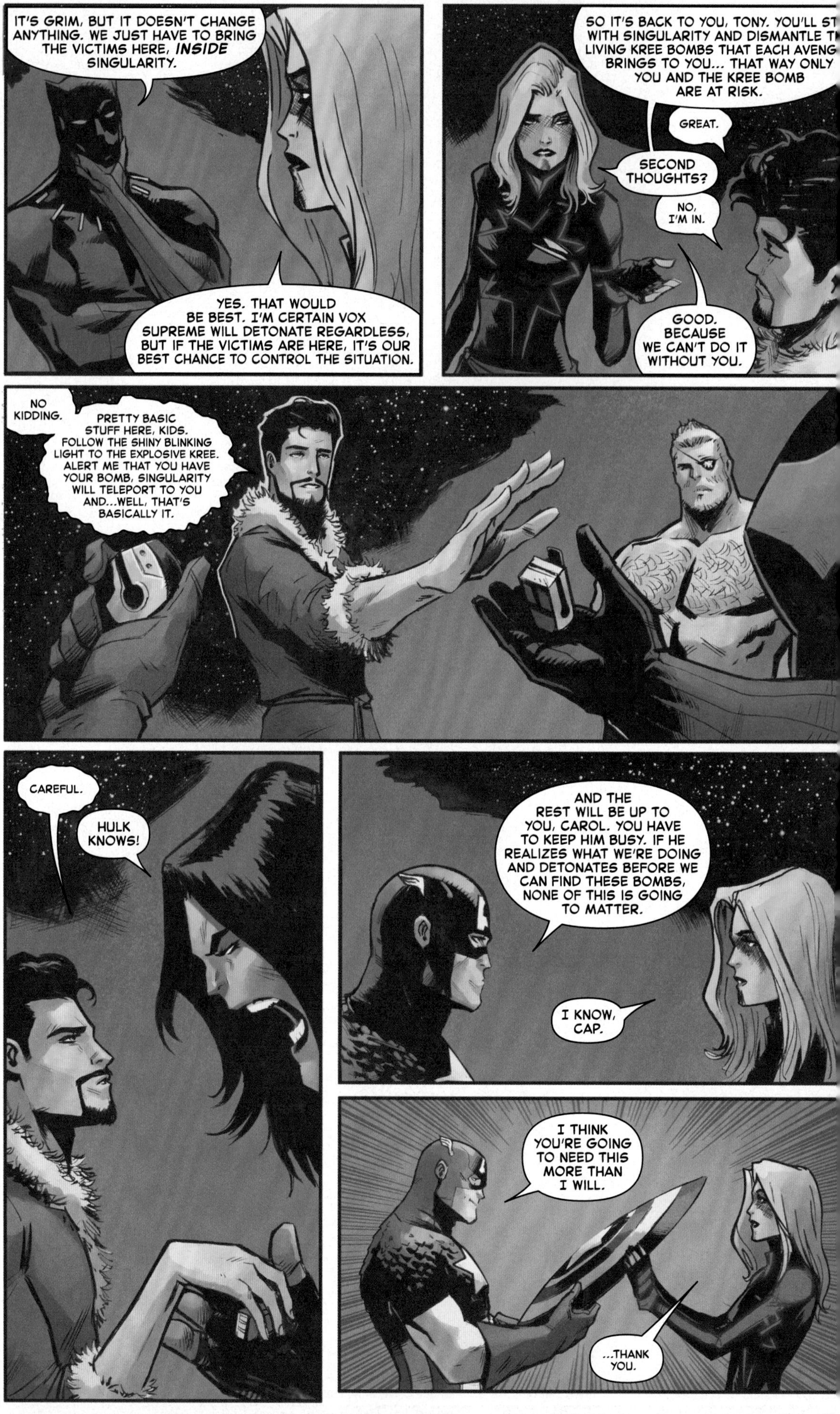

IT'S GRIM, BUT IT DOESN'T CHANGE ANYTHING. WE JUST HAVE TO BRING THE VICTIMS HERE, INSIDE SINGULARITY.
YES. THAT WOULD BE BEST. I'M CERTAIN VOX SUPREME WILL DETONATE REGARDLESS, BUT IF THE VICTIMS ARE HERE, IT'S OUR BEST CHANCE TO CONTROL THE SITUATION.
SO IT'S BACK TO YOU, TONY. YOU'LL ST WITH SINGULARITY AND DISMANTLE T LIVING KREE BOMBS THAT EACH AVENG BRINGS TO YOU... THAT WAY ONLY YOU AND THE KREE BOMB ARE AT RISK.
GREAT.
SECOND THOUGHTS?
NO, I'M IN.
GOOD. BECAUSE WE CAN'T DO IT WITHOUT YOU.
NO KIDDING.
PRETTY BASIC STUFF HERE, KIDS. FOLLOW THE SHINY BLINKING LIGHT TO THE EXPLOSIVE KREE. ALERT ME THAT YOU HAVE YOUR BOMB, SINGULARITY WILL TELEPORT TO YOU AND...WELL, THAT'S BASICALLY IT.
CAREFUL.
HULK KNOWS!
AND THE REST WILL BE UP TO YOU, CAROL. YOU HAVE TO KEEP HIM BUSY. IF HE REALIZES WHAT WE'RE DOING AND DETONATES BEFORE WE CAN FIND THESE BOMBS, NONE OF THIS IS GOING TO MATTER.
I KNOW, CAP.
I THINK YOU'RE GOING TO NEED THIS MORE THAN I WILL.
...THANK YOU.

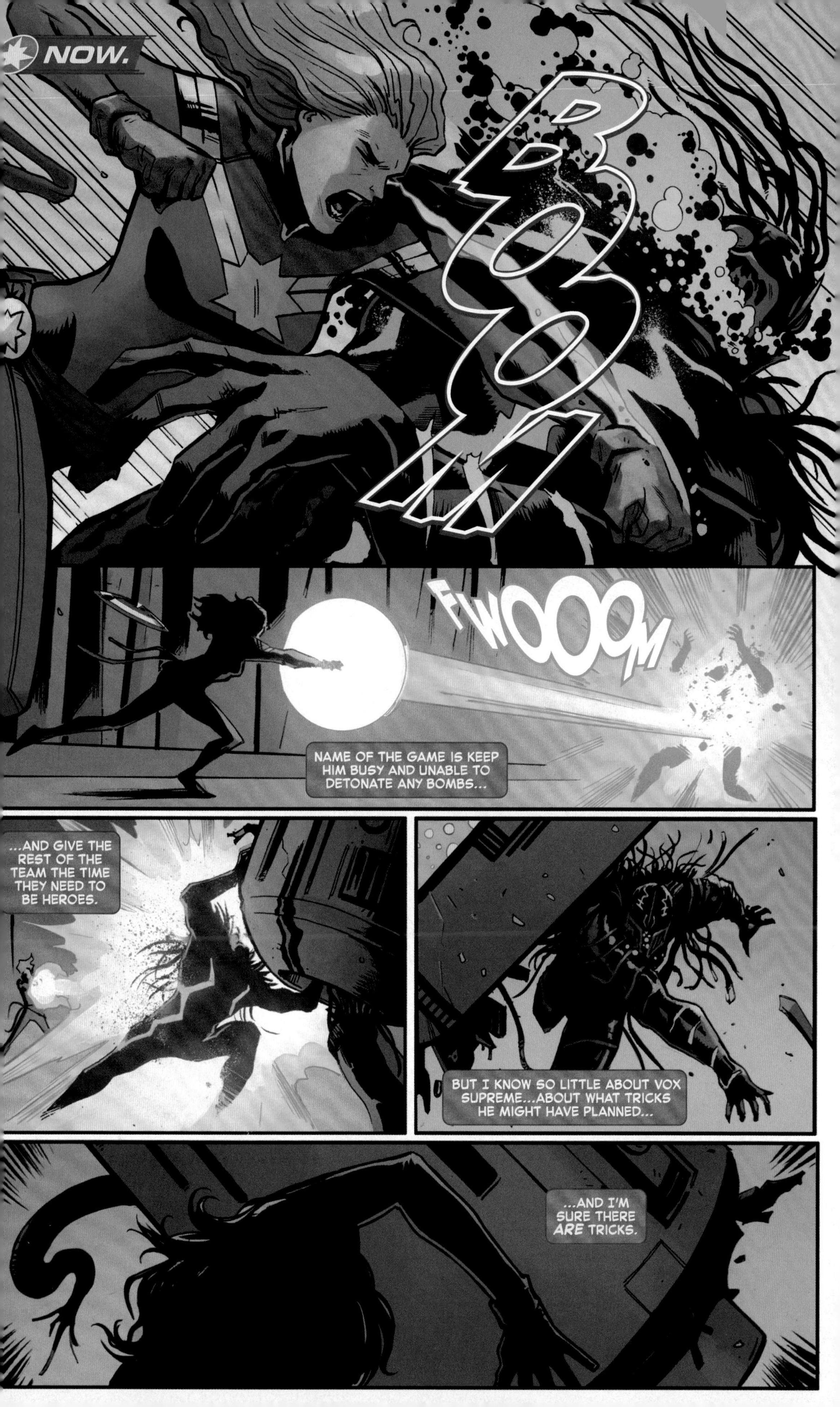
NOW.
BOOM
FWOOOM
NAME OF THE GAME IS KEEP HIM BUSY AND UNABLE TO DETONATE ANY BOMBS...
...AND GIVE THE REST OF THE TEAM THE TIME THEY NEED TO BE HEROES.
BUT I KNOW SO LITTLE ABOUT VOX SUPREME...ABOUT WHAT TRICKS HE MIGHT HAVE PLANNED...
...AND I'M SURE THERE *ARE* TRICKS.

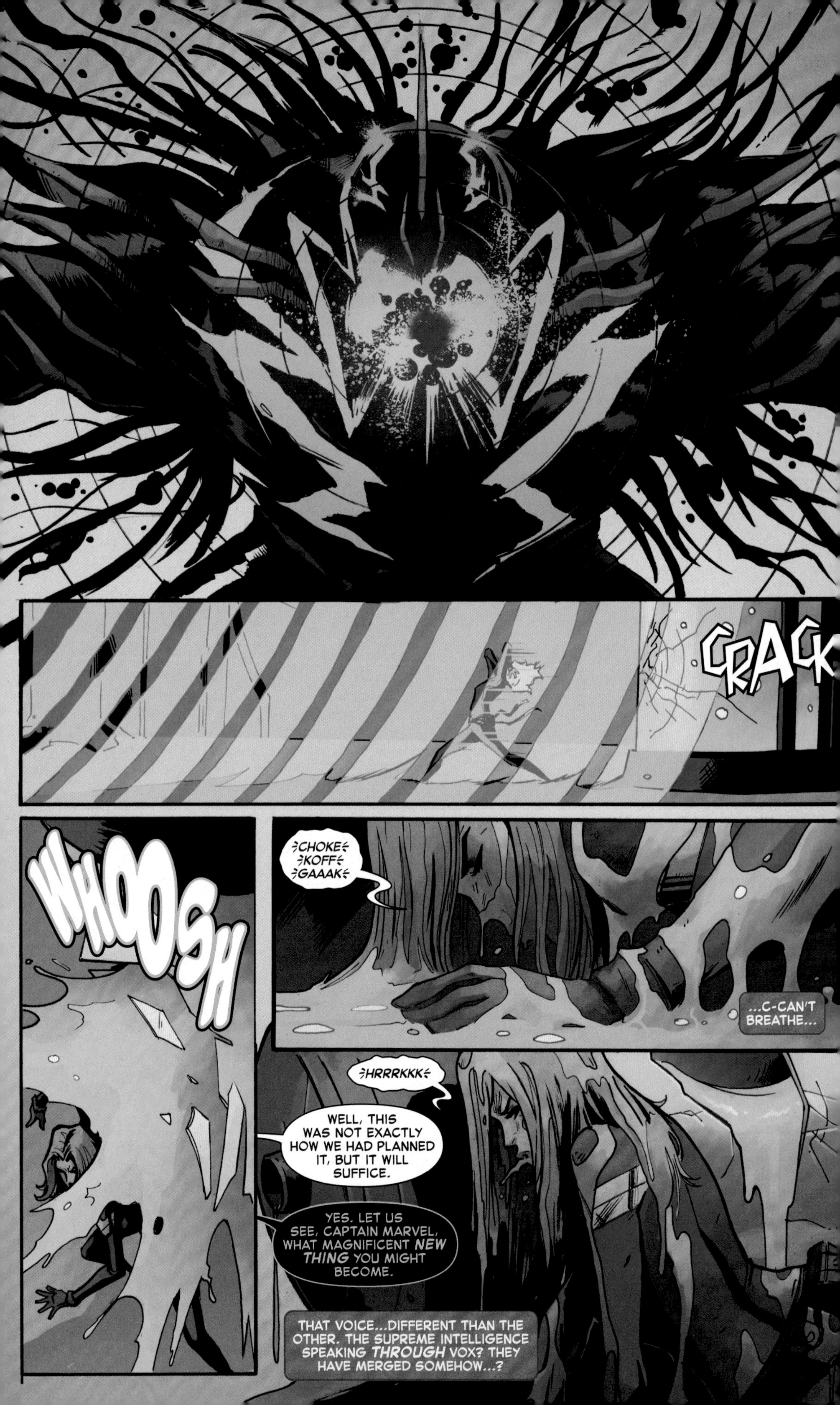
CRACK
WHOOSH
CHOKE
KOFF
GAAAK
...C-CAN'T BREATHE...
HRRRKKK
WELL, THIS WAS NOT EXACTLY HOW WE HAD PLANNED IT, BUT IT WILL SUFFICE.
YES. LET US SEE, CAPTAIN MARVEL, WHAT MAGNIFICENT *NEW THING* YOU MIGHT BECOME.
THAT VOICE...DIFFERENT THAN THE OTHER. THE SUPREME INTELLIGENCE SPEAKING *THROUGH* VOX? THEY HAVE MERGED SOMEHOW...?

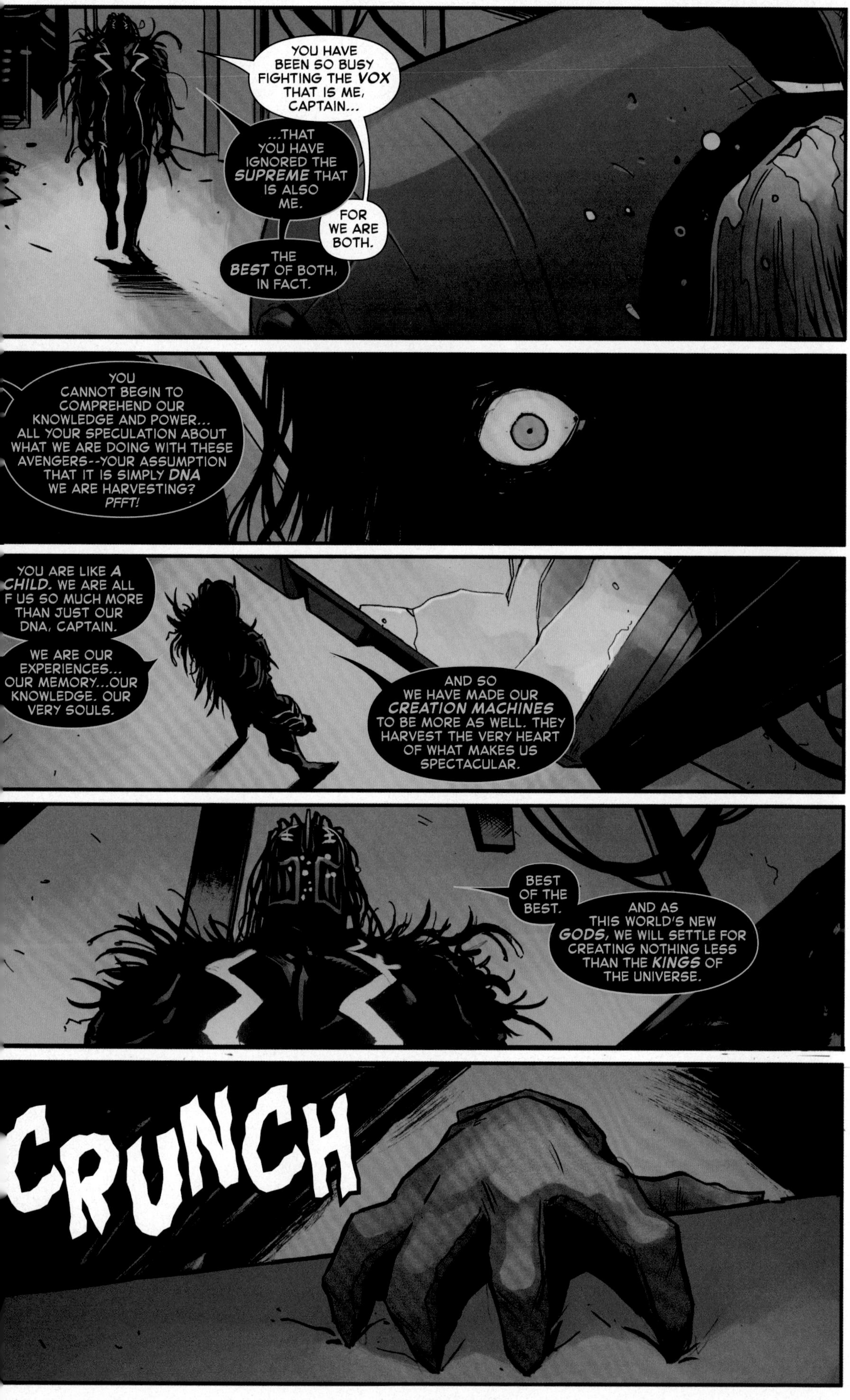
YOU HAVE BEEN SO BUSY FIGHTING THE VOX THAT IS ME, CAPTAIN...
...THAT YOU HAVE IGNORED THE SUPREME THAT IS ALSO ME.
FOR WE ARE BOTH.
THE BEST OF BOTH, IN FACT.
YOU CANNOT BEGIN TO COMPREHEND OUR KNOWLEDGE AND POWER... ALL YOUR SPECULATION ABOUT WHAT WE ARE DOING WITH THESE AVENGERS--YOUR ASSUMPTION THAT IT IS SIMPLY DNA WE ARE HARVESTING? PFFT!
YOU ARE LIKE A CHILD. WE ARE ALL F US SO MUCH MORE THAN JUST OUR DNA, CAPTAIN.
WE ARE OUR EXPERIENCES... OUR MEMORY...OUR KNOWLEDGE. OUR VERY SOULS.
AND SO WE HAVE MADE OUR CREATION MACHINES TO BE MORE AS WELL. THEY HARVEST THE VERY HEART OF WHAT MAKES US SPECTACULAR.
BEST OF THE BEST.
AND AS THIS WORLD'S NEW GODS, WE WILL SETTLE FOR CREATING NOTHING LESS THAN THE KINGS OF THE UNIVERSE.
CRUNCH

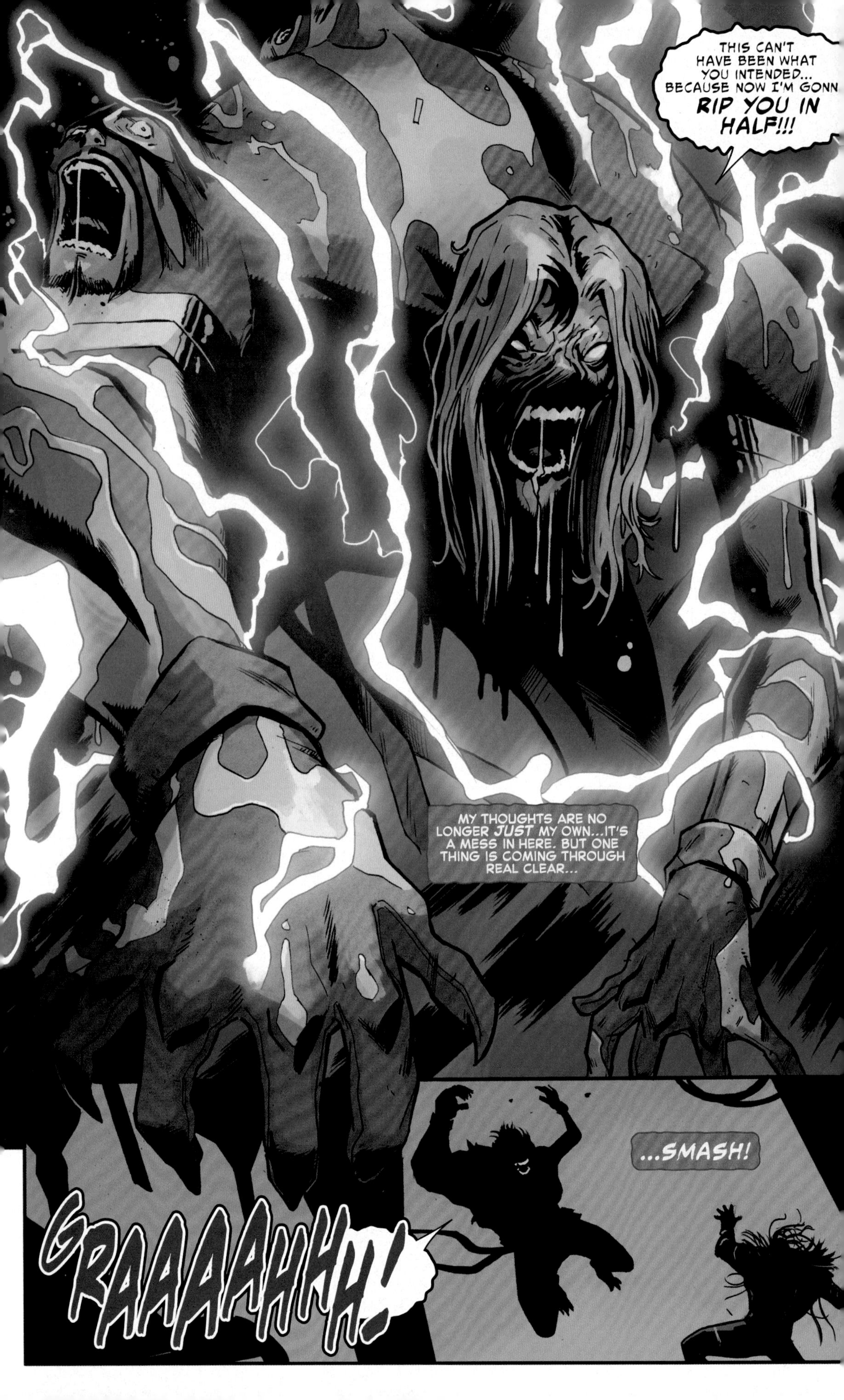
THIS CAN'T HAVE BEEN WHAT YOU INTENDED... BECAUSE NOW I'M GONN RIP YOU IN HALF!!!
MY THOUGHTS ARE NO LONGER JUST MY OWN...IT'S A MESS IN HERE. BUT ONE THING IS COMING THROUGH REAL CLEAR...
...SMASH!
GRAAAAHHH!

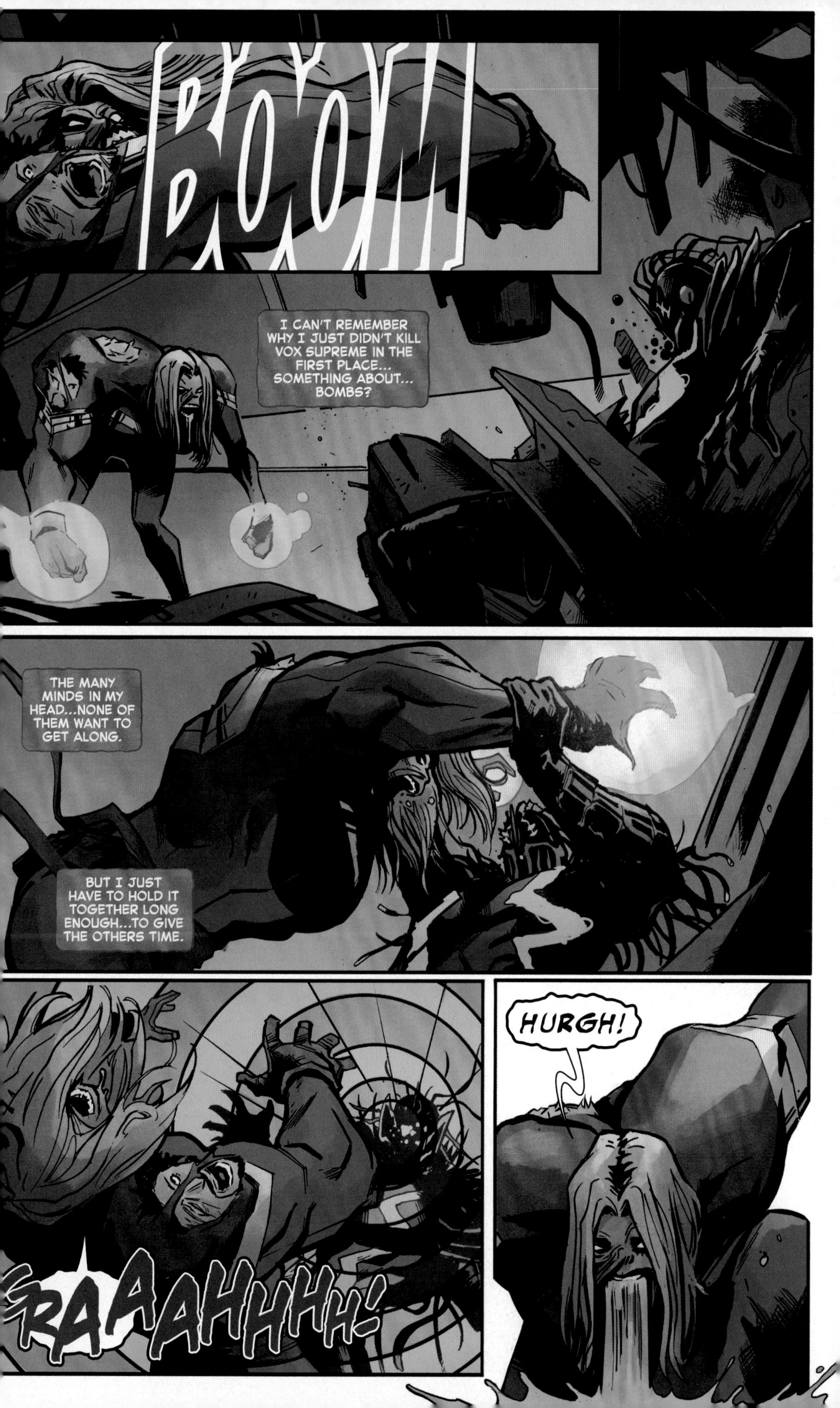
BOOM
I CAN'T REMEMBER WHY I JUST DIDN'T KILL VOX SUPREME IN THE FIRST PLACE... SOMETHING ABOUT... BOMBS?
THE MANY MINDS IN MY HEAD...NONE OF THEM WANT TO GET ALONG.
BUT I JUST HAVE TO HOLD IT TOGETHER LONG ENOUGH...TO GIVE THE OTHERS TIME.
RAAAHHHH!
HURGH!

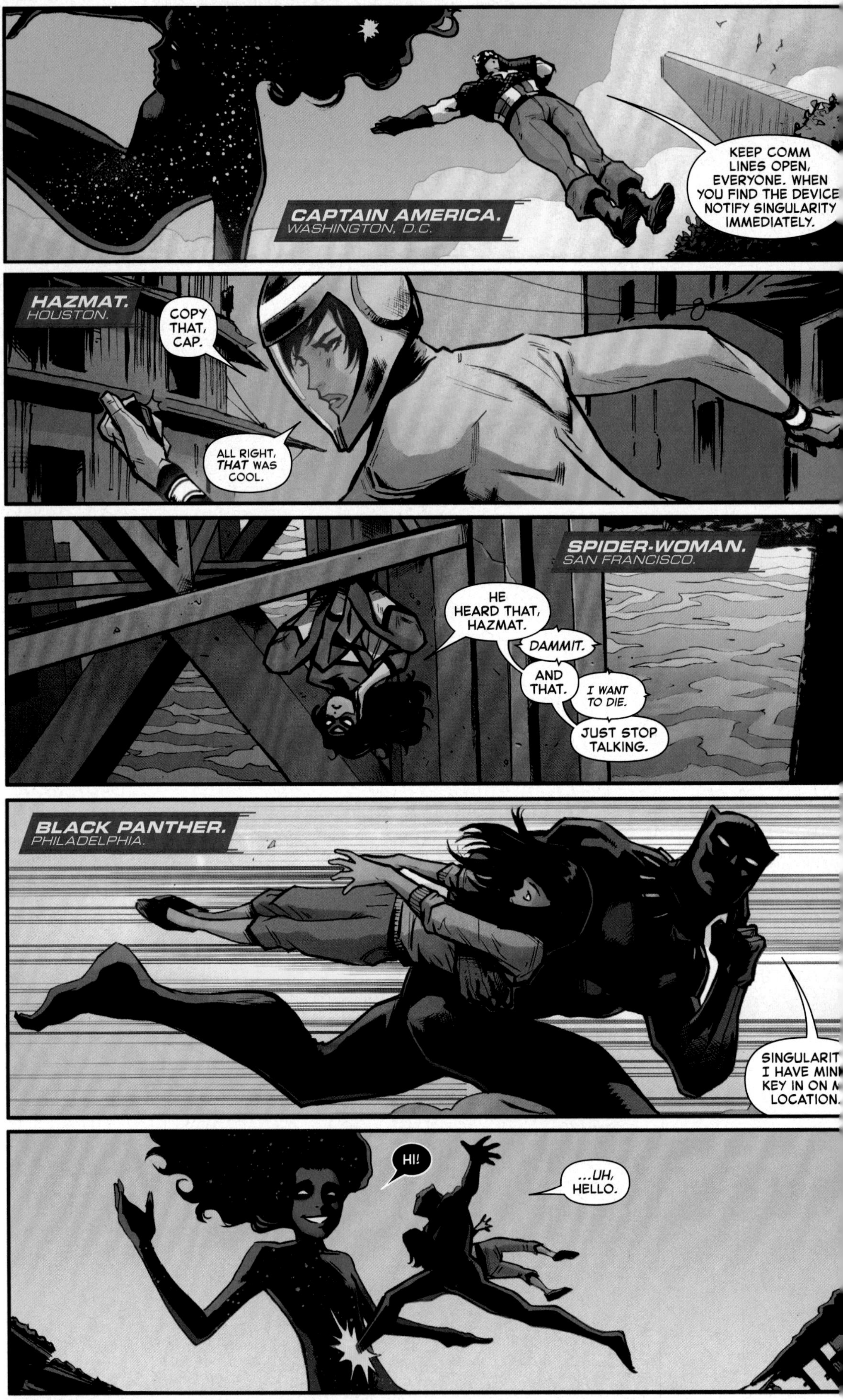

CAPTAIN AMERICA.
WASHINGTON, D.C.
KEEP COMM LINES OPEN, EVERYONE. WHEN YOU FIND THE DEVICE NOTIFY SINGULARITY IMMEDIATELY.
HAZMAT.
HOUSTON.
COPY THAT, CAP.
ALL RIGHT, THAT WAS COOL.
SPIDER-WOMAN.
SAN FRANCISCO.
HE HEARD THAT, HAZMAT.
DAMMIT.
AND THAT.
I WANT TO DIE.
JUST STOP TALKING.
BLACK PANTHER.
PHILADELPHIA.
HI!
...UH, HELLO.

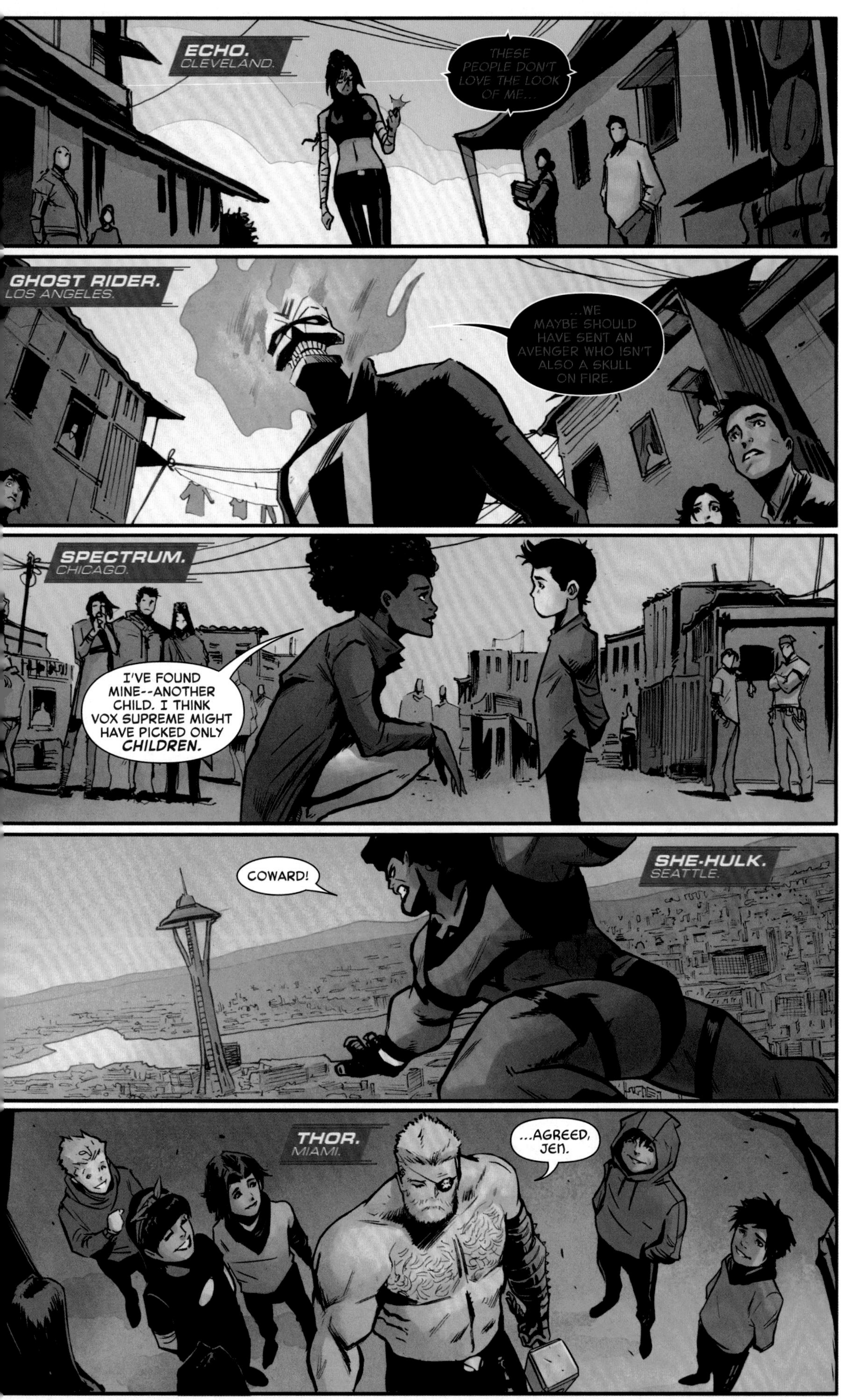
ECHO.
CLEVELAND.
THESE PEOPLE DON'T LOVE THE LOOK OF ME...
GHOST RIDER.
LOS ANGELES.
...WE MAYBE SHOULD HAVE SENT AN AVENGER WHO ISN'T ALSO A SKULL ON FIRE.
SPECTRUM.
CHICAGO.
I'VE FOUND MINE--ANOTHER CHILD. I THINK VOX SUPREME MIGHT HAVE PICKED ONLY CHILDREN.
SHE-HULK.
SEATTLE.
COWARD!
THOR.
MIAMI.
...AGREED, JEN.

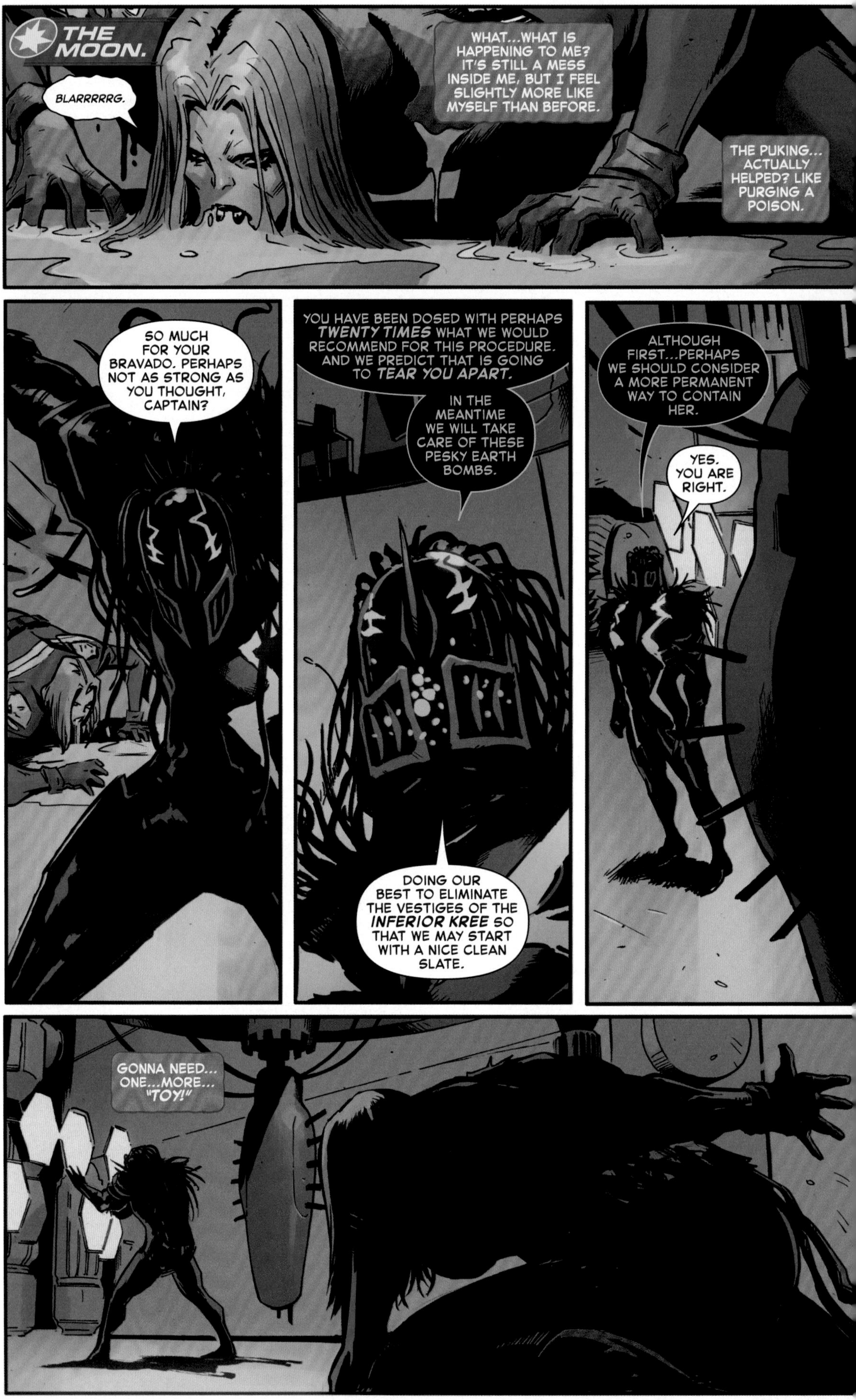
THE MOON.
BLARRRRRG.
WHAT...WHAT IS HAPPENING TO ME? IT'S STILL A MESS INSIDE ME, BUT I FEEL SLIGHTLY MORE LIKE MYSELF THAN BEFORE.
THE PUKING... ACTUALLY HELPED? LIKE PURGING A POISON.
SO MUCH FOR YOUR BRAVADO. PERHAPS NOT AS STRONG AS YOU THOUGHT, CAPTAIN?
YOU HAVE BEEN DOSED WITH PERHAPS TWENTY TIMES WHAT WE WOULD RECOMMEND FOR THIS PROCEDURE. AND WE PREDICT THAT IS GOING TO TEAR YOU APART.
IN THE MEANTIME WE WILL TAKE CARE OF THESE PESKY EARTH BOMBS.
DOING OUR BEST TO ELIMINATE THE VESTIGES OF THE INFERIOR KREE SO THAT WE MAY START WITH A NICE CLEAN SLATE.
ALTHOUGH FIRST...PERHAPS WE SHOULD CONSIDER A MORE PERMANENT WAY TO CONTAIN HER.
YES. YOU ARE RIGHT.
GONNA NEED... ONE...MORE... "TOY!"

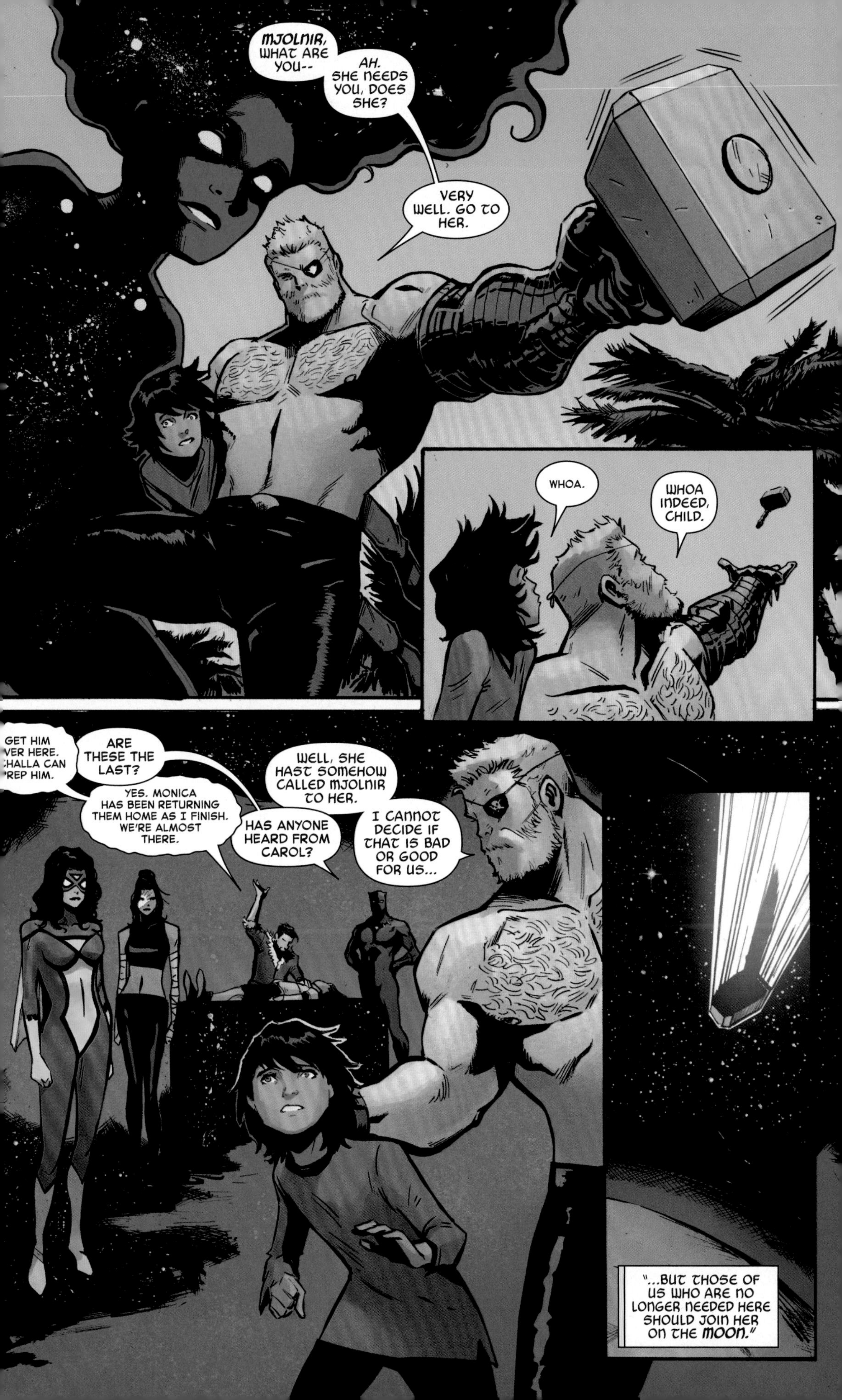
MJOLNIR, WHAT ARE YOU--
AH. SHE NEEDS YOU, DOES SHE?
VERY WELL. GO TO HER.
WHOA.
WHOA INDEED, CHILD.
GET HIM VER HERE. CHALLA CAN REP HIM.
ARE THESE THE LAST?
YES. MONICA HAS BEEN RETURNING THEM HOME AS I FINISH. WE'RE ALMOST THERE.
HAS ANYONE HEARD FROM CAROL?
WELL, SHE HAST SOMEHOW CALLED MJOLNIR TO HER.
I CANNOT DECIDE IF THAT IS BAD OR GOOD FOR US...
"...BUT THOSE OF US WHO ARE NO LONGER NEEDED HERE SHOULD JOIN HER ON THE MOON."

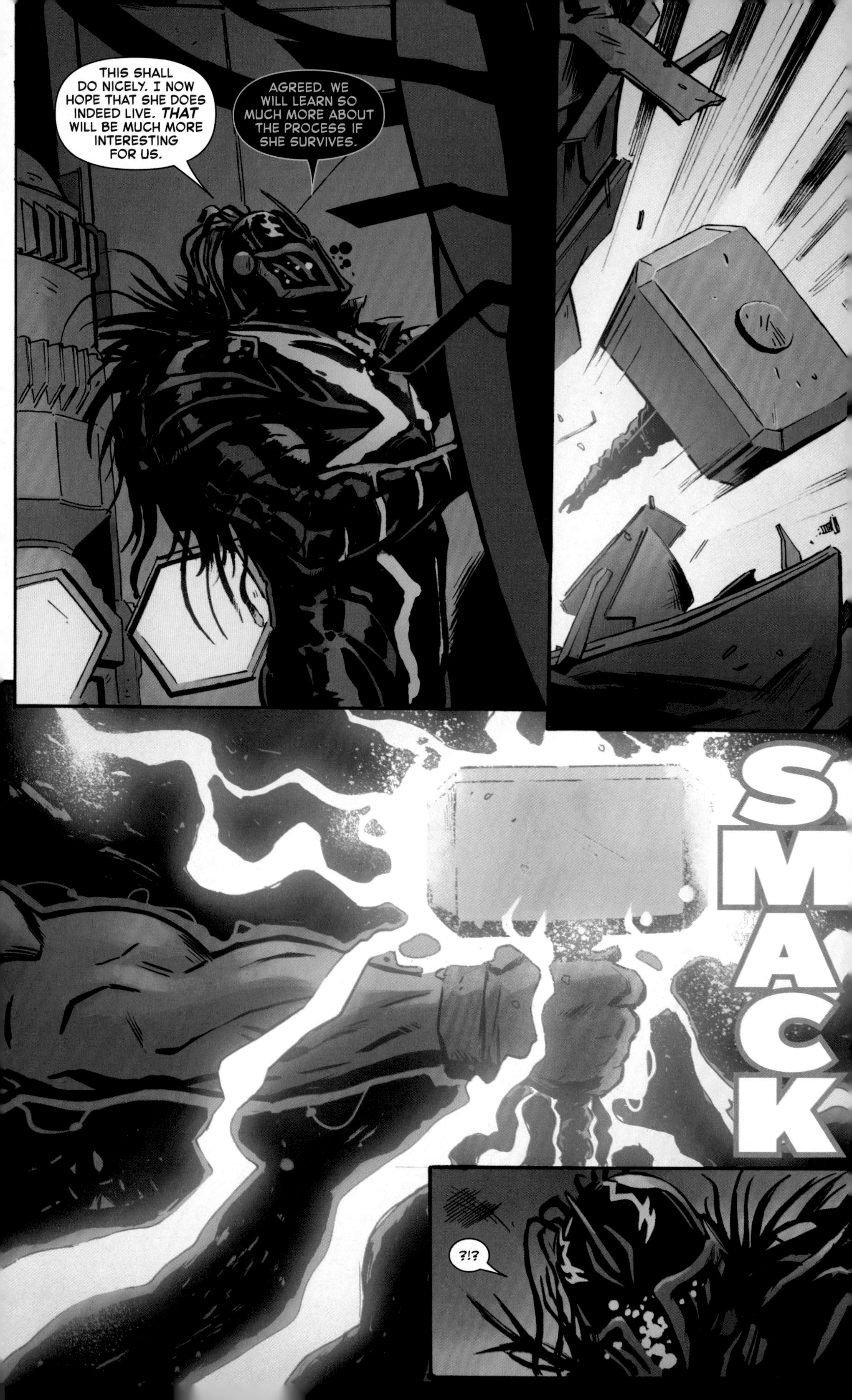
THIS SHALL DO NICELY. I NOW HOPE THAT SHE DOES INDEED LIVE. *THAT* WILL BE MUCH MORE INTERESTING FOR US.
AGREED. WE WILL LEARN SO MUCH MORE ABOUT THE PROCESS IF SHE SURVIVES.
SMACK
?!?

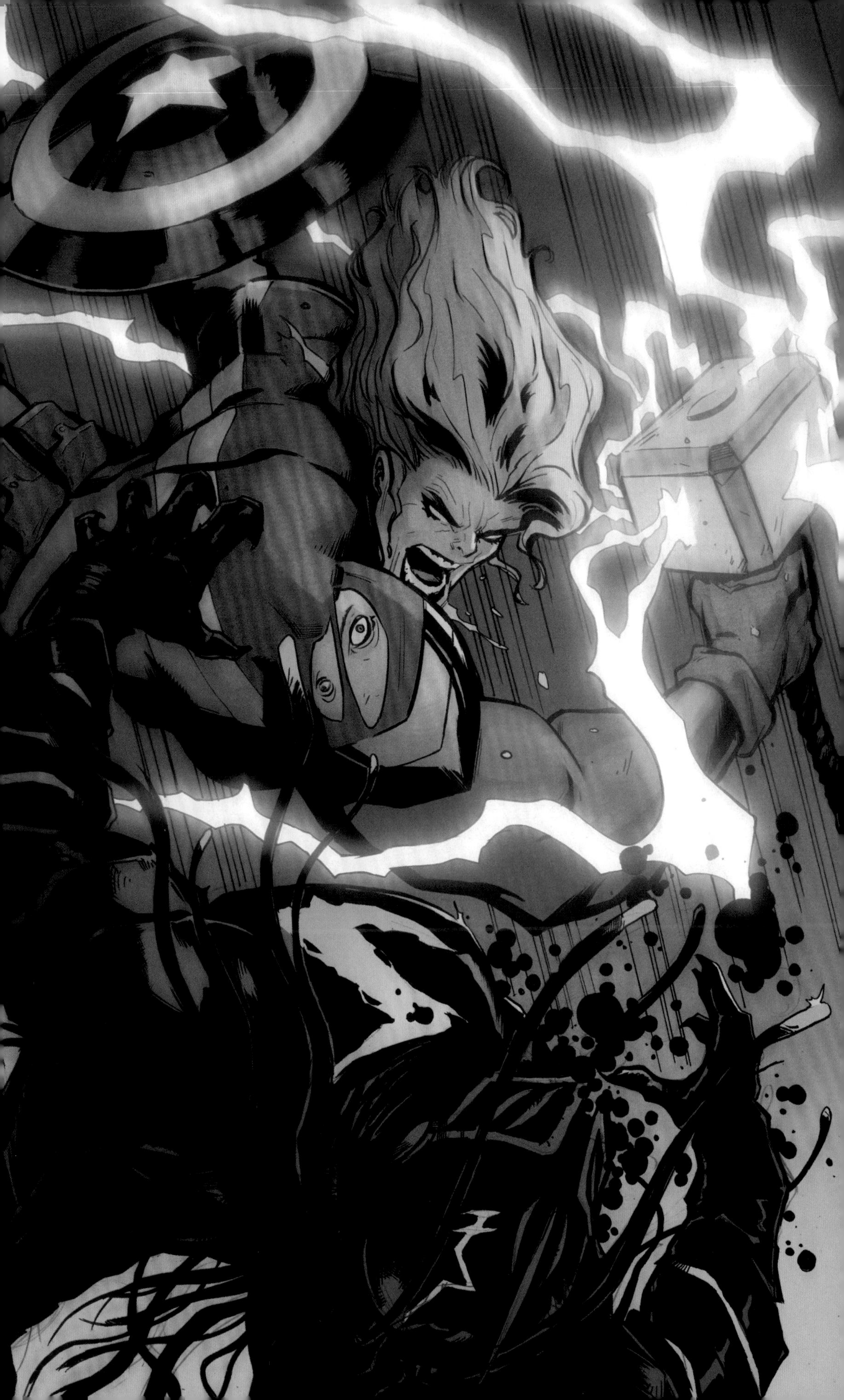

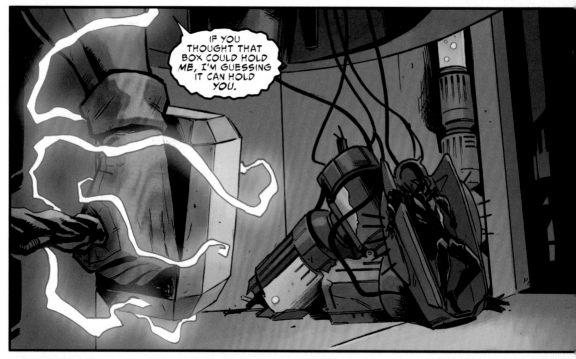

IF YOU THOUGHT THAT BOX COULD HOLD ME, I'M GUESSING IT CAN HOLD YOU.

SLAM

HEH. "THAT DAMN HAMMER."

I HAVE TO PURGE THE REST OF THIS POISON... BUT HOW?

I'LL BURN IT OUT.

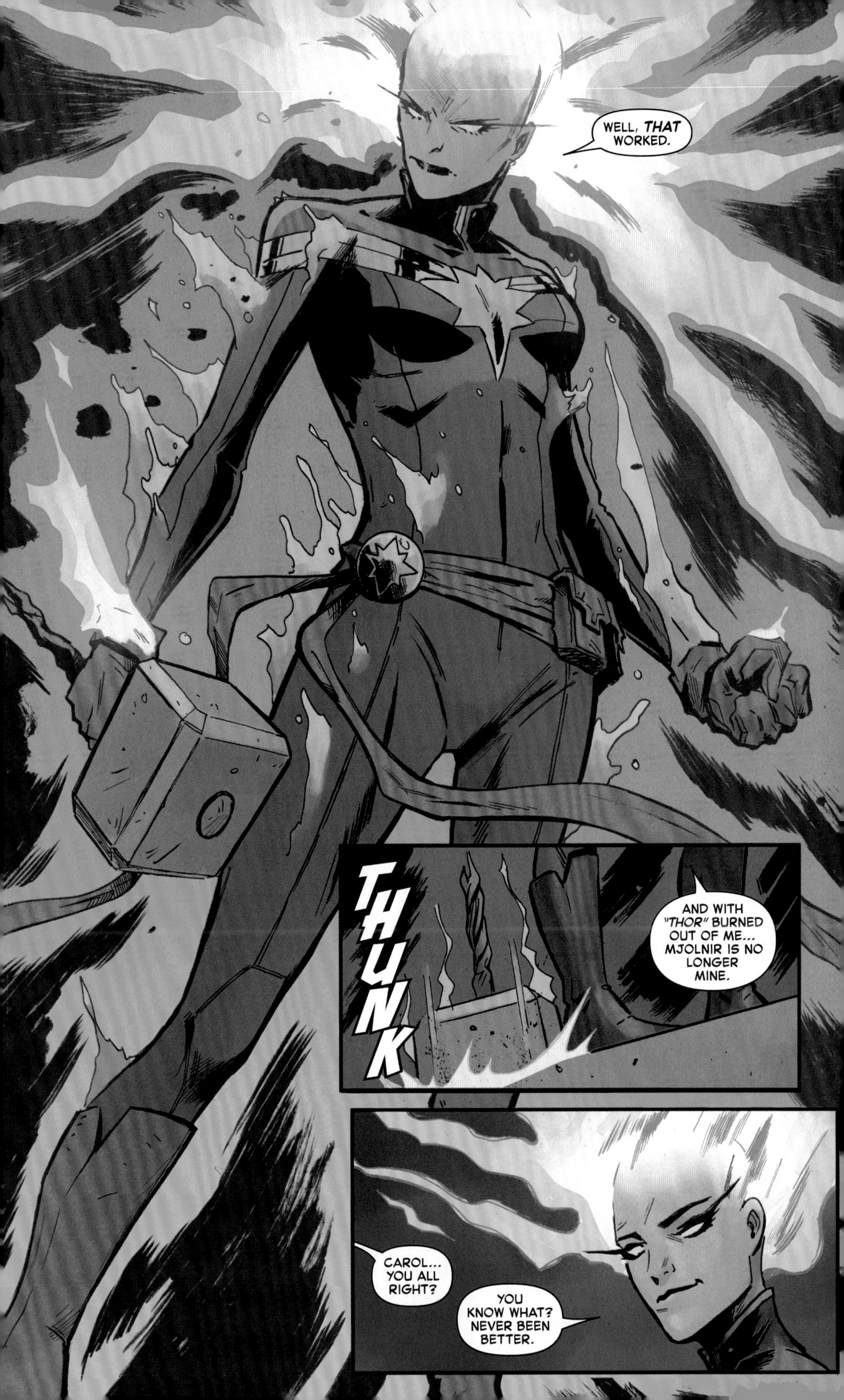
WELL, *THAT* WORKED.
THUNK
AND WITH "*THOR*" BURNED OUT OF ME... MJOLNIR IS NO LONGER MINE.
CAROL... YOU ALL RIGHT?
YOU KNOW WHAT? NEVER BEEN BETTER.

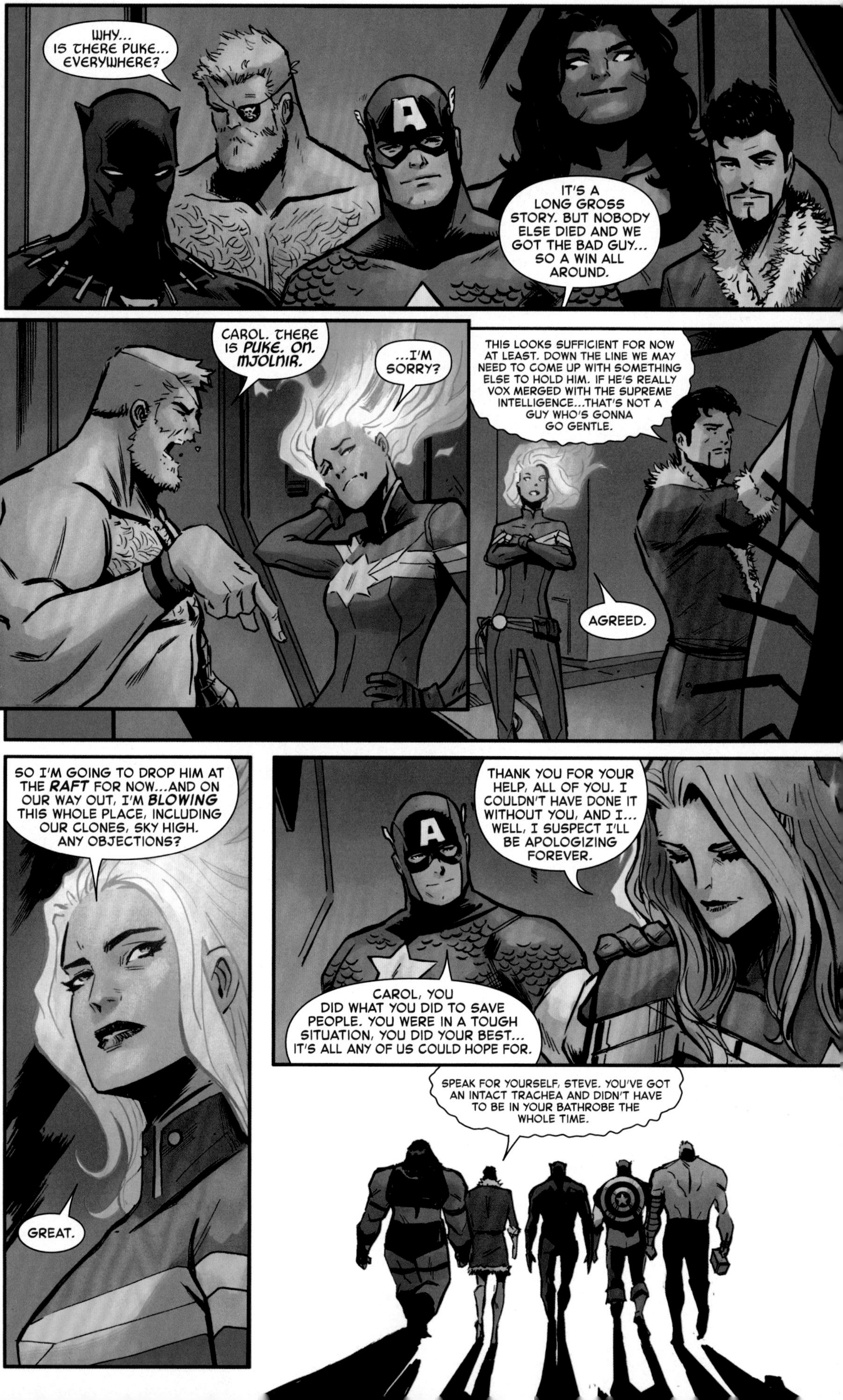

WHY... IS THERE PUKE... EVERYWHERE?
IT'S A LONG GROSS STORY. BUT NOBODY ELSE DIED AND WE GOT THE BAD GUY... SO A WIN ALL AROUND.
CAROL. THERE IS PUKE. ON. MJOLNIR.
...I'M SORRY?
THIS LOOKS SUFFICIENT FOR NOW AT LEAST. DOWN THE LINE WE MAY NEED TO COME UP WITH SOMETHING ELSE TO HOLD HIM. IF HE'S REALLY VOX MERGED WITH THE SUPREME INTELLIGENCE...THAT'S NOT A GUY WHO'S GONNA GO GENTLE.
AGREED.
SO I'M GOING TO DROP HIM AT THE RAFT FOR NOW...AND ON OUR WAY OUT, I'M BLOWING THIS WHOLE PLACE, INCLUDING OUR CLONES, SKY HIGH. ANY OBJECTIONS?
GREAT.
THANK YOU FOR YOUR HELP, ALL OF YOU. I COULDN'T HAVE DONE IT WITHOUT YOU, AND I... WELL, I SUSPECT I'LL BE APOLOGIZING FOREVER.
CAROL, YOU DID WHAT YOU DID TO SAVE PEOPLE. YOU WERE IN A TOUGH SITUATION, YOU DID YOUR BEST... IT'S ALL ANY OF US COULD HOPE FOR.
SPEAK FOR YOURSELF, STEVE. YOU'VE GOT AN INTACT TRACHEA AND DIDN'T HAVE TO BE IN YOUR BATHROBE THE WHOLE TIME.

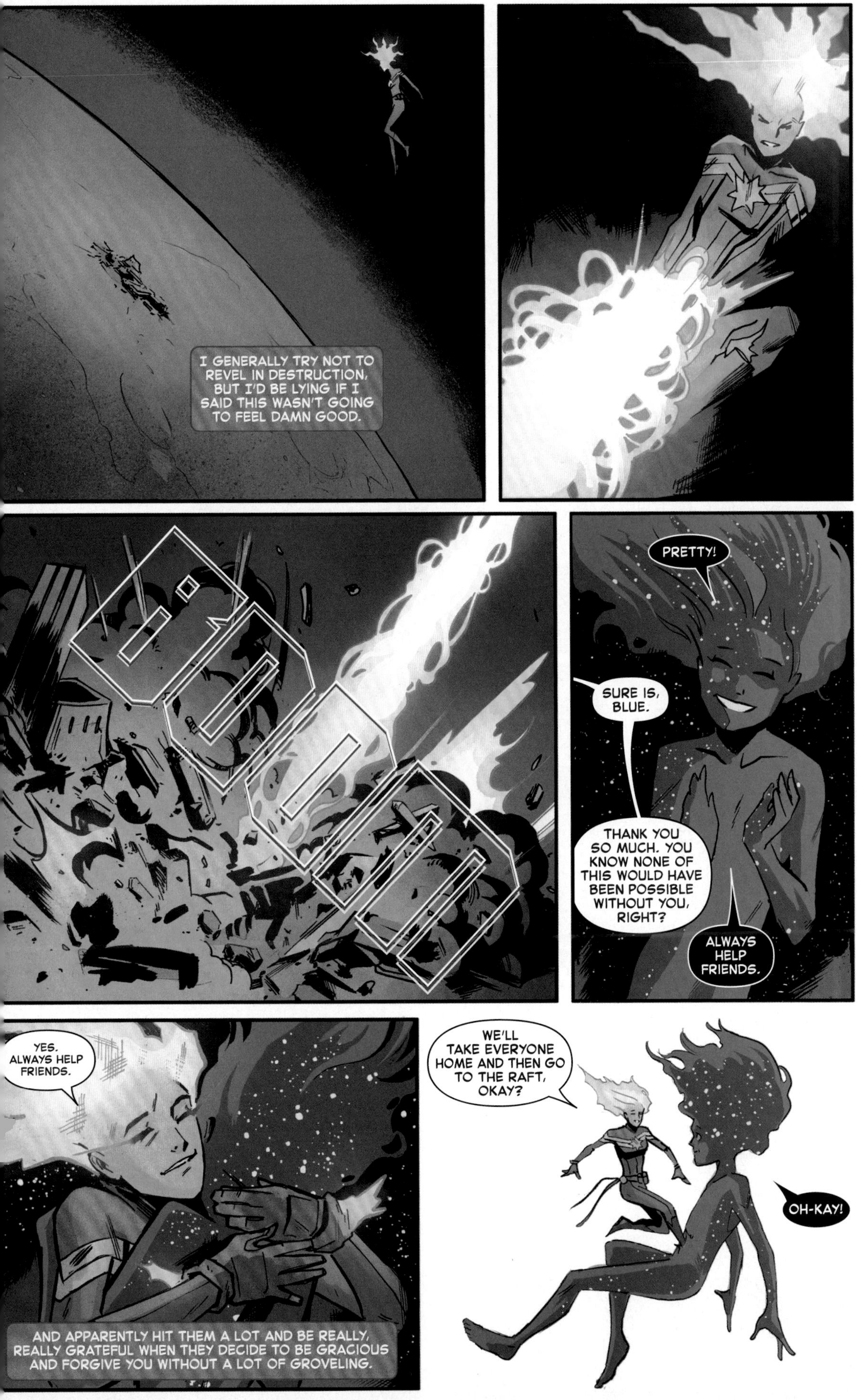
I GENERALLY TRY NOT TO REVEL IN DESTRUCTION, BUT I'D BE LYING IF I SAID THIS WASN'T GOING TO FEEL DAMN GOOD.
PRETTY!
SURE IS, BLUE.
THANK YOU SO MUCH. YOU KNOW NONE OF THIS WOULD HAVE BEEN POSSIBLE WITHOUT YOU, RIGHT?
ALWAYS HELP FRIENDS.
YES. ALWAYS HELP FRIENDS.
AND APPARENTLY HIT THEM A LOT AND BE REALLY, REALLY GRATEFUL WHEN THEY DECIDE TO BE GRACIOUS AND FORGIVE YOU WITHOUT A LOT OF GROVELING.
WE'LL TAKE EVERYONE HOME AND THEN GO TO THE RAFT, OKAY?
OH-KAY!

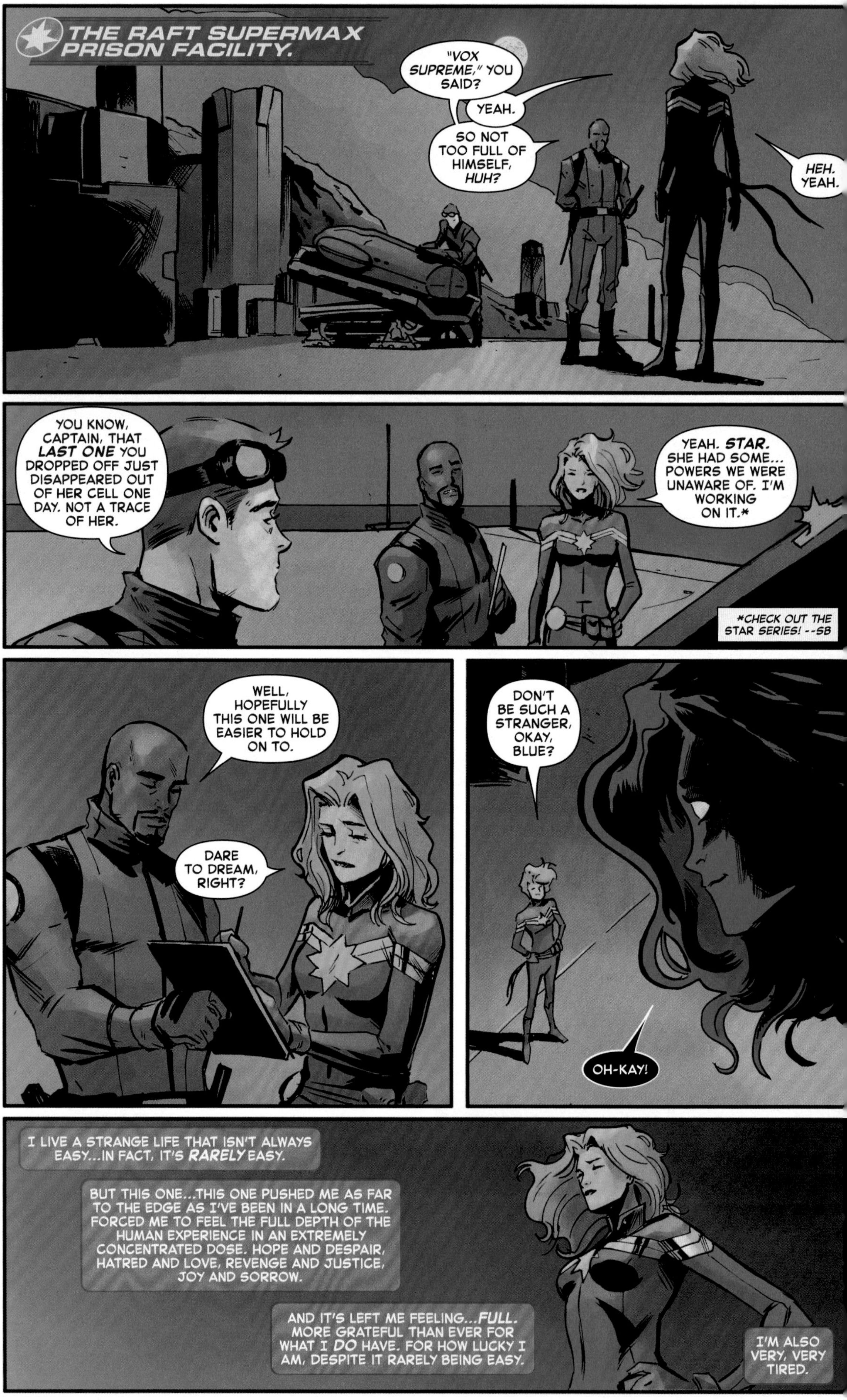
THE RAFT SUPERMAX PRISON FACILITY.
"VOX SUPREME," YOU SAID?
YEAH.
SO NOT TOO FULL OF HIMSELF, HUH?
HEH. YEAH.
YOU KNOW, CAPTAIN, THAT LAST ONE YOU DROPPED OFF JUST DISAPPEARED OUT OF HER CELL ONE DAY. NOT A TRACE OF HER.
YEAH. STAR. SHE HAD SOME... POWERS WE WERE UNAWARE OF. I'M WORKING ON IT.*
*CHECK OUT THE STAR SERIES! --SB
WELL, HOPEFULLY THIS ONE WILL BE EASIER TO HOLD ON TO.
DARE TO DREAM, RIGHT?
DON'T BE SUCH A STRANGER, OKAY, BLUE?
OH-KAY!
I LIVE A STRANGE LIFE THAT ISN'T ALWAYS EASY...IN FACT, IT'S RARELY EASY.
BUT THIS ONE...THIS ONE PUSHED ME AS FAR TO THE EDGE AS I'VE BEEN IN A LONG TIME. FORCED ME TO FEEL THE FULL DEPTH OF THE HUMAN EXPERIENCE IN AN EXTREMELY CONCENTRATED DOSE. HOPE AND DESPAIR, HATRED AND LOVE, REVENGE AND JUSTICE, JOY AND SORROW.
AND IT'S LEFT ME FEELING...FULL. MORE GRATEFUL THAN EVER FOR WHAT I DO HAVE. FOR HOW LUCKY I AM, DESPITE IT RARELY BEING EASY.
I'M ALSO VERY, VERY TIRED.

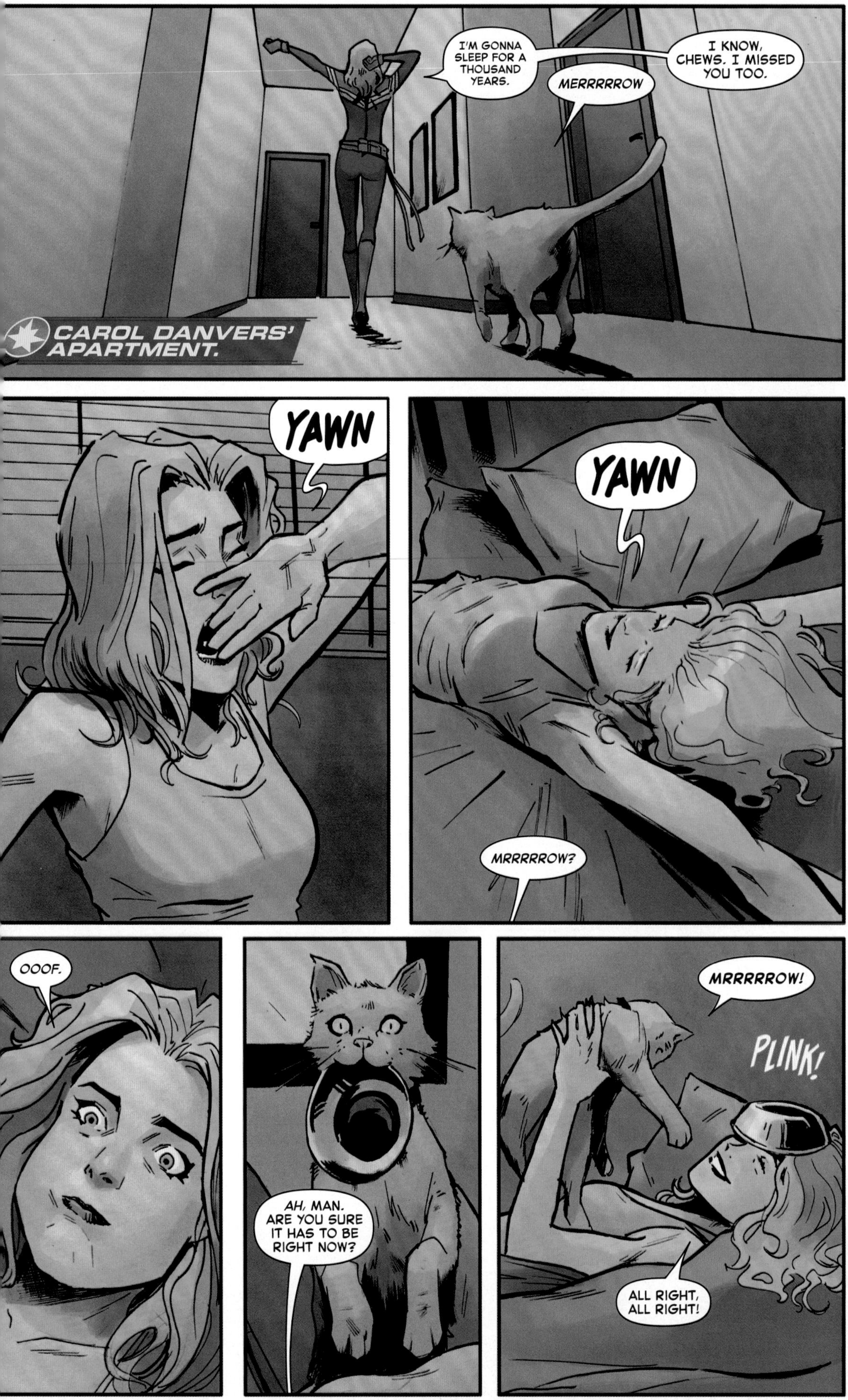
CAROL DANVERS' APARTMENT.
I'M GONNA SLEEP FOR A THOUSAND YEARS.
MERRRRROW
I KNOW, CHEWS. I MISSED YOU TOO.
YAWN
YAWN
MRRRRROW?
OOOF.
AH, MAN. ARE YOU SURE IT HAS TO BE RIGHT NOW?
MRRRRROW!
PLINK!
ALL RIGHT, ALL RIGHT!

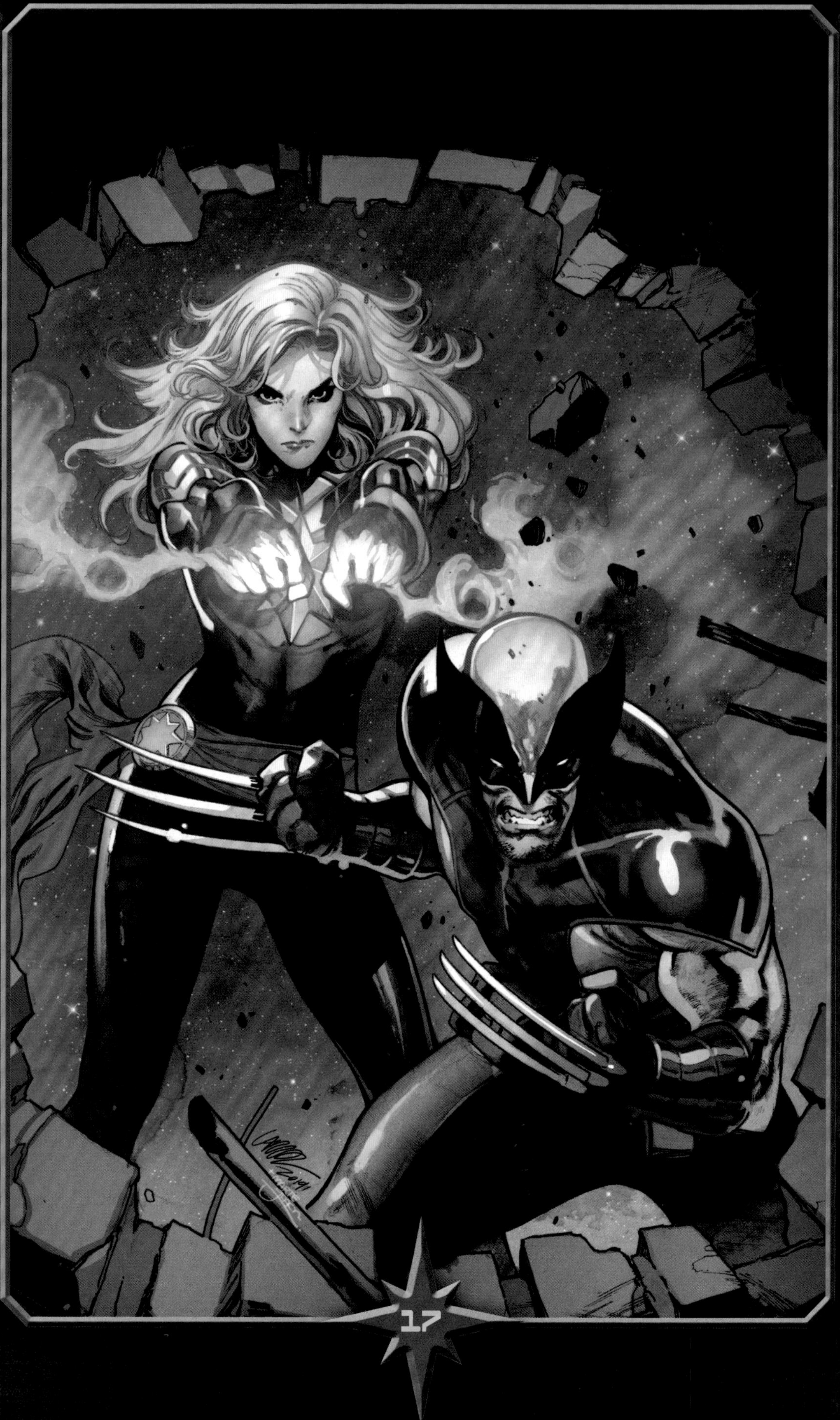
17

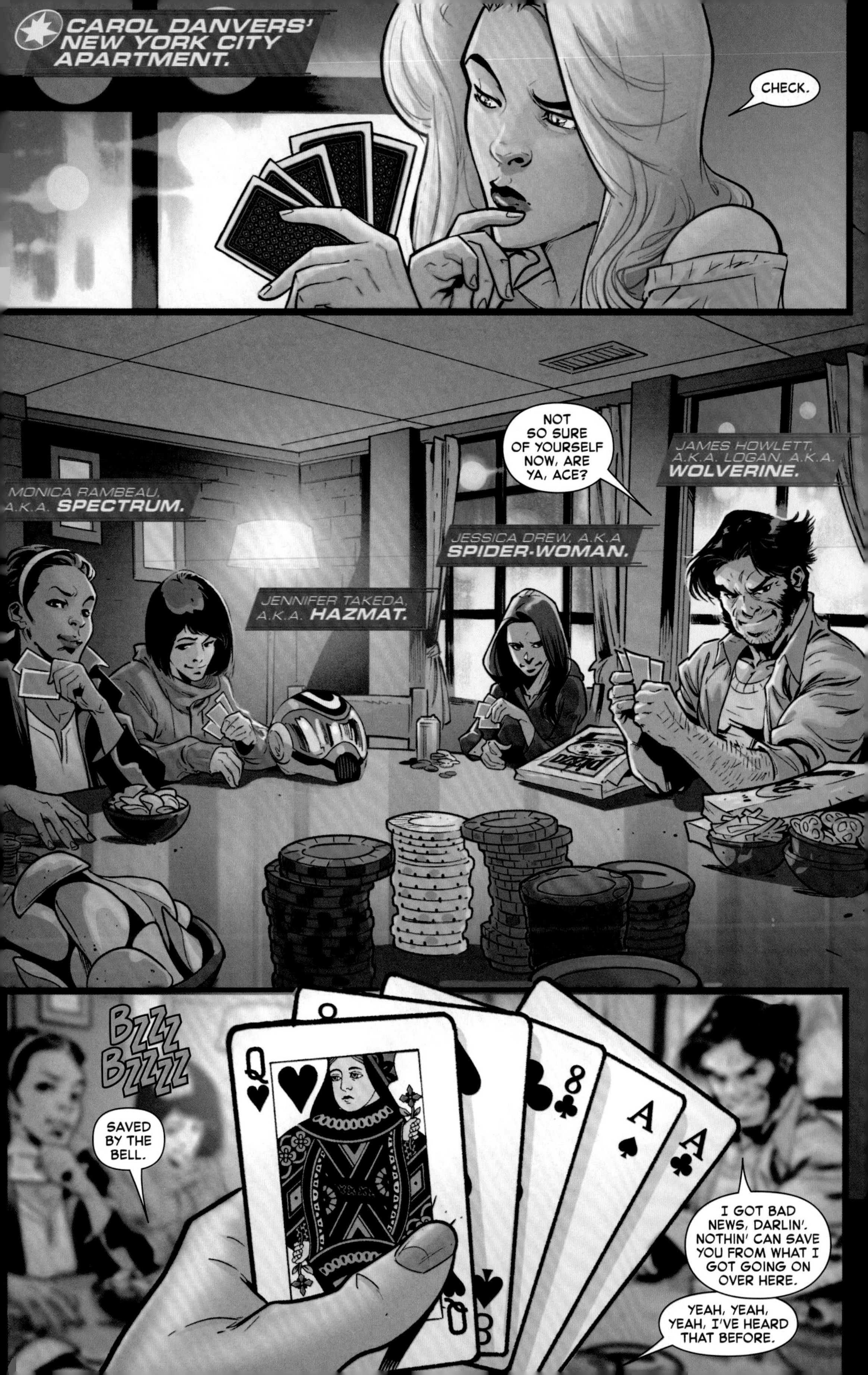
CAROL DANVERS' NEW YORK CITY APARTMENT.
CHECK.
MONICA RAMBEAU, A.K.A. SPECTRUM.
JENNIFER TAKEDA, A.K.A. HAZMAT.
NOT SO SURE OF YOURSELF NOW, ARE YA, ACE?
JESSICA DREW, A.K.A SPIDER-WOMAN.
JAMES HOWLETT, A.K.A. LOGAN, A.K.A. WOLVERINE.
BZZZ BZZZZ
SAVED BY THE BELL.
I GOT BAD NEWS, DARLIN'. NOTHIN' CAN SAVE YOU FROM WHAT I GOT GOING ON OVER HERE.
YEAH, YEAH, YEAH, I'VE HEARD THAT BEFORE.

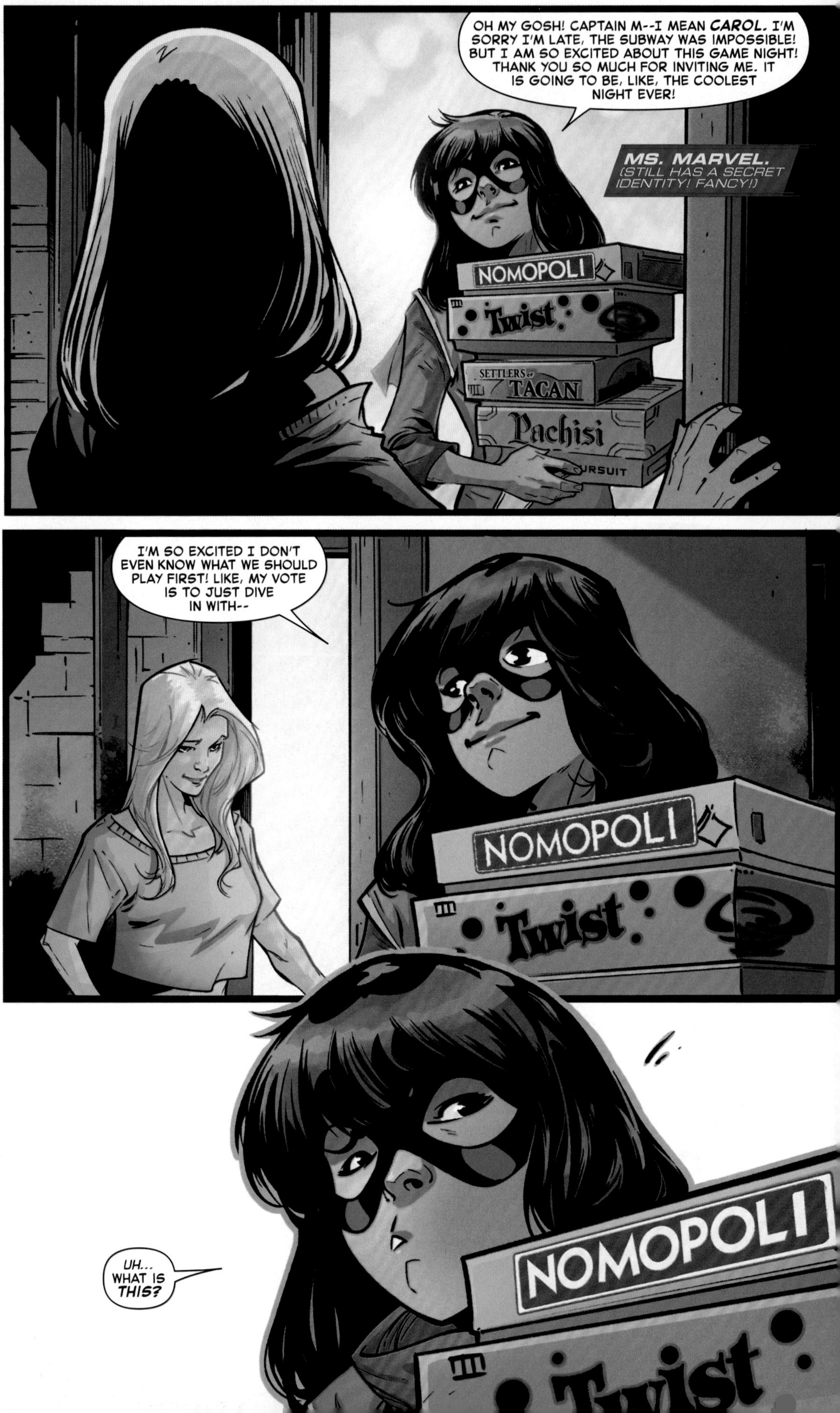
OH MY GOSH! CAPTAIN M--I MEAN CAROL. I'M SORRY I'M LATE, THE SUBWAY WAS IMPOSSIBLE! BUT I AM SO EXCITED ABOUT THIS GAME NIGHT! THANK YOU SO MUCH FOR INVITING ME. IT IS GOING TO BE, LIKE, THE COOLEST NIGHT EVER!
MS. MARVEL. (STILL HAS A SECRET IDENTITY! FANCY!)
NOMOPOLI
Twist
SETTLERS of TACAN
Pachisi
URSUIT
I'M SO EXCITED I DON'T EVEN KNOW WHAT WE SHOULD PLAY FIRST! LIKE, MY VOTE IS TO JUST DIVE IN WITH--
NOMOPOLI
Twist
UH... WHAT IS THIS?
NOMOPOLI
Twist

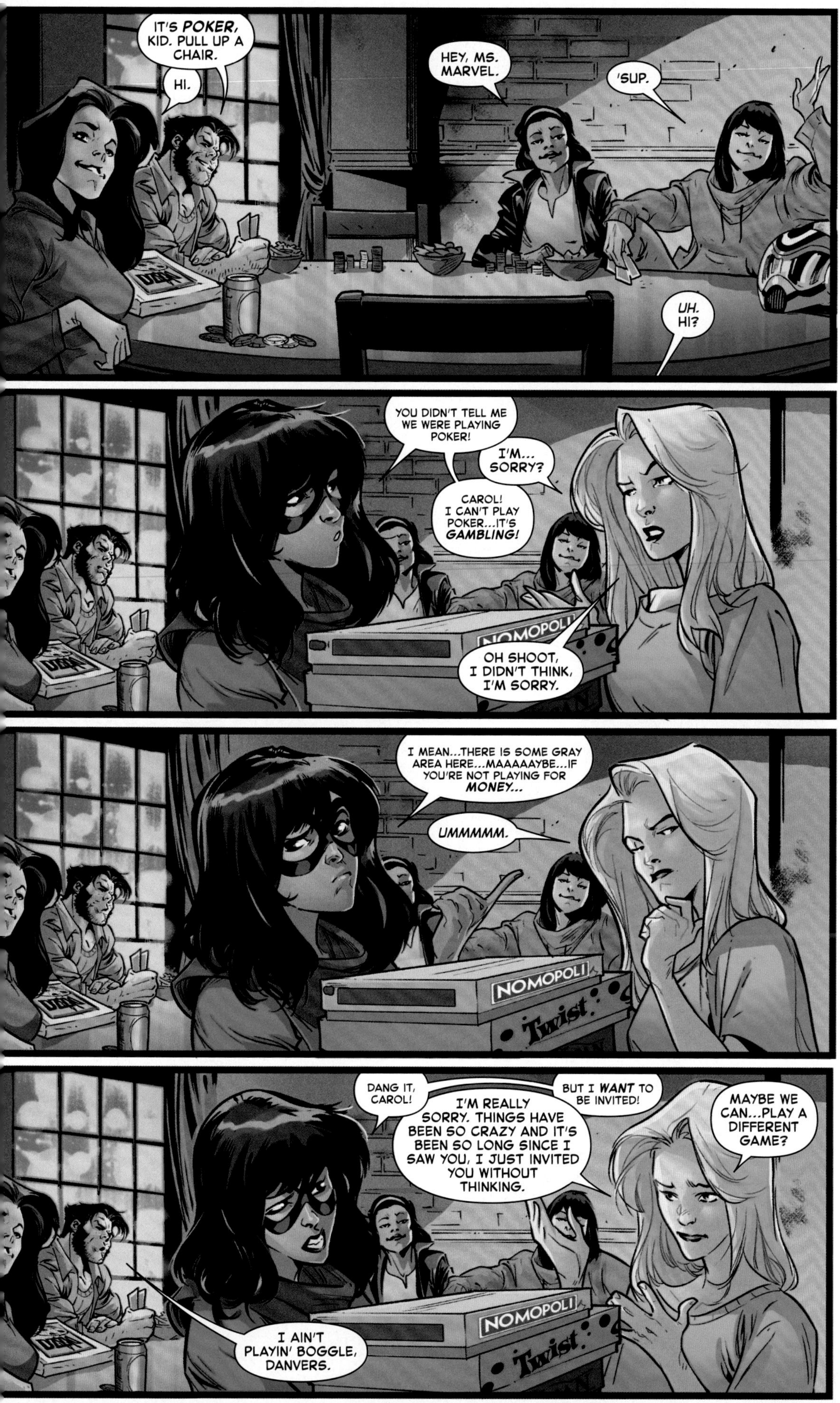
IT'S POKER, KID. PULL UP A CHAIR.
HI.
HEY, MS. MARVEL.
'SUP.
UH. HI?
YOU DIDN'T TELL ME WE WERE PLAYING POKER!
I'M... SORRY?
CAROL! I CAN'T PLAY POKER...IT'S GAMBLING!
NOMOPOLI
OH SHOOT, I DIDN'T THINK, I'M SORRY.
I MEAN...THERE IS SOME GRAY AREA HERE...MAAAAAYBE...IF YOU'RE NOT PLAYING FOR MONEY...
UMMMMM.
NOMOPOLI
Twist
DANG IT, CAROL!
BUT I WANT TO BE INVITED!
I'M REALLY SORRY. THINGS HAVE BEEN SO CRAZY AND IT'S BEEN SO LONG SINCE I SAW YOU, I JUST INVITED YOU WITHOUT THINKING.
MAYBE WE CAN...PLAY A DIFFERENT GAME?
I AIN'T PLAYIN' BOGGLE, DANVERS.
NOMOPOLI
Twist

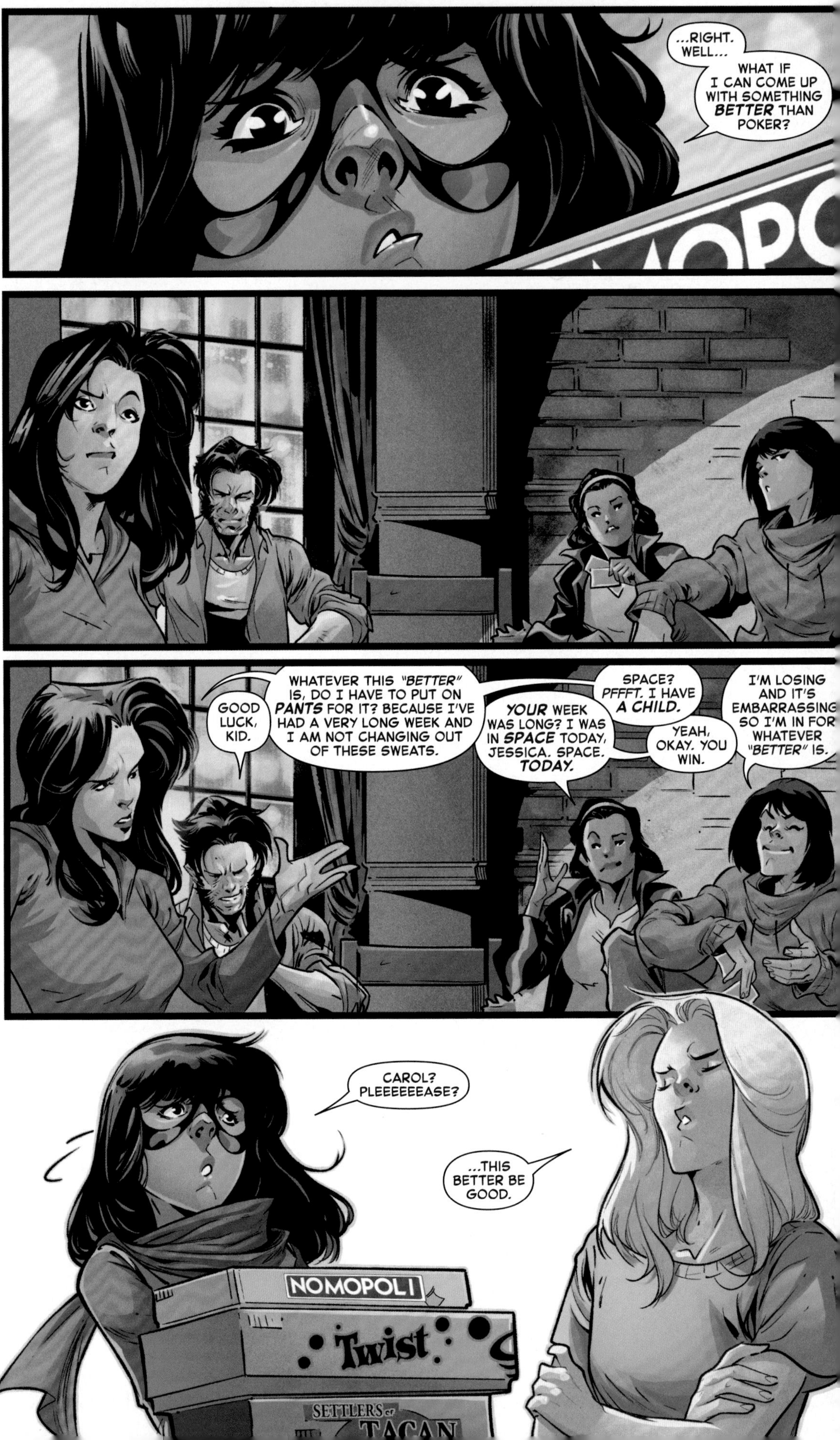
...RIGHT. WELL...
WHAT IF I CAN COME UP WITH SOMETHING BETTER THAN POKER?
GOOD LUCK, KID.
WHATEVER THIS "BETTER" IS, DO I HAVE TO PUT ON PANTS FOR IT? BECAUSE I'VE HAD A VERY LONG WEEK AND I AM NOT CHANGING OUT OF THESE SWEATS.
YOUR WEEK WAS LONG? I WAS IN SPACE TODAY, JESSICA. SPACE. TODAY.
SPACE? PFFFT. I HAVE A CHILD.
YEAH, OKAY. YOU WIN.
I'M LOSING AND IT'S EMBARRASSING SO I'M IN FOR WHATEVER "BETTER" IS.
CAROL? PLEEEEEEASE?
...THIS BETTER BE GOOD.
NOMOPOLI
Twist
SETTLERS of TACAN

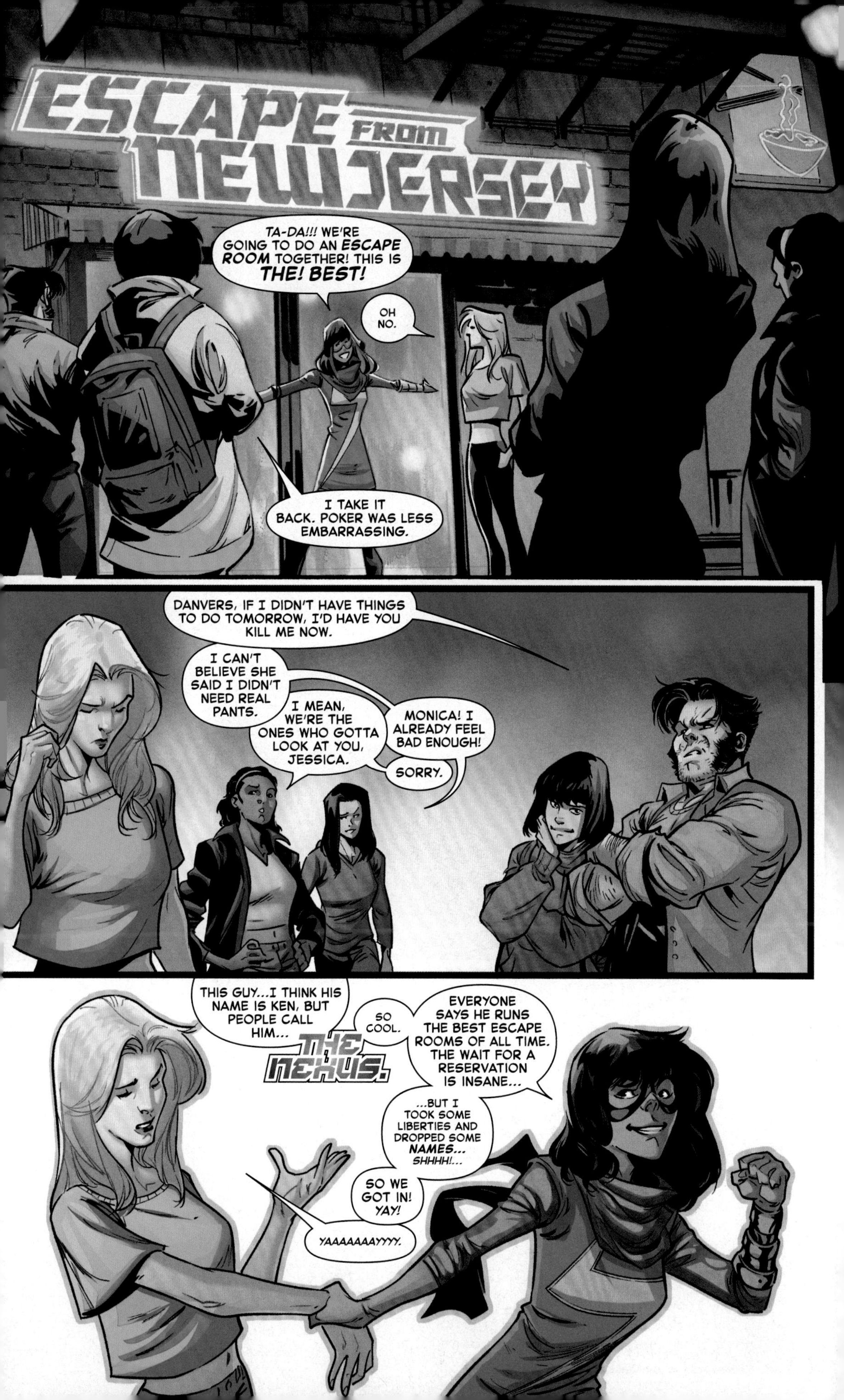
ESCAPE FROM NEW JERSEY
TA-DA!!! WE'RE GOING TO DO AN ESCAPE ROOM TOGETHER! THIS IS THE! BEST!
OH NO.
I TAKE IT BACK. POKER WAS LESS EMBARRASSING.
DANVERS, IF I DIDN'T HAVE THINGS TO DO TOMORROW, I'D HAVE YOU KILL ME NOW.
I CAN'T BELIEVE SHE SAID I DIDN'T NEED REAL PANTS.
I MEAN, WE'RE THE ONES WHO GOTTA LOOK AT YOU, JESSICA.
MONICA! I ALREADY FEEL BAD ENOUGH!
SORRY.
THIS GUY...I THINK HIS NAME IS KEN, BUT PEOPLE CALL HIM...
THE NEXUS.
SO COOL.
EVERYONE SAYS HE RUNS THE BEST ESCAPE ROOMS OF ALL TIME. THE WAIT FOR A RESERVATION IS INSANE...
...BUT I TOOK SOME LIBERTIES AND DROPPED SOME NAMES... SHHHH!...
SO WE GOT IN! YAY!
YAAAAAAAYYYY.

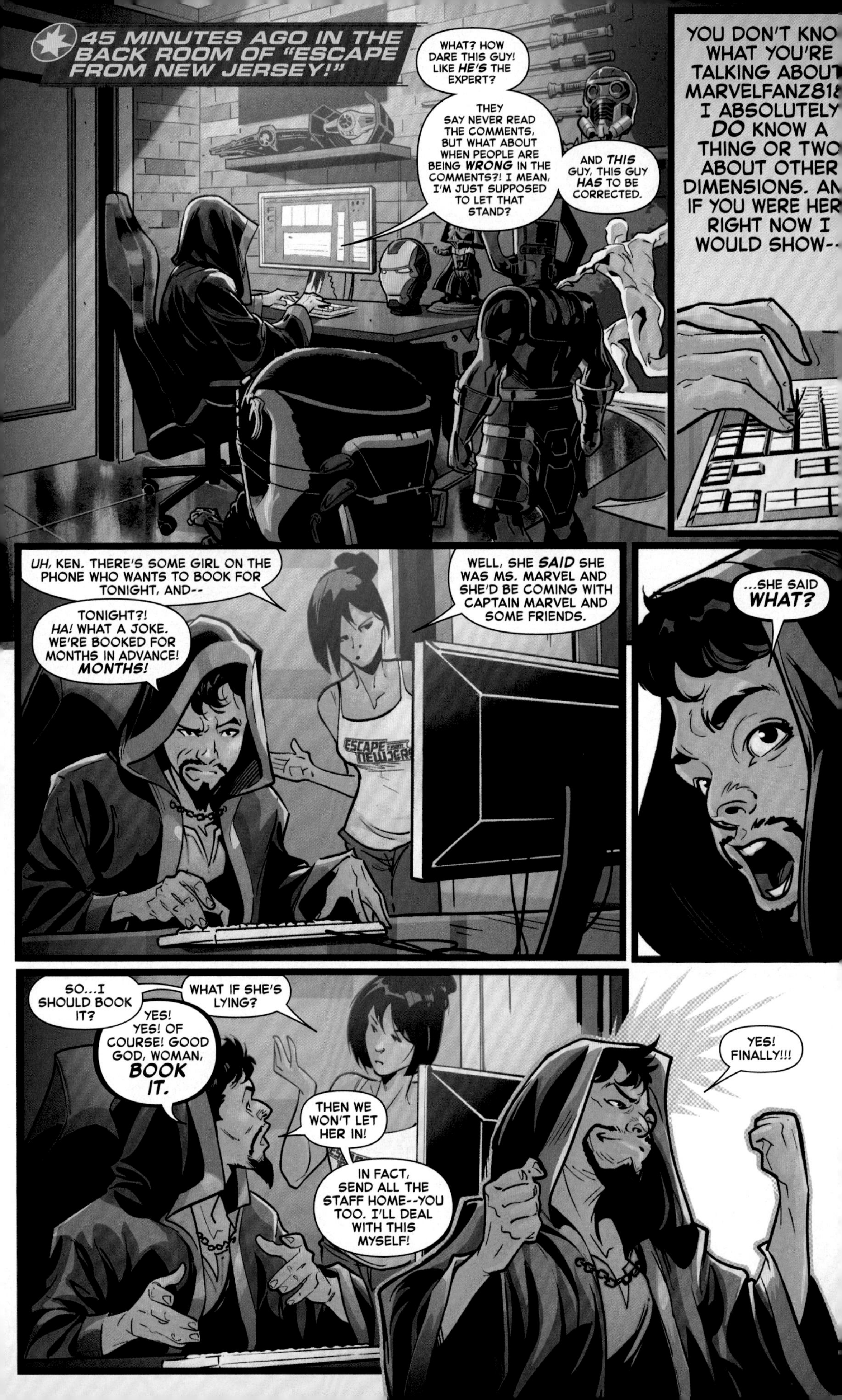

45 MINUTES AGO IN THE BACK ROOM OF "ESCAPE FROM NEW JERSEY!"
WHAT? HOW DARE THIS GUY! LIKE *HE'S* THE EXPERT?
THEY SAY NEVER READ THE COMMENTS, BUT WHAT ABOUT WHEN PEOPLE ARE BEING ***WRONG*** IN THE COMMENTS?! I MEAN, I'M JUST SUPPOSED TO LET THAT STAND?
AND ***THIS*** GUY, THIS GUY ***HAS*** TO BE CORRECTED.
YOU DON'T KNO WHAT YOU'RE TALKING ABOUT MARVELFANZ81 I ABSOLUTELY *DO* KNOW A THING OR TWO ABOUT OTHER DIMENSIONS. AN IF YOU WERE HER RIGHT NOW I WOULD SHOW--
UH, KEN. THERE'S SOME GIRL ON THE PHONE WHO WANTS TO BOOK FOR TONIGHT, AND--
TONIGHT?! *HA!* WHAT A JOKE. WE'RE BOOKED FOR MONTHS IN ADVANCE! ***MONTHS!***
WELL, SHE ***SAID*** SHE WAS MS. MARVEL AND SHE'D BE COMING WITH CAPTAIN MARVEL AND SOME FRIENDS.
ESCAPE FROM NEW JERS
...SHE SAID ***WHAT?***
SO...I SHOULD BOOK IT?
YES! YES! OF COURSE! GOOD GOD, WOMAN, ***BOOK IT.***
WHAT IF SHE'S LYING?
THEN WE WON'T LET HER IN!
IN FACT, SEND ALL THE STAFF HOME--YOU TOO. I'LL DEAL WITH THIS MYSELF!
YES! FINALLY!!!

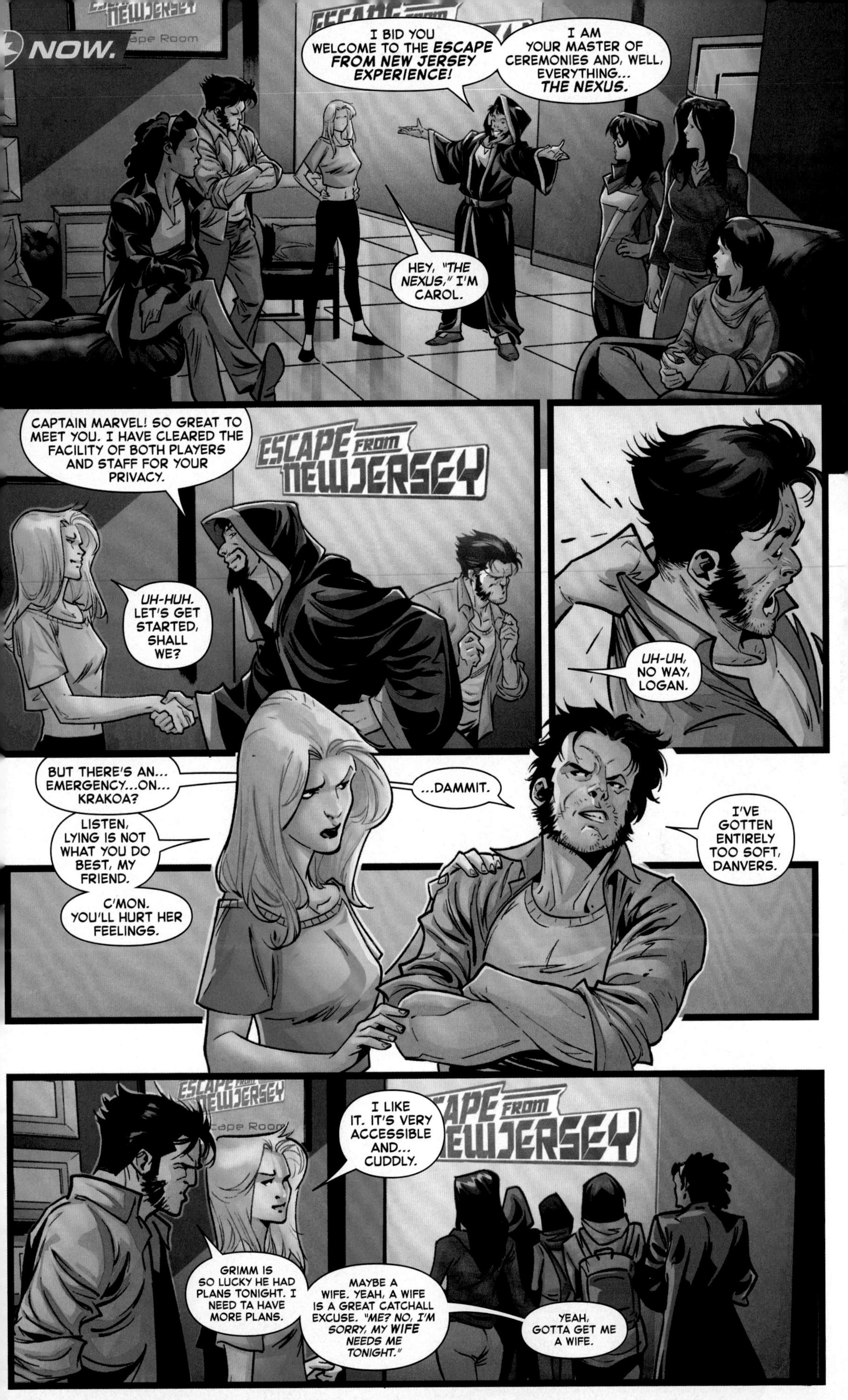
NOW.
ESCAPE FROM NEW JERSEY
Escape Room
I BID YOU WELCOME TO THE *ESCAPE FROM NEW JERSEY EXPERIENCE!*
I AM YOUR MASTER OF CEREMONIES AND, WELL, EVERYTHING... *THE NEXUS.*
HEY, *"THE NEXUS,"* I'M CAROL.
CAPTAIN MARVEL! SO GREAT TO MEET YOU. I HAVE CLEARED THE FACILITY OF BOTH PLAYERS AND STAFF FOR YOUR PRIVACY.
ESCAPE FROM NEW JERSEY
UH-HUH. LET'S GET STARTED, SHALL WE?
UH-UH, NO WAY, LOGAN.
BUT THERE'S AN... EMERGENCY...ON... KRAKOA?
...DAMMIT.
I'VE GOTTEN ENTIRELY TOO SOFT, DANVERS.
LISTEN, LYING IS NOT WHAT YOU DO BEST, MY FRIEND.
C'MON. YOU'LL HURT HER FEELINGS.
ESCAPE FROM NEW JERSEY
Escape Room
I LIKE IT. IT'S VERY ACCESSIBLE AND... CUDDLY.
ESCAPE FROM NEW JERSEY
GRIMM IS SO LUCKY HE HAD PLANS TONIGHT. I NEED TA HAVE MORE PLANS.
MAYBE A WIFE. YEAH, A WIFE IS A GREAT CATCHALL EXCUSE. *"ME? NO, I'M SORRY, MY WIFE NEEDS ME TONIGHT."*
YEAH, GOTTA GET ME A WIFE.

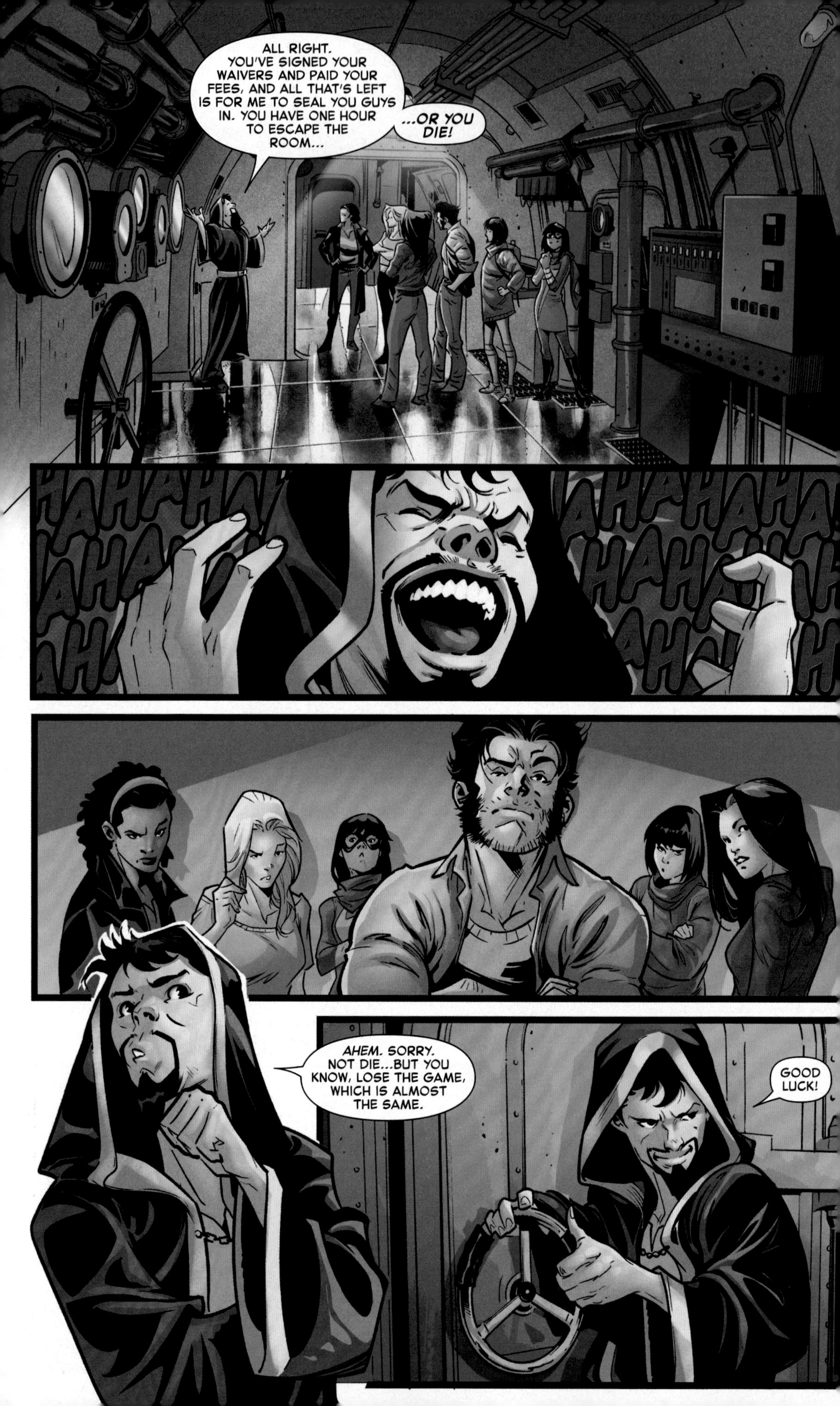

ALL RIGHT. YOU'VE SIGNED YOUR WAIVERS AND PAID YOUR FEES, AND ALL THAT'S LEFT IS FOR ME TO SEAL YOU GUYS IN. YOU HAVE ONE HOUR TO ESCAPE THE ROOM...
...OR YOU DIE!
HAHAHAHAHAHAHAHA
AHEM. SORRY. NOT DIE...BUT YOU KNOW, LOSE THE GAME, WHICH IS ALMOST THE SAME.
GOOD LUCK!

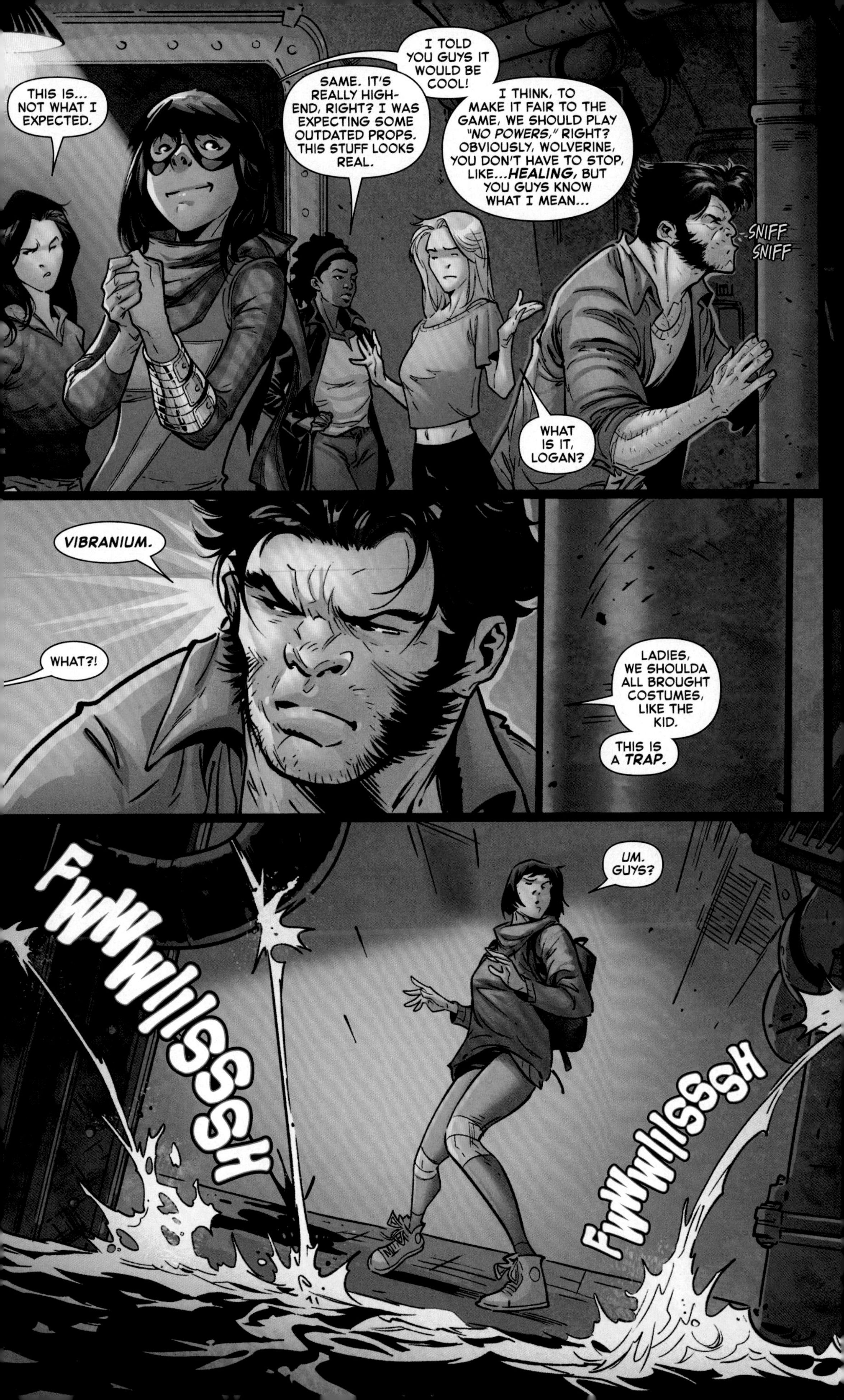

THIS IS... NOT WHAT I EXPECTED.
SAME. IT'S REALLY HIGH-END, RIGHT? I WAS EXPECTING SOME OUTDATED PROPS. THIS STUFF LOOKS REAL.
I TOLD YOU GUYS IT WOULD BE COOL!
I THINK, TO MAKE IT FAIR TO THE GAME, WE SHOULD PLAY "NO POWERS," RIGHT? OBVIOUSLY, WOLVERINE, YOU DON'T HAVE TO STOP, LIKE...HEALING, BUT YOU GUYS KNOW WHAT I MEAN...
SNIFF SNIFF
WHAT IS IT, LOGAN?
VIBRANIUM.
WHAT?!
LADIES, WE SHOULDA ALL BROUGHT COSTUMES, LIKE THE KID.
THIS IS A TRAP.
UM. GUYS?
FWWIISSSH
FWWIISSSH

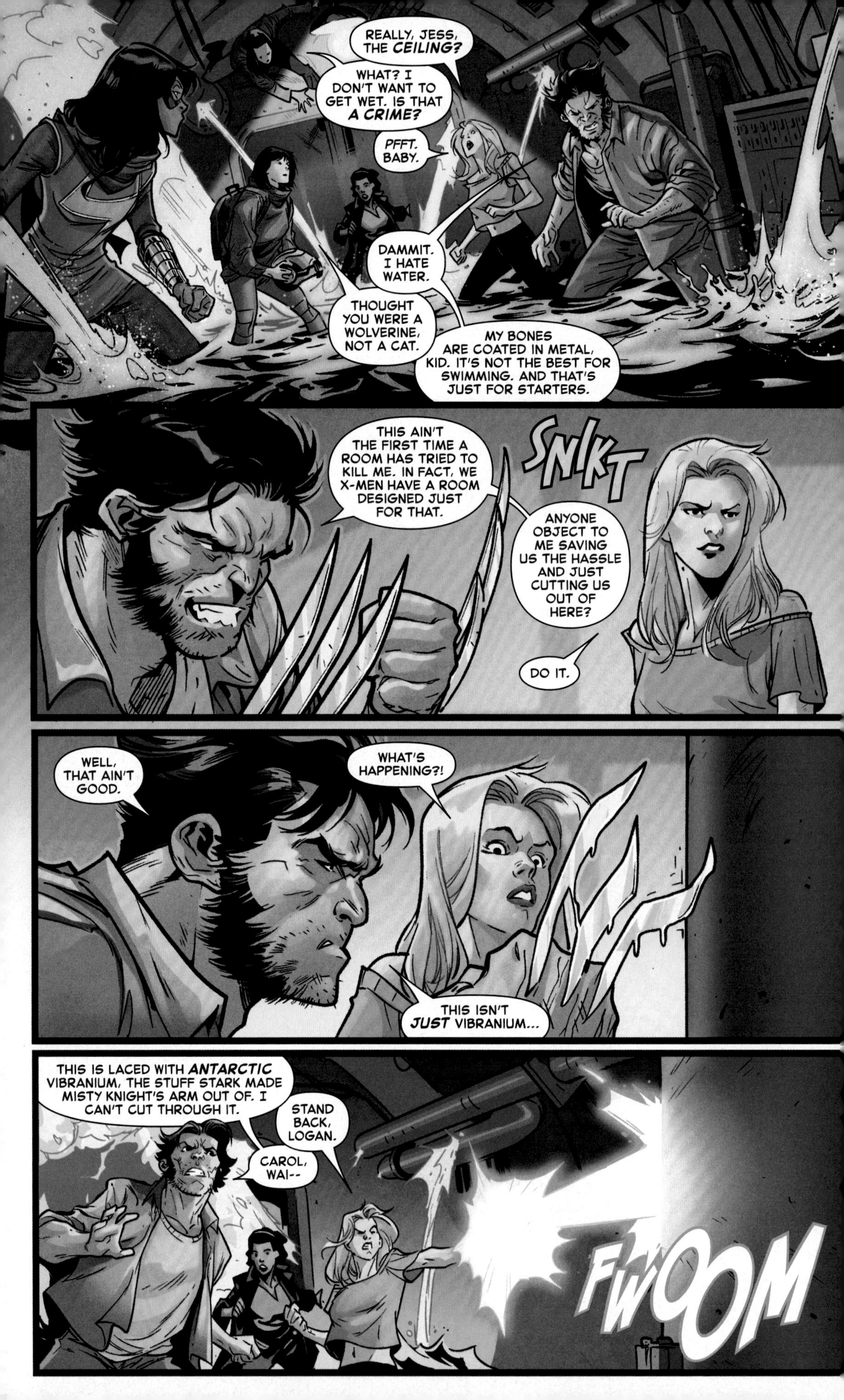

REALLY, JESS, THE CEILING?
WHAT? I DON'T WANT TO GET WET. IS THAT A CRIME?
PFFT. BABY.
DAMMIT. I HATE WATER.
THOUGHT YOU WERE A WOLVERINE, NOT A CAT.
MY BONES ARE COATED IN METAL, KID. IT'S NOT THE BEST FOR SWIMMING. AND THAT'S JUST FOR STARTERS.
THIS AIN'T THE FIRST TIME A ROOM HAS TRIED TO KILL ME. IN FACT, WE X-MEN HAVE A ROOM DESIGNED JUST FOR THAT.
SNIKT
ANYONE OBJECT TO ME SAVING US THE HASSLE AND JUST CUTTING US OUT OF HERE?
DO IT.
WELL, THAT AIN'T GOOD.
WHAT'S HAPPENING?!
THIS ISN'T JUST VIBRANIUM...
THIS IS LACED WITH ANTARCTIC VIBRANIUM, THE STUFF STARK MADE MISTY KNIGHT'S ARM OUT OF. I CAN'T CUT THROUGH IT.
STAND BACK, LOGAN.
CAROL, WAI--
FWOOM

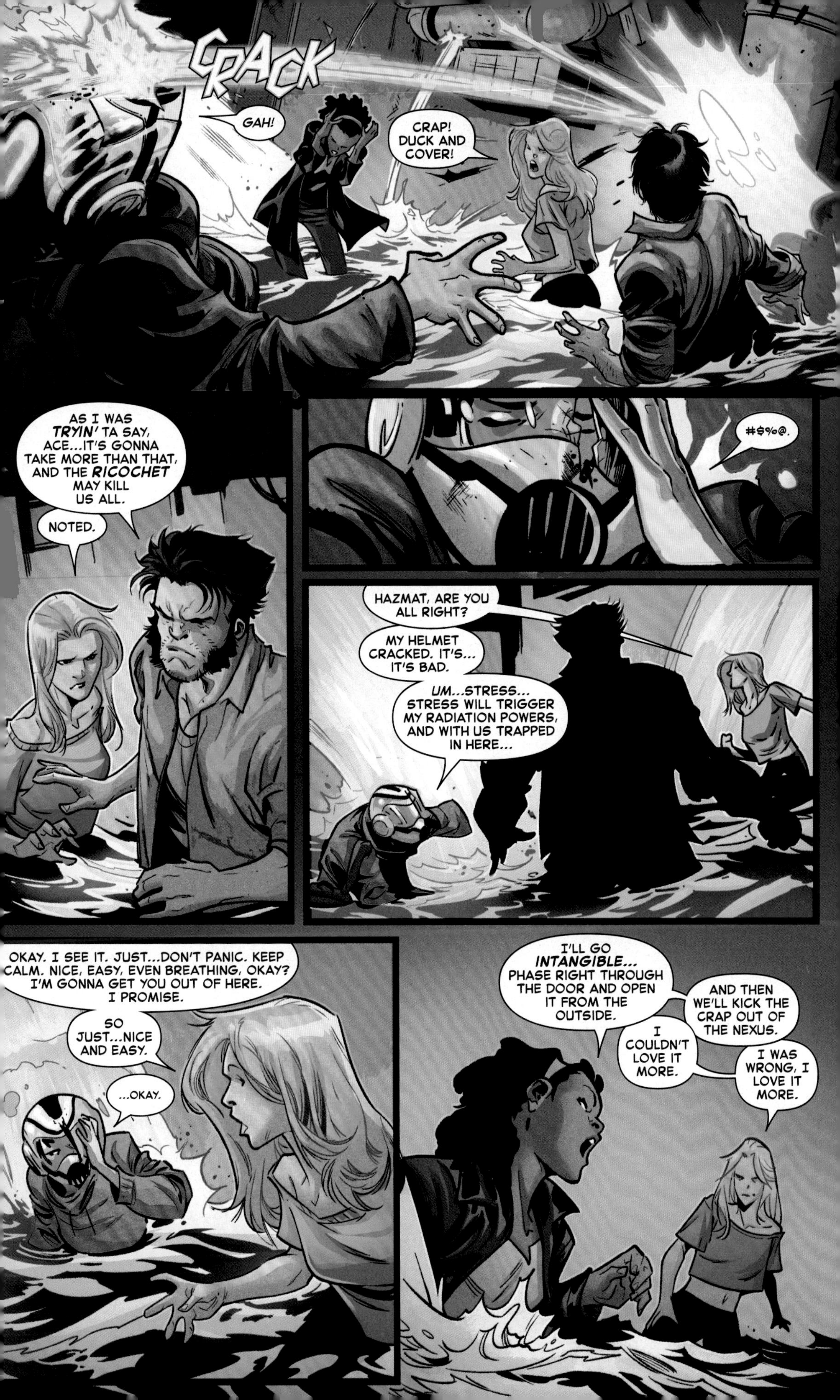
CRACK
GAH!
CRAP! DUCK AND COVER!
AS I WAS TRYIN' TA SAY, ACE...IT'S GONNA TAKE MORE THAN THAT, AND THE RICOCHET MAY KILL US ALL.
NOTED.
#$%@.
HAZMAT, ARE YOU ALL RIGHT?
MY HELMET CRACKED. IT'S... IT'S BAD.
UM...STRESS... STRESS WILL TRIGGER MY RADIATION POWERS, AND WITH US TRAPPED IN HERE...
OKAY. I SEE IT. JUST...DON'T PANIC. KEEP CALM. NICE, EASY, EVEN BREATHING, OKAY? I'M GONNA GET YOU OUT OF HERE. I PROMISE.
SO JUST...NICE AND EASY.
...OKAY.
I'LL GO INTANGIBLE... PHASE RIGHT THROUGH THE DOOR AND OPEN IT FROM THE OUTSIDE.
AND THEN WE'LL KICK THE CRAP OUT OF THE NEXUS.
I COULDN'T LOVE IT MORE.
I WAS WRONG, I LOVE IT MORE.

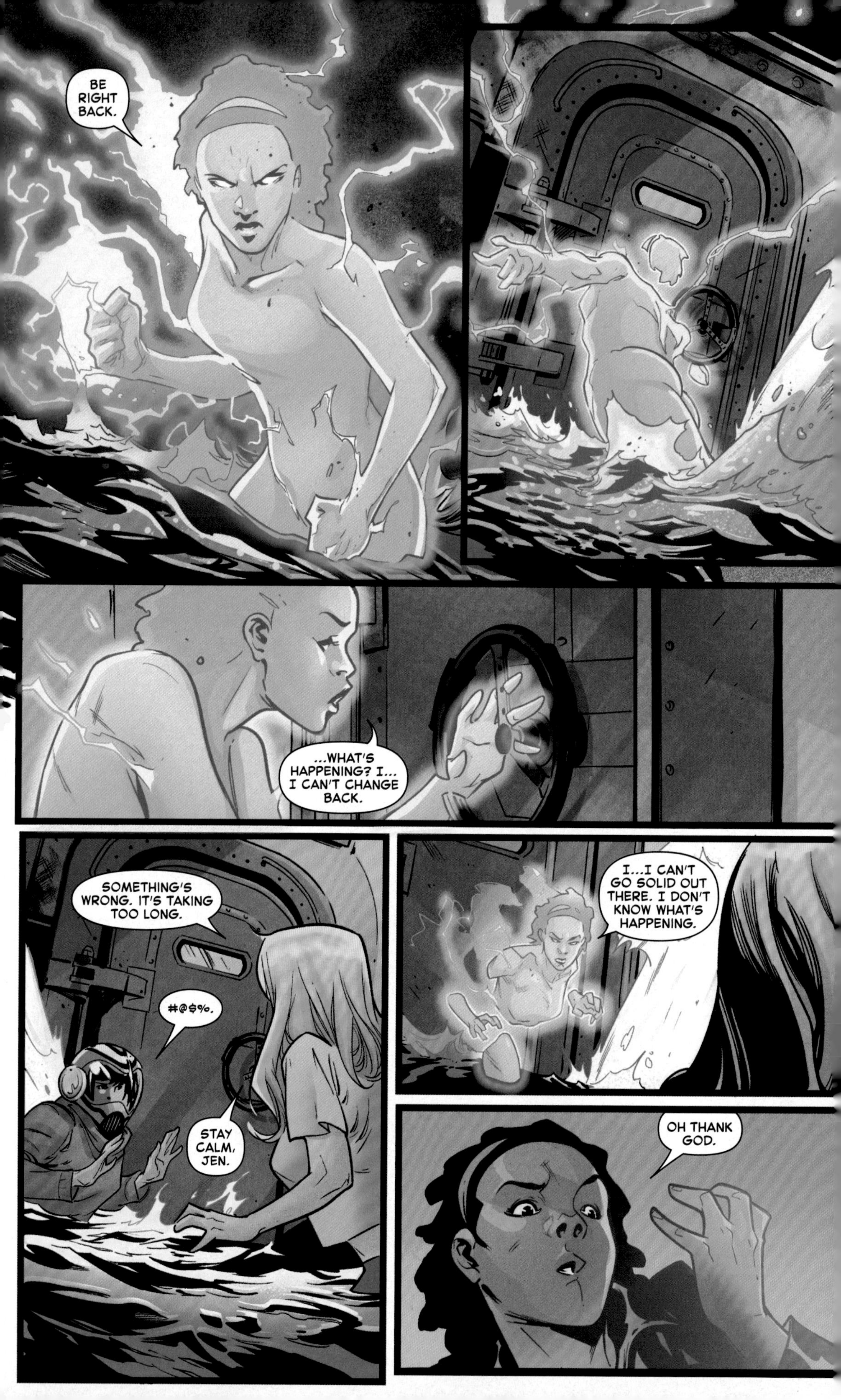
BE RIGHT BACK.
...WHAT'S HAPPENING? I... I CAN'T CHANGE BACK.
SOMETHING'S WRONG. IT'S TAKING TOO LONG.
#@$%.
STAY CALM, JEN.
I...I CAN'T GO SOLID OUT THERE. I DON'T KNOW WHAT'S HAPPENING.
OH THANK GOD.

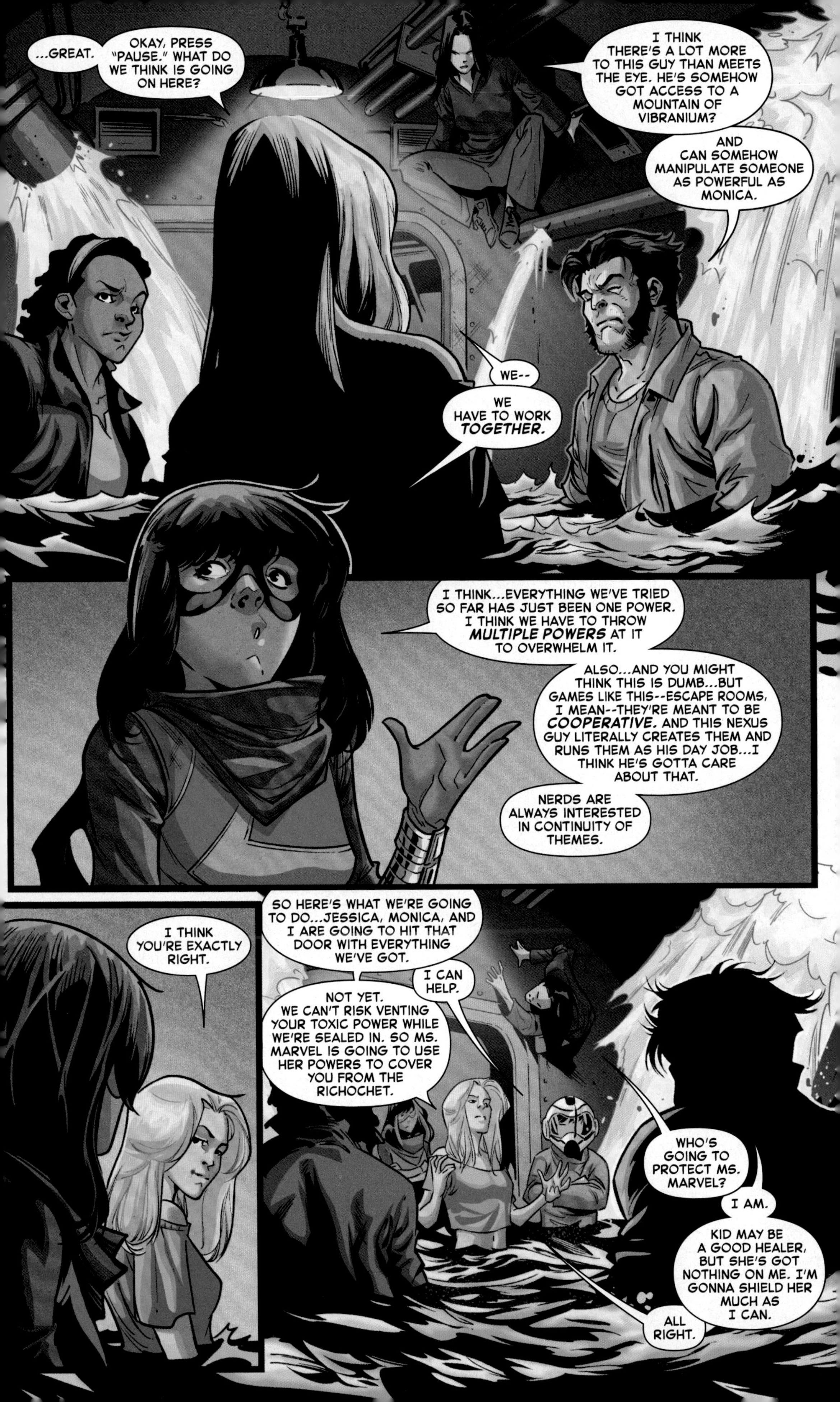

...GREAT.
OKAY, PRESS "PAUSE." WHAT DO WE THINK IS GOING ON HERE?
I THINK THERE'S A LOT MORE TO THIS GUY THAN MEETS THE EYE. HE'S SOMEHOW GOT ACCESS TO A MOUNTAIN OF VIBRANIUM?
AND CAN SOMEHOW MANIPULATE SOMEONE AS POWERFUL AS MONICA.
WE--
WE HAVE TO WORK TOGETHER.
I THINK...EVERYTHING WE'VE TRIED SO FAR HAS JUST BEEN ONE POWER. I THINK WE HAVE TO THROW MULTIPLE POWERS AT IT TO OVERWHELM IT.
ALSO...AND YOU MIGHT THINK THIS IS DUMB...BUT GAMES LIKE THIS--ESCAPE ROOMS, I MEAN--THEY'RE MEANT TO BE COOPERATIVE. AND THIS NEXUS GUY LITERALLY CREATES THEM AND RUNS THEM AS HIS DAY JOB...I THINK HE'S GOTTA CARE ABOUT THAT.
NERDS ARE ALWAYS INTERESTED IN CONTINUITY OF THEMES.
I THINK YOU'RE EXACTLY RIGHT.
SO HERE'S WHAT WE'RE GOING TO DO...JESSICA, MONICA, AND I ARE GOING TO HIT THAT DOOR WITH EVERYTHING WE'VE GOT.
I CAN HELP.
NOT YET. WE CAN'T RISK VENTING YOUR TOXIC POWER WHILE WE'RE SEALED IN. SO MS. MARVEL IS GOING TO USE HER POWERS TO COVER YOU FROM THE RICHOCHET.
WHO'S GOING TO PROTECT MS. MARVEL?
I AM.
KID MAY BE A GOOD HEALER, BUT SHE'S GOT NOTHING ON ME. I'M GONNA SHIELD HER MUCH AS I CAN.
ALL RIGHT.

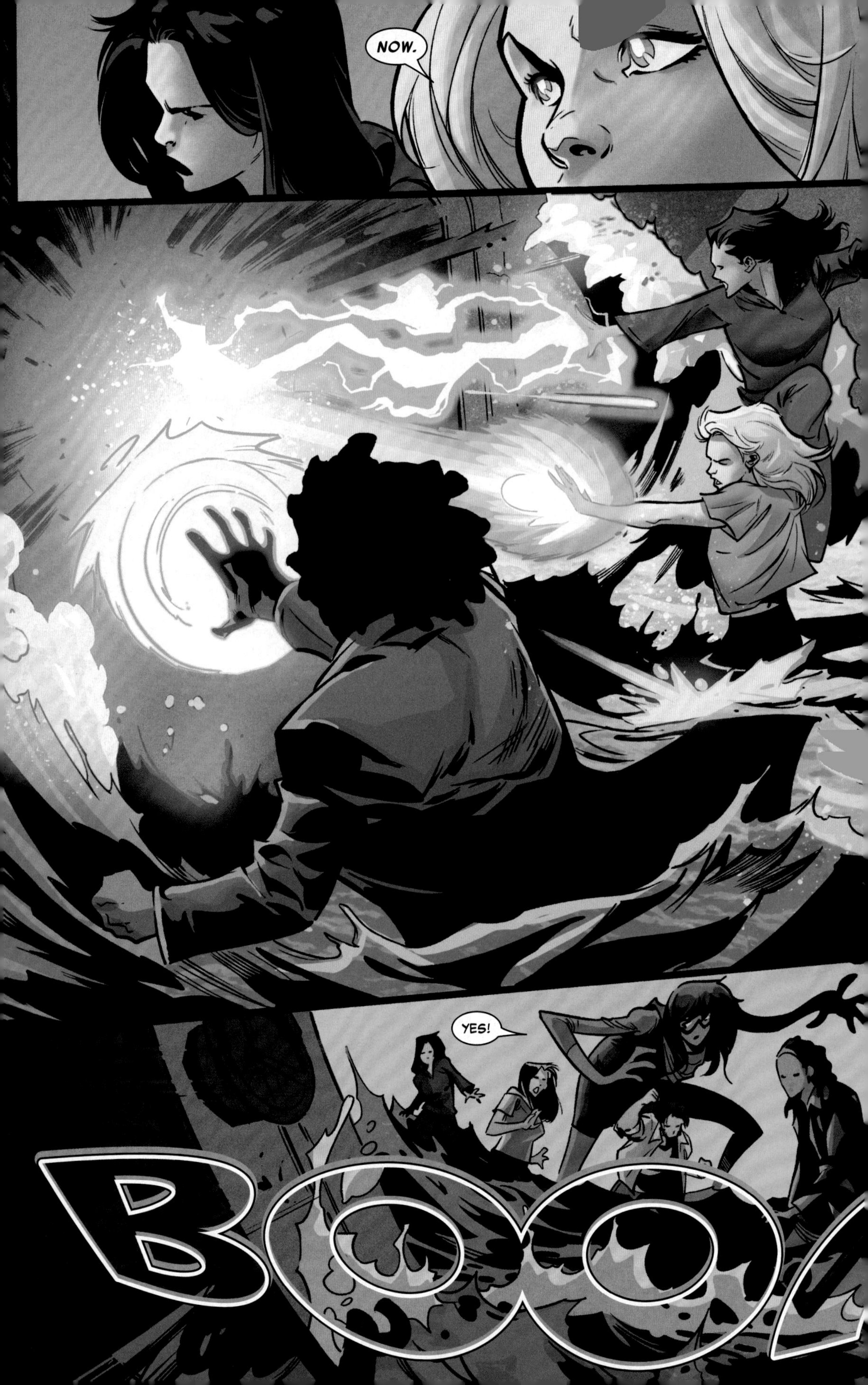
NOW.
YES!
BOO

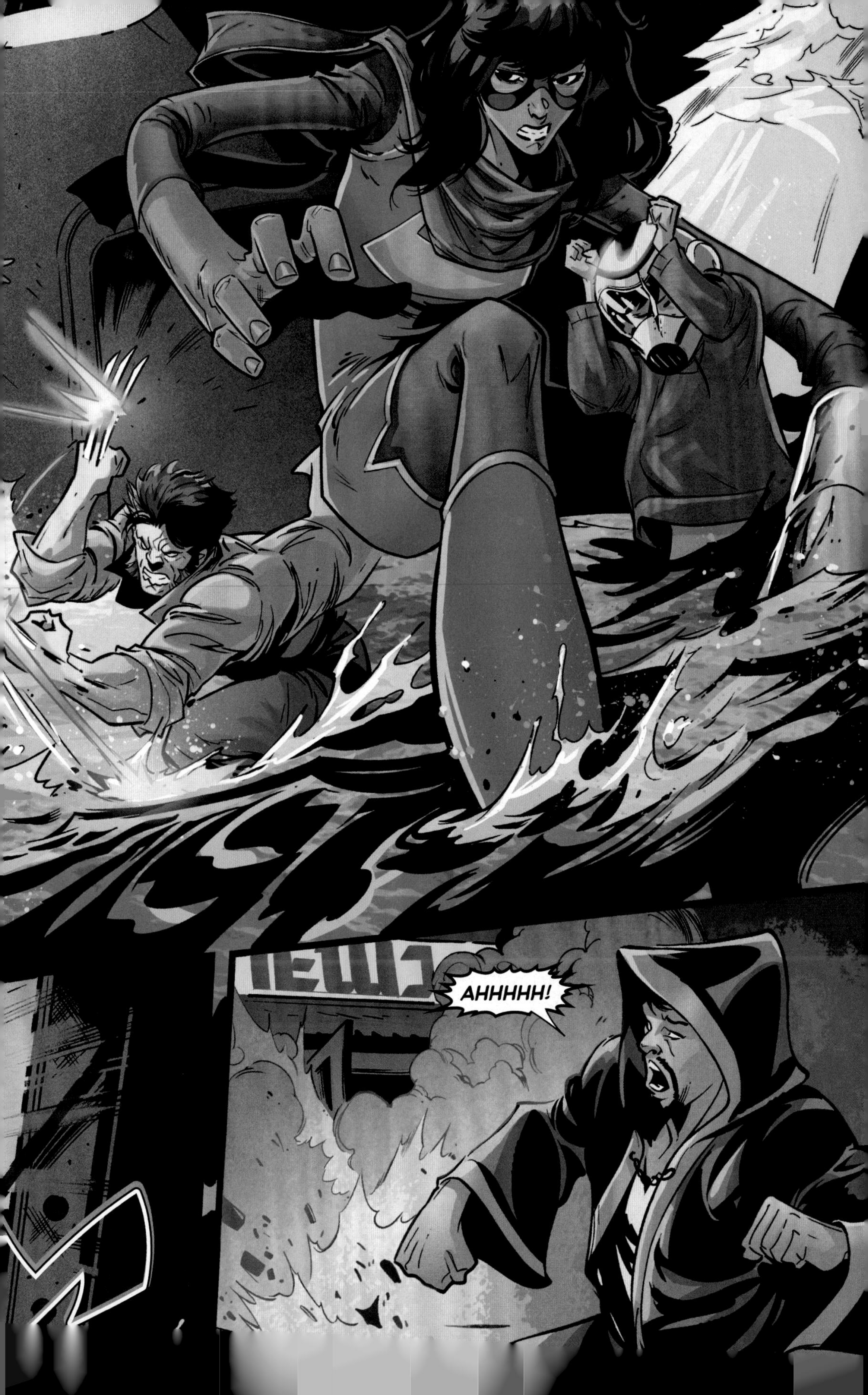
AHHHHH!

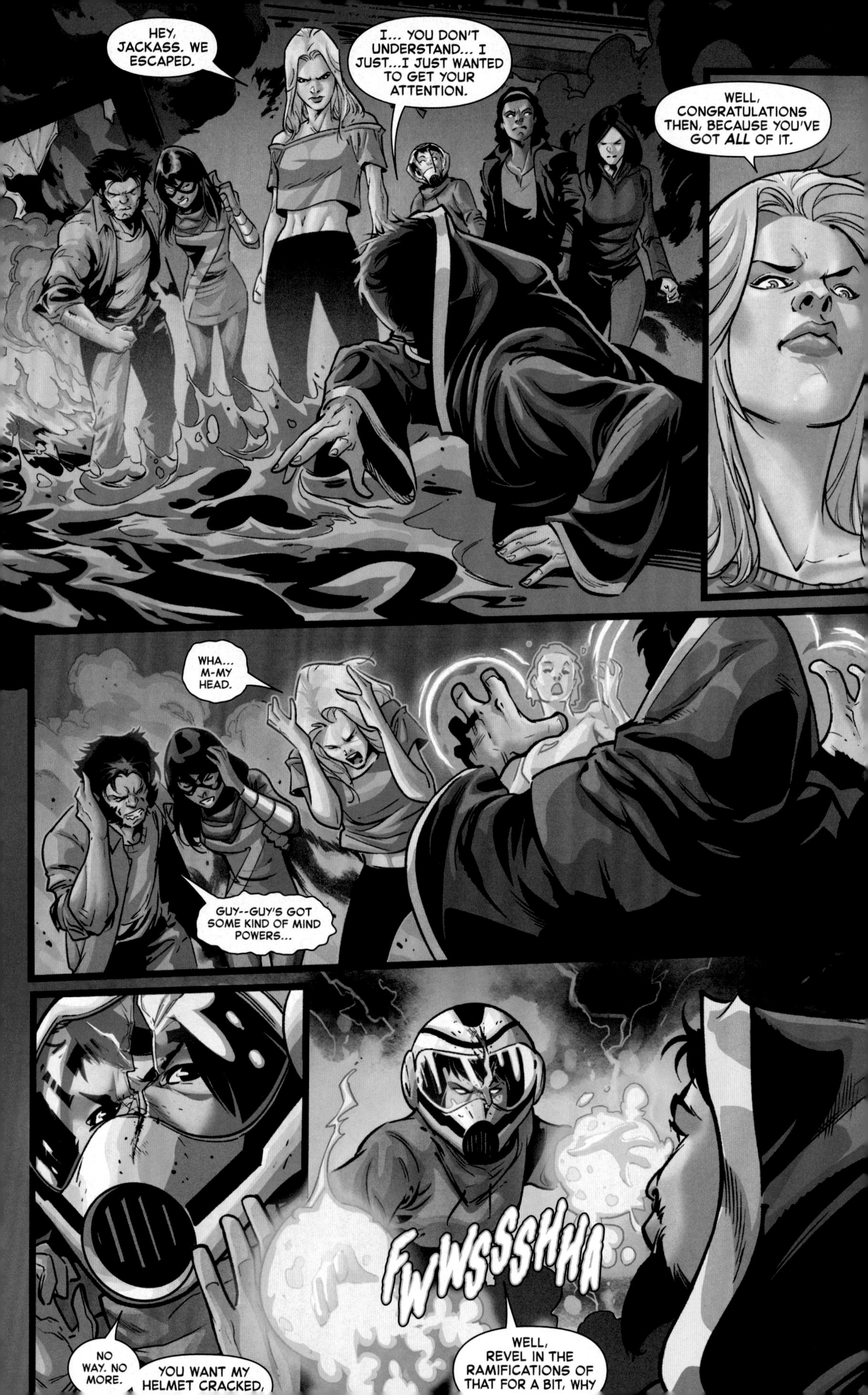
HEY, JACKASS. WE ESCAPED.
I... YOU DON'T UNDERSTAND... I JUST...I JUST WANTED TO GET YOUR ATTENTION.
WELL, CONGRATULATIONS THEN, BECAUSE YOU'VE GOT ALL OF IT.
WHA... M-MY HEAD.
GUY--GUY'S GOT SOME KIND OF MIND POWERS...
NO WAY. NO MORE.
YOU WANT MY HELMET CRACKED,
FWWSSSHHA
WELL, REVEL IN THE RAMIFICATIONS OF THAT FOR A BIT, WHY

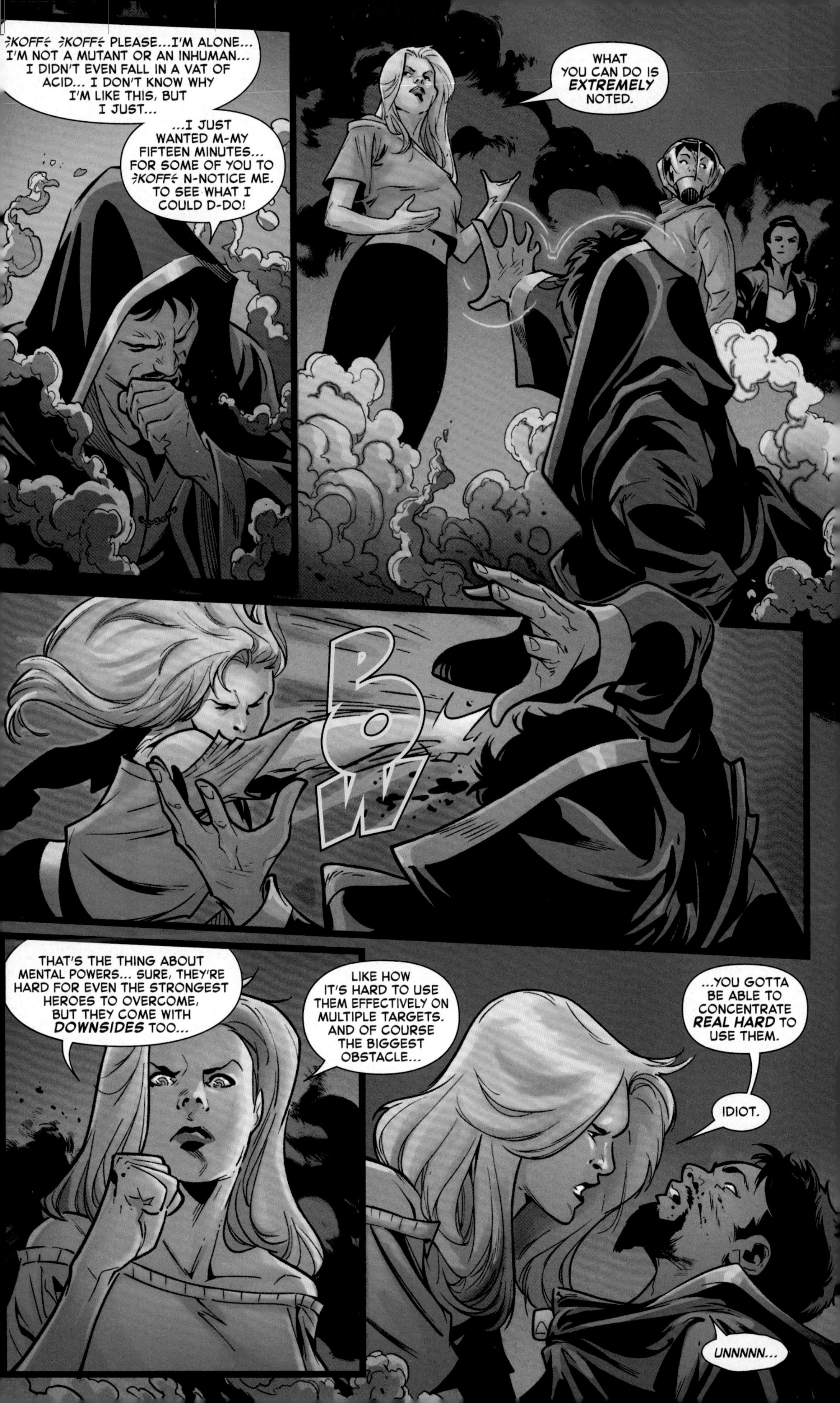
KOFF *KOFF* PLEASE...I'M ALONE... I'M NOT A MUTANT OR AN INHUMAN... I DIDN'T EVEN FALL IN A VAT OF ACID... I DON'T KNOW WHY I'M LIKE THIS, BUT I JUST...
...I JUST WANTED M-MY FIFTEEN MINUTES... FOR SOME OF YOU TO *KOFF* N-NOTICE ME. TO SEE WHAT I COULD D-DO!
WHAT YOU CAN DO IS EXTREMELY NOTED.
POW
THAT'S THE THING ABOUT MENTAL POWERS... SURE, THEY'RE HARD FOR EVEN THE STRONGEST HEROES TO OVERCOME, BUT THEY COME WITH DOWNSIDES TOO...
LIKE HOW IT'S HARD TO USE THEM EFFECTIVELY ON MULTIPLE TARGETS. AND OF COURSE THE BIGGEST OBSTACLE...
...YOU GOTTA BE ABLE TO CONCENTRATE REAL HARD TO USE THEM.
IDIOT.
UNNNNN...

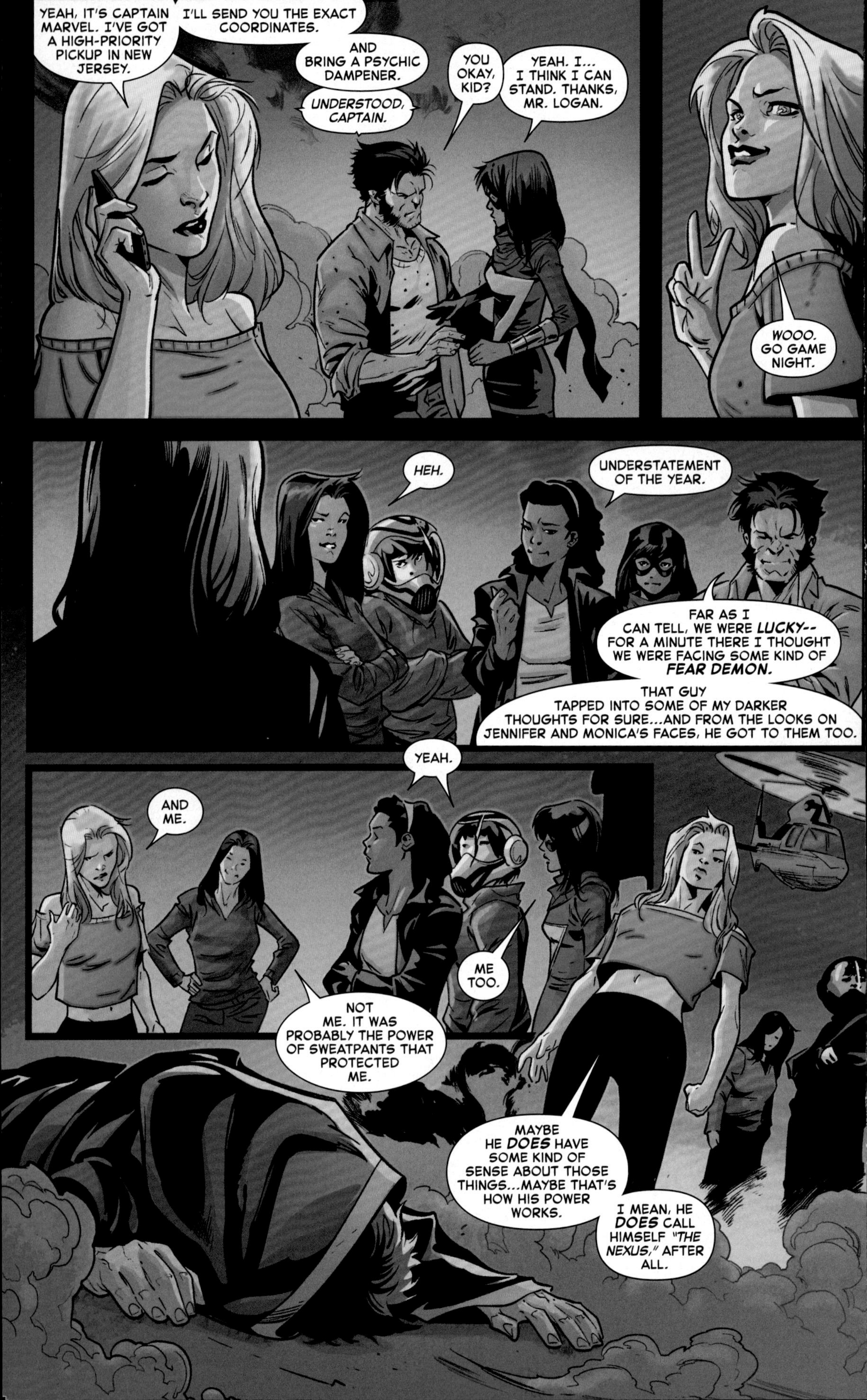

YEAH, IT'S CAPTAIN MARVEL. I'VE GOT A HIGH-PRIORITY PICKUP IN NEW JERSEY.
I'LL SEND YOU THE EXACT COORDINATES.
AND BRING A PSYCHIC DAMPENER.
UNDERSTOOD, CAPTAIN.
YOU OKAY, KID?
YEAH. I... I THINK I CAN STAND. THANKS, MR. LOGAN.
WOOO. GO GAME NIGHT.
HEH.
UNDERSTATEMENT OF THE YEAR.
FAR AS I CAN TELL, WE WERE LUCKY-- FOR A MINUTE THERE I THOUGHT WE WERE FACING SOME KIND OF FEAR DEMON.
THAT GUY TAPPED INTO SOME OF MY DARKER THOUGHTS FOR SURE...AND FROM THE LOOKS ON JENNIFER AND MONICA'S FACES, HE GOT TO THEM TOO.
YEAH.
AND ME.
ME TOO.
NOT ME. IT WAS PROBABLY THE POWER OF SWEATPANTS THAT PROTECTED ME.
MAYBE HE DOES HAVE SOME KIND OF SENSE ABOUT THOSE THINGS...MAYBE THAT'S HOW HIS POWER WORKS.
I MEAN, HE DOES CALL HIMSELF "THE NEXUS," AFTER ALL.

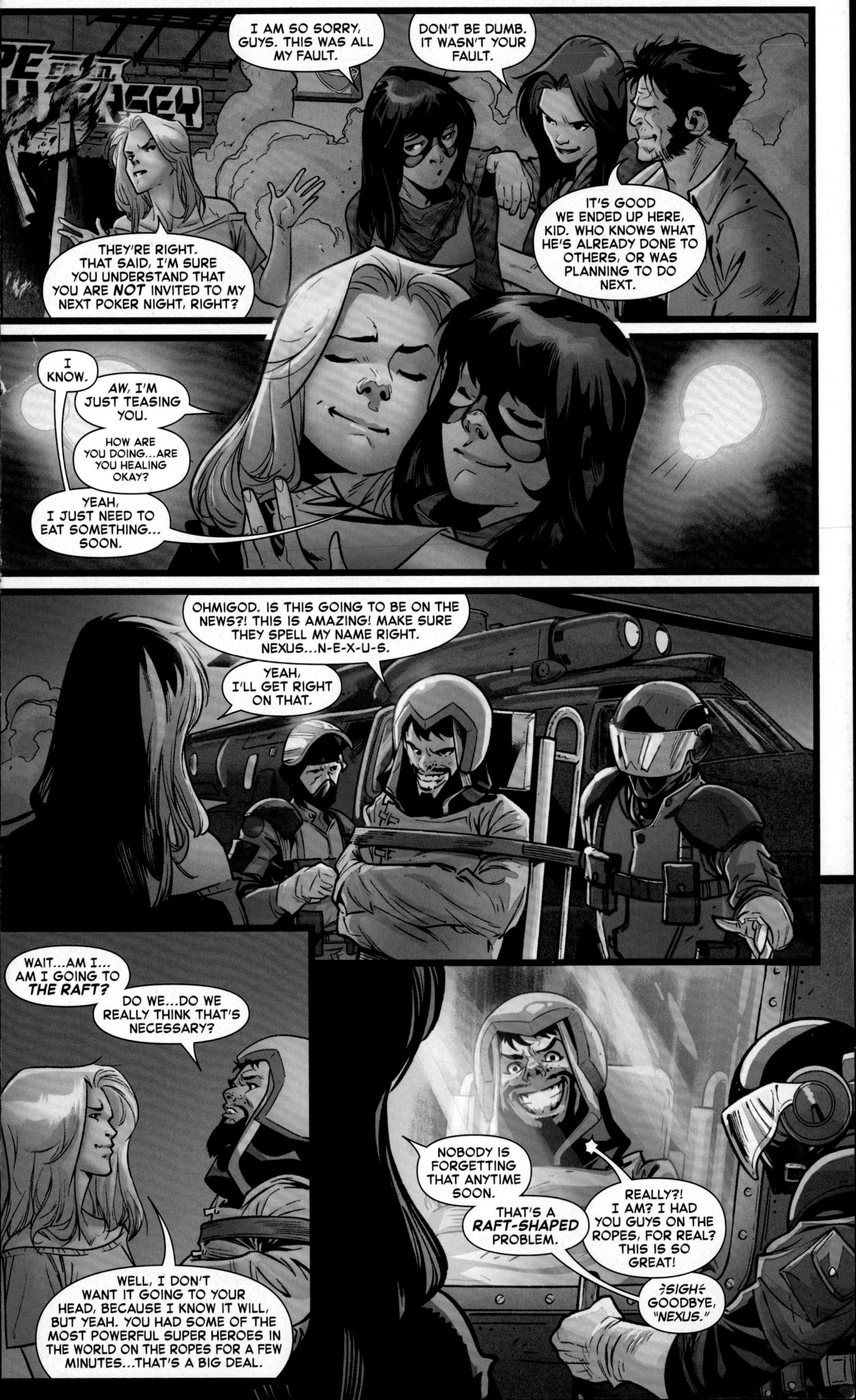
I AM SO SORRY, GUYS. THIS WAS ALL MY FAULT.
DON'T BE DUMB. IT WASN'T YOUR FAULT.
THEY'RE RIGHT. THAT SAID, I'M SURE YOU UNDERSTAND THAT YOU ARE *NOT* INVITED TO MY NEXT POKER NIGHT, RIGHT?
IT'S GOOD WE ENDED UP HERE, KID. WHO KNOWS WHAT HE'S ALREADY DONE TO OTHERS, OR WAS PLANNING TO DO NEXT.
I KNOW.
AW, I'M JUST TEASING YOU.
HOW ARE YOU DOING...ARE YOU HEALING OKAY?
YEAH, I JUST NEED TO EAT SOMETHING... SOON.
OHMIGOD. IS THIS GOING TO BE ON THE NEWS?! THIS IS AMAZING! MAKE SURE THEY SPELL MY NAME RIGHT. NEXUS...N-E-X-U-S.
YEAH, I'LL GET RIGHT ON THAT.
WAIT...AM I... AM I GOING TO *THE RAFT?*
DO WE...DO WE REALLY THINK THAT'S NECESSARY?
WELL, I DON'T WANT IT GOING TO YOUR HEAD, BECAUSE I KNOW IT WILL, BUT YEAH. YOU HAD SOME OF THE MOST POWERFUL SUPER HEROES IN THE WORLD ON THE ROPES FOR A FEW MINUTES...THAT'S A BIG DEAL.
NOBODY IS FORGETTING THAT ANYTIME SOON.
THAT'S A *RAFT-SHAPED* PROBLEM.
REALLY?! I AM? I HAD YOU GUYS ON THE ROPES, FOR REAL? THIS IS SO GREAT!
SIGH GOODBYE, *"NEXUS."*

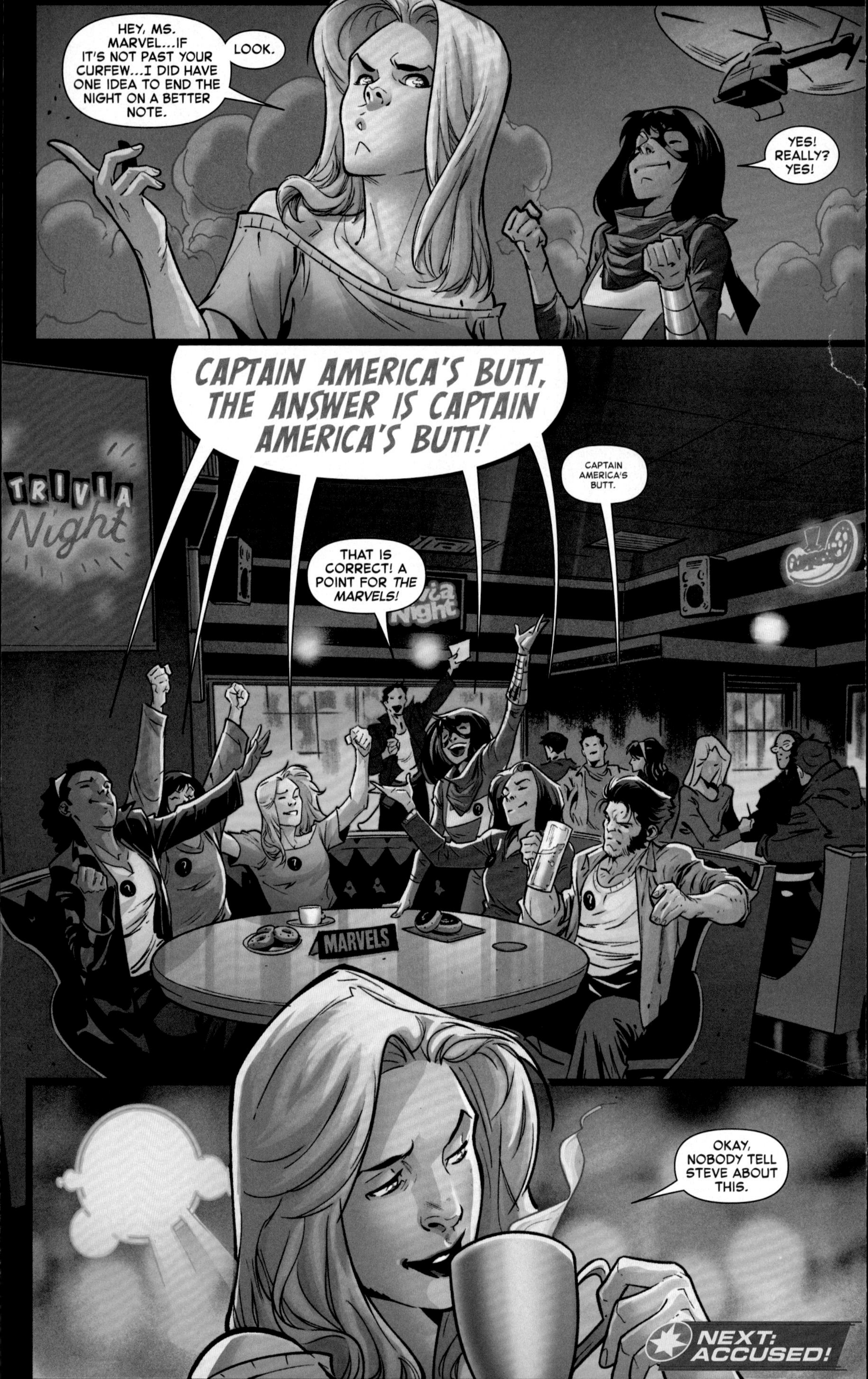
HEY, MS. MARVEL...IF IT'S NOT PAST YOUR CURFEW...I DID HAVE ONE IDEA TO END THE NIGHT ON A BETTER NOTE.
LOOK.
YES! REALLY? YES!
TRIVIA Night
CAPTAIN AMERICA'S BUTT, THE ANSWER IS CAPTAIN AMERICA'S BUTT!
CAPTAIN AMERICA'S BUTT.
THAT IS CORRECT! A POINT FOR THE MARVELS!
MARVELS
OKAY, NOBODY TELL STEVE ABOUT THIS.
NEXT: ACCUSED!

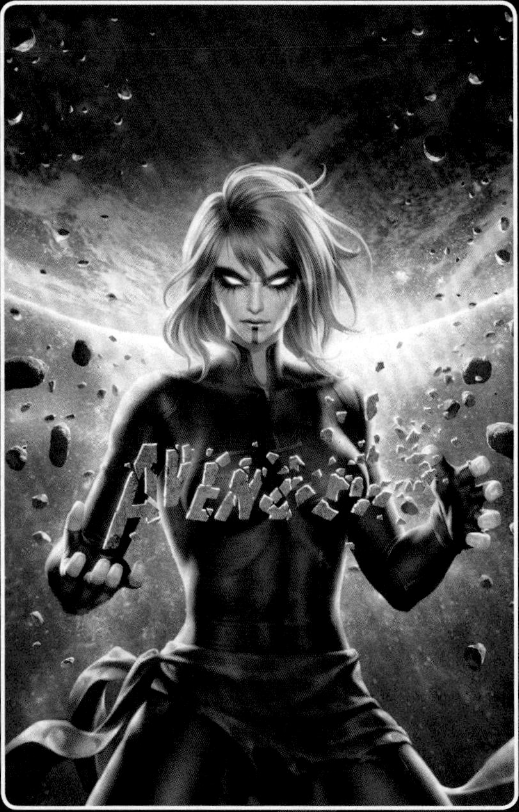

JUNGGEUN YOON
12 VARIANT

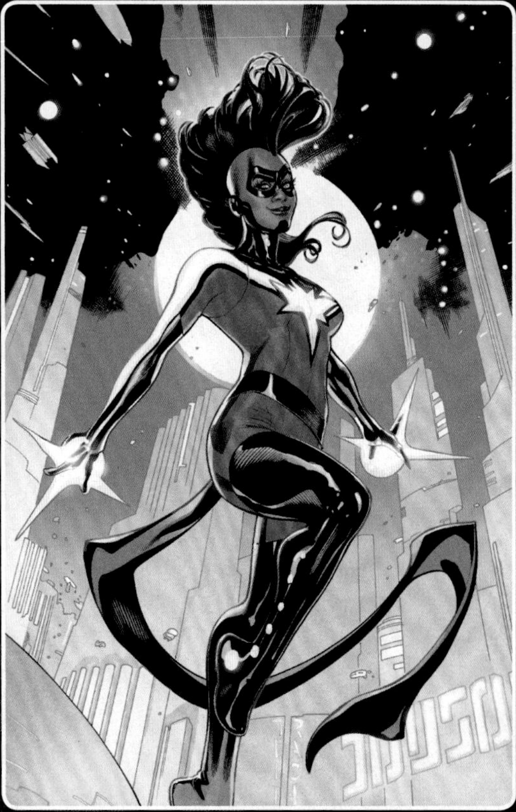

TERRY DODSON & RACHEL DODSON
12 2099 VARIANT

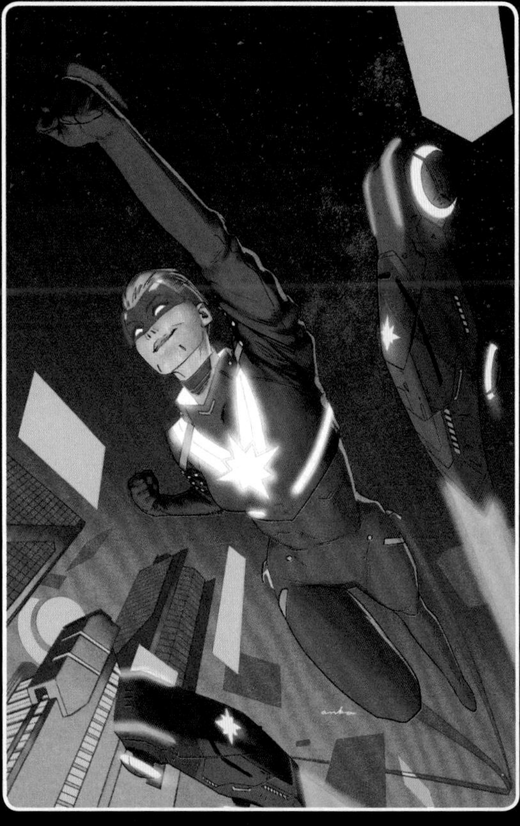

KRIS ANKA
13 2020 VARIANT

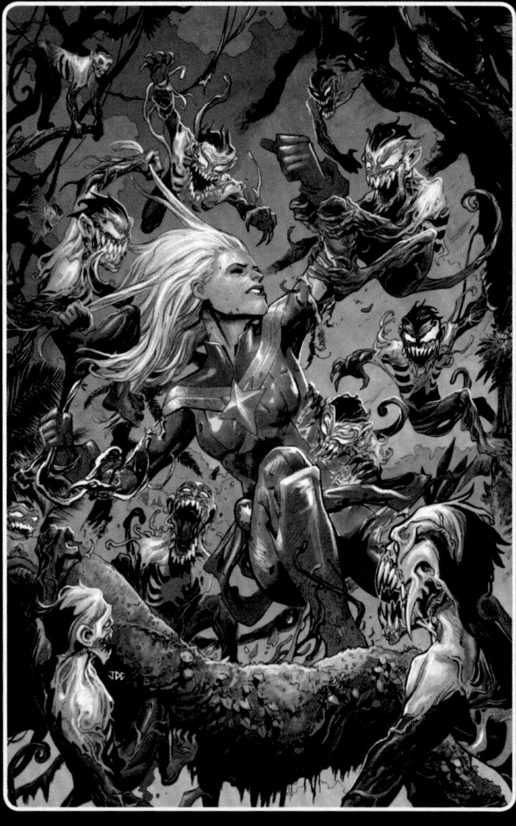

JOSH CASSARA & RAIN BEREDO
13 VENOM ISLAND VARIANT

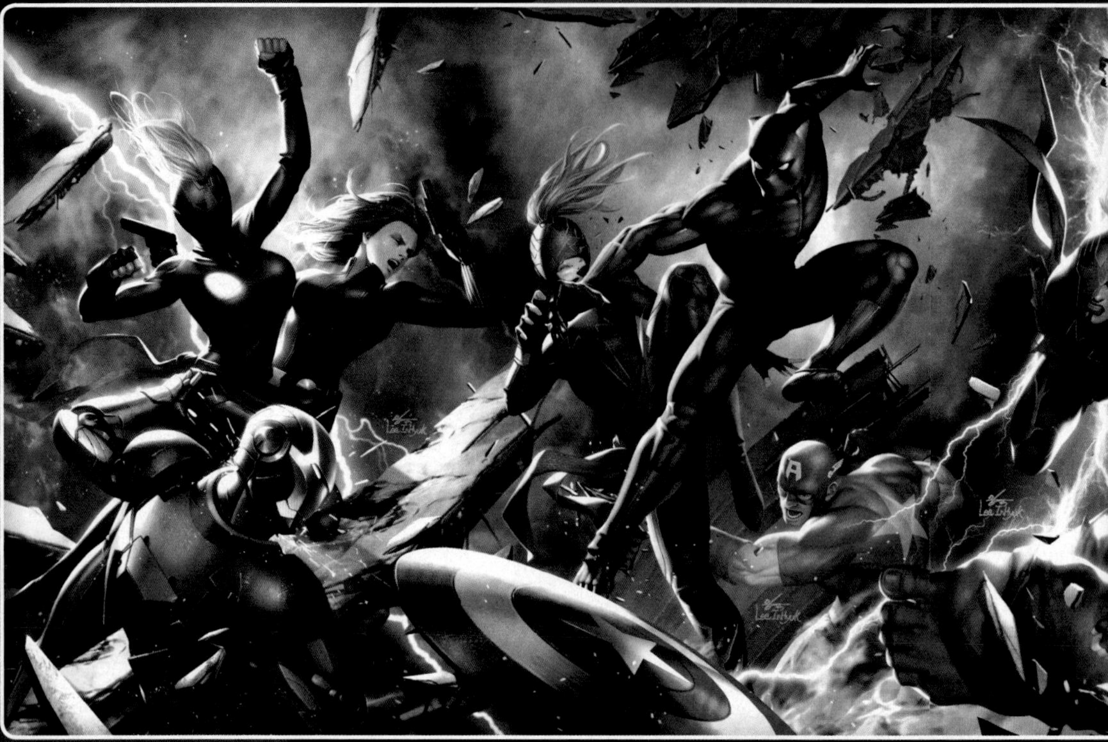

INHYUK LEE
12-16 COMBINED VARIANTS

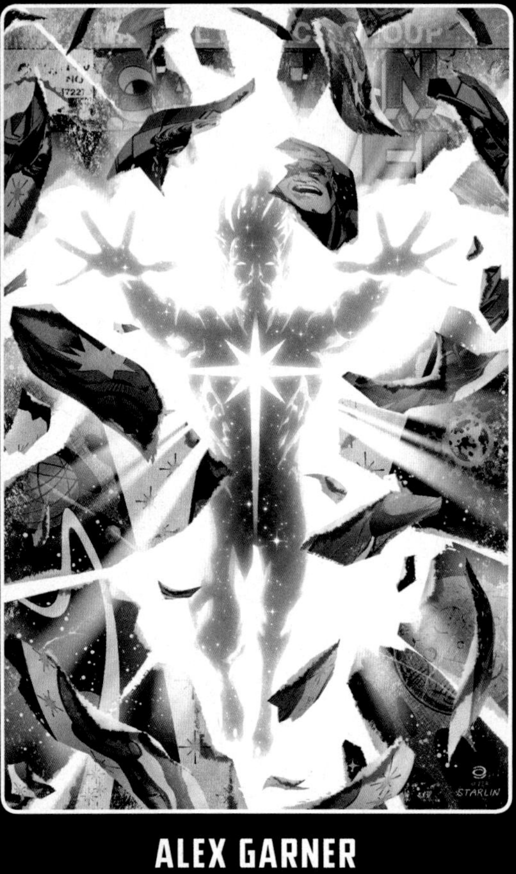
STARLIN

ALEX GARNER

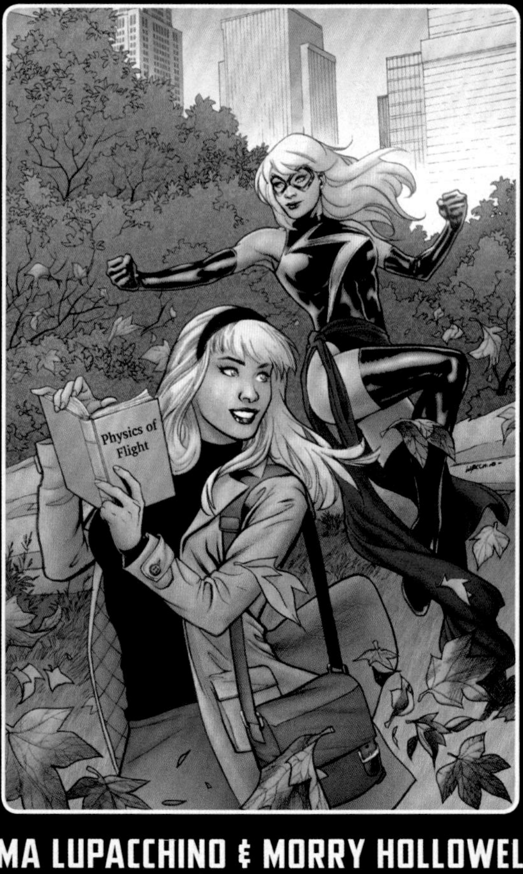
Physics of
Flight

EMA LUPACCHINO & MORRY HOLLOWEL

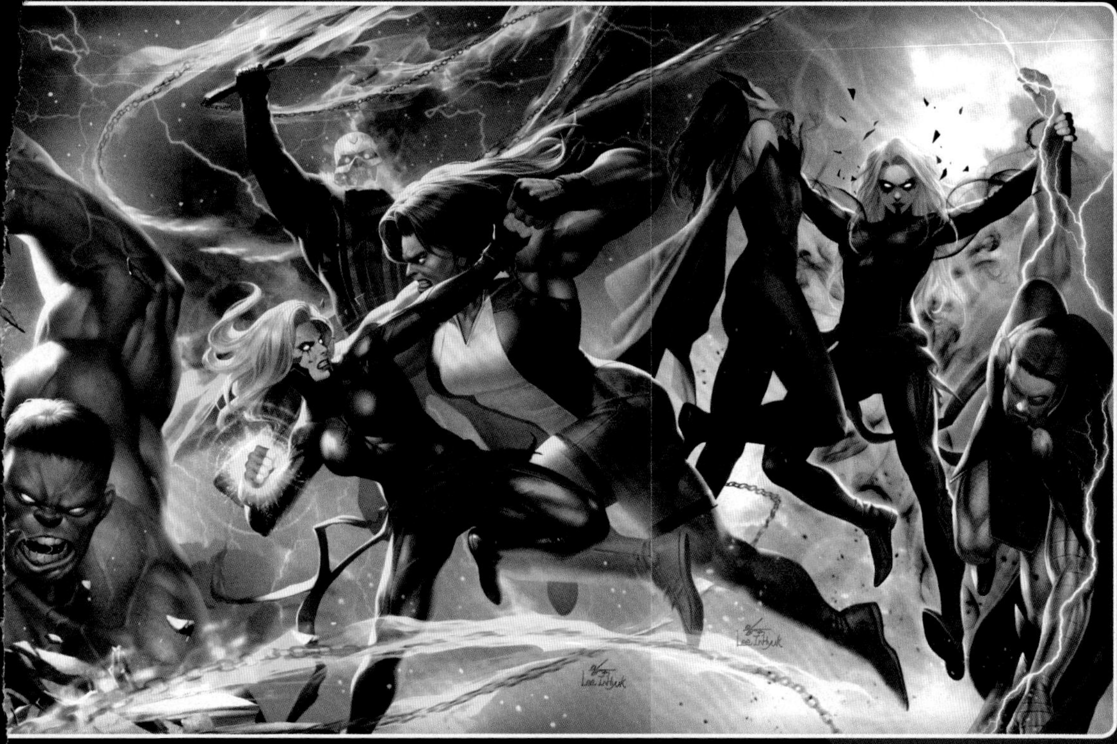
Lee InHyuk

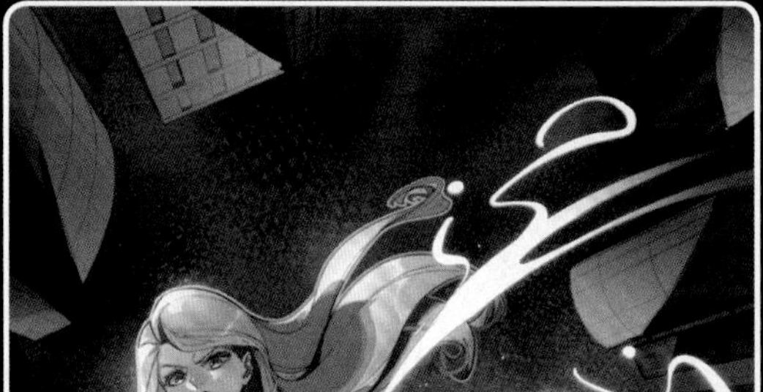

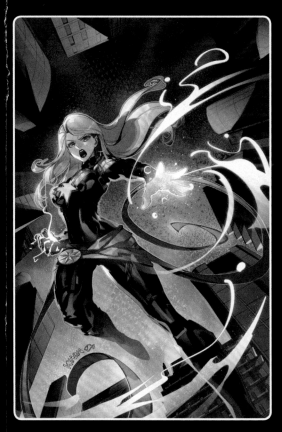

ZILI YU
15 VARIANT

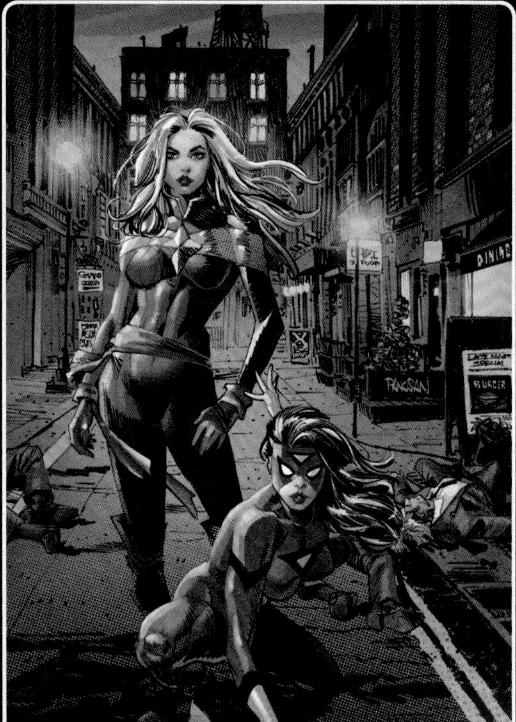
DINING
BURGER
PANOSIAN

DAN PANOSIAN
16 SPIDER-WOMAN VARIANT

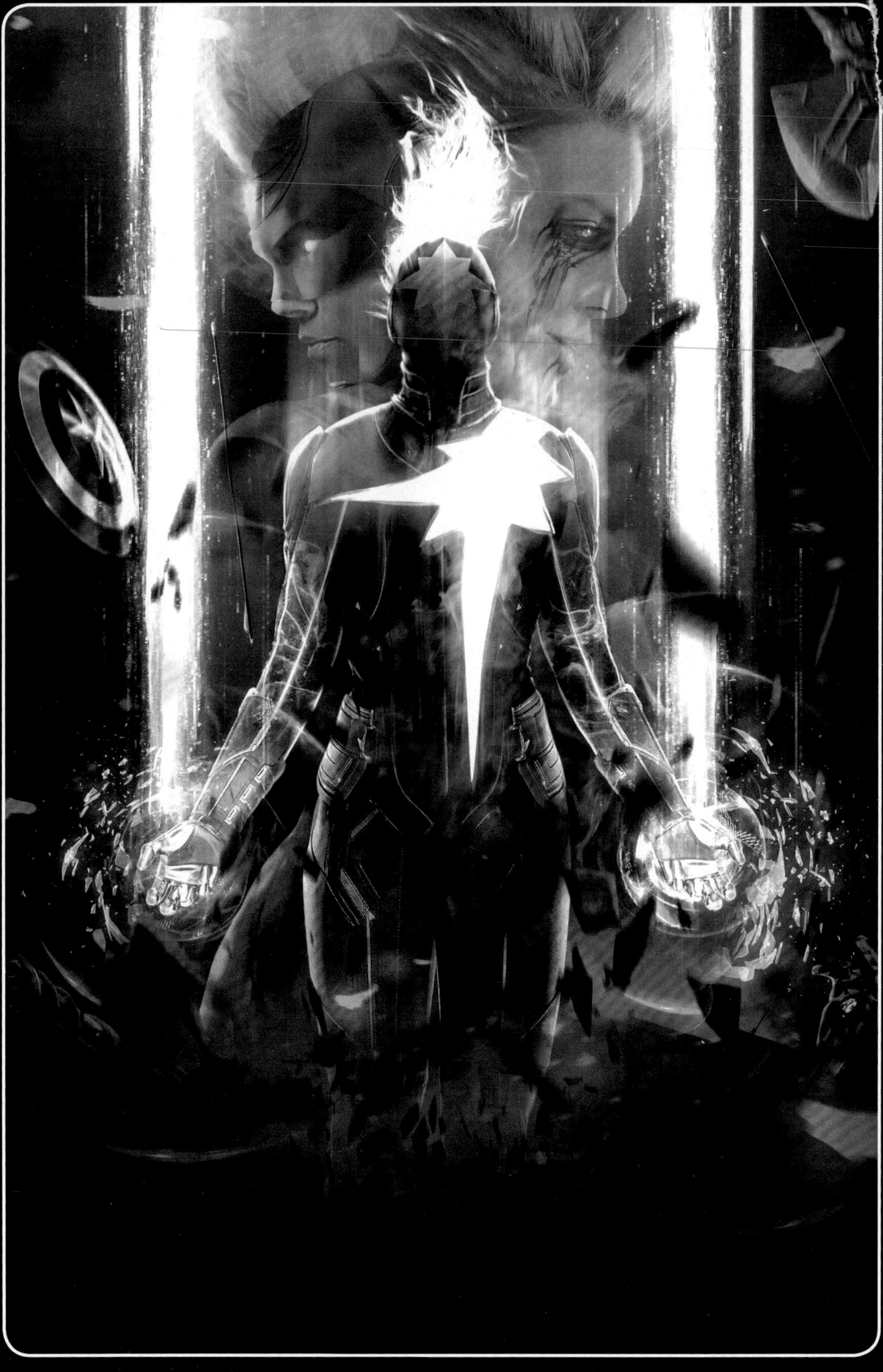

BOSSLOGIC
16 VARIANT